BIBLE MODELS

BIBLE MODELS

THE SHINING LIGHTS OF SCRIPTURE

RICHARD NEWTON

SOLID GROUND CHRISTIAN BOOKS
BIRMINGHAM, ALABAMA USA

Solid Ground Christian Books
PO Box 660132
Vestavia Hills AL 35266
205-443-0311
sgcb@charter.net
www.solid-ground-books.com

BIBLE MODELS
The Shining Lights of Scripture

Richard Newton (1813-1887)

Taken from the 1884 edition by George Barrie Publishing, Philadelphia

Cover image is taken from the Barrie edition and pictures Elijah being fed by the Brook Cherith.

Cover design by Borgo Design
Contact them at borgogirl@bellsouth.net

ISBN- 978-159925-154-7

Introduction to New Edition

With the publication of *Bible Models* there are now a full dozen volumes available from the pen of Richard Newton (1813-1887), the man known as "the Prince of Preachers to children." Solid Ground is planning to reprint at least another ten volumes for today's children and those who love them.

A quick glance through this volume will instantly convince the reader that he is holding a rare and precious book. *Bible Models* was published toward the end of Newton's fruitful life and ministry, and it became an instant favorite in households throughout the world. Like his other books, it was translated into numerous languages and spoke to the hearts of people all over the world.

Tragically, in our day, most books for children are trivial and childish. It becomes evident that books that profess to be Christian in nature are often shallow and weak. The primary goal of many of today's books is to entertain the young. While Newton books will entertain, they will do so by engaging the mind, will and affections by means of the truth. This is why they are so badly needed in our day.

When you turn this page you will get the rare privilege of reading the author's original Preface in his own handwriting. Take a few minutes to read each of these words and ponder what he has to say before you move into the body of the book.

Another suggestion: get on your knees and seek the face of the Almighty as you take your first steps onto this holy ground. We can never understand or benefit from God's truth without the aid of the Holy Spirit, and the ministry of the Spirit will be withheld from those who are proud and self-sufficient. Let us imitate the words of our Lord in Isaiah 66:2, "But to this one I will look, to him who is humble and contrite in spirit, and who trembles at My word."

The Publisher
March 26, 2008

[The following PREFACE is a Fac-simile of Dr. Newton's hand-writing.]

Preface.

Among the ancient Romans, it used to be the custom for fathers, who were well off, to have in the halls of their dwellings, busts, and statues of the great and good men of their nation. The object in placing them there, was to give their children an opportunity of becoming acquainted with those men, and of trying to imitate the good points of their characters.

This was a wise thing to do; for no doubt, it led many of the Roman boys and girls to think about the famous characters in the past history of their nation, and try to become like them.

And our Father in heaven has done something like this, for the church which is his family. He has filled His blessed book, the Bible, with interesting sketches of the lives and characters of the great and good men, who have been His servants and followers, from the beginning of the world.

And the apostle James shows us the use God intends that we should make of the accounts given us of the lives of those good men, when he says,—"Take my brethren, the prophets <u>for an example</u>." James 5:10. This means that we should meditate on the lives of the holy men of whom we read in the Bible, till we get the model points of their characters distinctly before us, and then try, by the help of God, to have them brought forth in our own hearts and lives. This is one of the very best things for us to do.

In one of the beautiful collects of the Episcopal Church, there is a prayer which may be offered here. It asks that—"God would give us grace to follow His blessed saints in all virtuous and godly living, that we may come to the unspeakable joys which He has prepared for those who unfeignedly love Him."

And as we study these "Bible Models", let our hearts go out in the earnest prayer, that, by God's blessing, we may be able to follow the good examples here set before us. And, if such results shall attend this volume, as it goes on its quiet way, then it will not have been written in vain.

Richd Newton

ABEL'S OFFERING.

ABEL, THE MODEL SPEAKER.

"By it, he being dead, yet speaketh."—HEBREWS xi: 4.

HE apostle is speaking here of Abel. He was the brother of Cain—the second son of our first parents, Adam and Eve. This carries us back to the very beginning of the world's history. Here we have an account given us of the sacrifice that was offered by these two brothers. This is the first time that we find anything said about a sacrifice in the Bible. And as Abel was the first person to offer a sacrifice, so far as we know, so he was the first person, belonging to our race, who died, and the first who entered heaven.

The apostle tells us that Abel offered a better sacrifice than his brother did; and then he says that *"By it, he being dead, yet speaketh."*

This is the first of a new course of sermons for the young. I propose to call them BIBLE MODELS. In this course we shall take up some of the leading persons whose histories are given in the Bible, and call attention to certain points in connection with each.

From what the apostle says of Abel in our text, we may consider him as *The Model Speaker*.

It may seem strange to take this view of him when we do not know a single word that he ever spoke. But then we must remember that we speak by our *lives*, as well as with our *lips;* and that, as the old proverb says, "*Actions* speak louder than *words*." And it is by his life, or actions, that we are now to look at Abel as speaking, while we consider him as "the model speaker." And in thus considering him, there are two things for us to notice: one of these is *the matter* of his speaking; the other is *the manner* of it.

Now let us look at *the matter* of Abel's speaking—or what he spoke about.

When a person is going to make a speech, it is very important for him to choose a good subject. Abel did this. The thing to which the apostle here refers, as that by which Abel speaks to us, is the sacrifice which he offered. When God gave Adam and Eve the first promise, about "the seed of the woman,"—which referred to Christ; there can be no doubt that He told them to offer sacrifices, in connection with their daily worship. These sacrifices were intended as types, or figures of our Saviour Christ, and of the one great sacrifice which He was to offer, in the fullness of time, for the sins of the whole world. They pointed to Him as "the lamb slain from the foundation of the world."

Cain paid no attention to what God had said on this subject. He brought only the fruits of the ground for his offering. But Abel minded what

God had said, and brought a lamb for an offering. The blood of this lamb was shed, and its body offered as a burnt sacrifice upon the altar. And it is by *this action*, that "he being dead, yet speaketh." Abel was a model speaker because, by what he did, he spoke about Christ and his death. And this is the most important thing that any one can ever speak about. And there are *three* reasons why this subject is so important:

In the first place, this is an important subject to speak about, because we cannot—BE GOOD—*till we know about Jesus, and his death.* Here, for instance, is my watch. Suppose that its main-spring were broken; could it keep good time? No. I might wind it up, and make the fingers point to the right hour; but it would be of no use. It could not keep good time. The only thing to do with such a watch would be to take it to a watch-maker, and let him put a new main-spring in it.

Now our hearts are to us what the main-spring is to a watch. But sin has made our hearts wicked. This is like breaking the main-spring of a watch. And Jesus is the only One who can put our hearts right. And we never can be, really, and truly good, till we take our hearts to Jesus, and ask him to make them right. Then, we shall be like the watch, that has a new main-spring in it. It will keep good time.

A gentleman, very well known in this country, died not long ago. He tried for awhile to be good without the help of Jesus. But at last he gave it up, and asked him to make his heart right. And before he died, in talking to his minister, he said, "The great mistake of my life has been that I tried to be moral, or good, without the help of Christ; but I have learned that we can only be truly moral, or good, by the help of that grace which Jesus gives." This shows us that Abel was a model speaker, in the *matter* of his speaking, because by his sacrifice he spoke about Christ and his death, and we cannot BE GOOD *till we know about this*.

But we cannot—BE HAPPY—till we know about Christ and his death. And this is another reason why Abel was a model speaker, when by his sacrifice he spoke about him.

Here is one of good Bishop Whipple's stories, to illustrate this part of our subject.

"One day," says the Bishop, "an Indian came to my house. As soon as he entered, he kneeled at my feet. 'My father,' he said, 'I have come six hundred miles to thank you for your love to the Indians. I was a wild man, living beyond Turtle Mountain. I knew that my people were perishing. Every time I looked in the face of my child, it made my heart sick. My father told me there was a Great Spirit. Sometimes I went into the woods, and asked this Spirit to help me. But there was no answer. It was like standing in the dark, and reaching out my hands to take hold of nothing.

"'One day an Indian came to my wigwam. He said he had heard you tell a wonderful story at Red Lake. You said that the Great Spirit's Son had come down to earth, to save all the people that need help; and that the reason why the white man was so much happier than the red man, was because he had the true religion of the Great Spirit's Son. Then I said I must see that man. They told me you would be at Red Lake Crossing. I went two hundred miles to see you. I asked for you. They told me you were sick, and could not come. Then I said where can I find a missionary? I went one hundred and fifty miles more. I found that the missionary was a red man, like myself. My father, I have been with him three months. He has told me the wonderful story. I have it all in my heart. It is no longer dark here. My heart laughs all the time.'"

But there is nothing that can lighten up the dark heart of the poor Indian, or any other poor sinner, and make it laugh all the time, as the story of Jesus can do. And Abel was a model speaker, because by what he did, he was speaking of Christ and his death, and we cannot be happy till we know this.

But then we cannot—Be Safe—till we know about Jesus and his death. And this is the third reason why Abel was a model speaker, because, when he offered his sacrifice, *this*, was what he was speaking about.

We may get a good illustration of this point of our subject, from what took place among the Israelites, in the night of their deliverance from the land of Egypt. God told them, that at midnight, he would send his angel, to pass over all the land, and destroy in a moment, the first-born, or oldest child, in every Egyptian family. And then he told them what to do, in order that they might be kept in safety, while the angel of death was doing his terrible work among the Egyptians. The Israelites were to take a lamb, for every family. They were to kill the lamb in the evening, and, with a bunch of hyssop, sprinkle its blood on the door-posts of their houses. Every family, that had this blood sprinkled on their doors, God said would be safe from the stroke of the destroying angel.

The Jews tell this story in connection with that dreadful night. A Jewish father had one little girl, about ten years old. She was his only child, and he was very fond of her. As the first-born child, in that family, she would be the one to die, if the angel's stroke should fall on their dwelling. Before going to sleep, she asked her father if the blood had been sprinkled on their door-posts. He said it was, and she fell asleep. But her sleep was disturbed. She awoke several times, through the evening, and each time she asked anxiously, if it was all right about the blood. Assured that it was she tried to sleep on, but in vain. A little while before midnight, she woke again, in great alarm. She asked her father to take her in his arms, and carry her to the door, that she might see the blood. He did so; but found, to his horror, that there was *no blood on the door-posts!* It had been left to a servant to attend to it, and he had neglected it. Her father ran to get the blood, and then sprinkled it on the door-posts, with his own hand. His dear child saw the blood there. Then she knew that they were safe; and she went sweetly to sleep. That blood protected them when the destroying angel passed over.

And so, it is only seeing the blood of Christ, by faith, that makes our souls safe now. This is the most important thing to speak about, because it is the only thing that can make us good, and happy, and safe.

ABEL, THE MODEL SPEAKER.

Abel was a model speaker because of the *matter* of his speaking, or what he spoke about.

But Abel was a model speaker also, because of the —MANNER—*of his speaking.*

He spoke by his life, or actions; and there are three ways in which this made him a model speaker. 1. *In the first place it made him*—A PLAIN—*speaker.*

Every body who has heard what the apostle Paul says about Abel's sacrifice, understands what it meant. When he spoke by that action Abel was speaking *plainly.*

As he built his altar, and offered the lamb upon it, and stood by his sacrifice, to worship God, he was speaking very plainly, about the importance of the great sacrifice, which Christ was coming to offer. He was telling, as plainly as possible, that *his* only hope of being pardoned, and of going to heaven, was through that sacrifice. And what was true of Abel, is true of us all. When we speak by our actions, it is the best, and plainest way of speaking. We can find plenty of illustrations of this.

The best recommendations. A gentleman once advertised for a boy, to assist him in his office. Nearly fifty boys applied for the place the next day. Out of the whole number, in a little while, he chose one, and sent the rest away.

A friend of his was in the office with him, at the time. When the choice had been made, and the other boys sent away, this friend said to him: "I am quite curious to know on what grounds you selected this boy. He had no letter of recommendation, while some of the others had several."

"You are mistaken," said the gentleman; "this boy had better recommendations than any of the others. Let me tell you about them. When he came into the office, he wiped his feet, and closed the door after him. By this I knew that he was tidy and orderly. He gave up his seat in a moment, to that old lame man, who came in. This showed that he was kind and thoughtful. He took off his cap when he came in, and answered my questions promptly. This showed that he was polite and respectful. He lifted up the book, which I had purposely laid on the floor, and placed it on the table, while all the rest stepped over it, or thrust it aside with their feet. This showed that he was careful. He waited for his turn, instead of pushing the others aside; and this showed that he was modest. When I talked with him, I noticed that his clothes were carefully brushed; his shoes were polished, his hair well combed, and his teeth as white as milk. When he wrote his name, I noticed that his finger-nails were clean, instead of being black with dirt, as was the case with some of the boys who were better dressed than he. Don't you call these good letters of recommendation? I do. What I learn about a boy, in watching him for a few minutes, is worth more than all the fine letters he can bring with him." That boy was speaking by those little acts. And you see how *plainly* he spoke. The gentleman understood him, and he got the place.

A little pedlar speaking plainly. Robbie was a little fellow about ten or eleven years old. He used to go about with a basket on his arm, and sell pins, and tapes, and pocket-combs, and such things. One day he came into the waiting-room connected with the railway station, crying out—"Pins and pocket-combs! Pins and pocket-combs!" His voice was low, for he was tired, and faint for want of food. The busy crowd took no notice of the little pedlar. But, there was a lady there, who had been unfortunate enough to tear her silk dress.

"Here, my boy," she said to him, "you have just what I want. Give me a paper of pins, that I may pin up this ugly rent, till I get home." And then, turning to the gentleman with her, who was her brother, she said, "Harry, will you pay this little fellow, for a paper of pins?"

He was picking out some change, when Robbie said to the lady:

"No, no, ma'am! Don't take that paper; it isn't a whole one. I cut off a row of pins from it, this morning for my little sister, to dress her doll with."

"Never mind, my little man," said the lady, "there are more than I want now, and I shall only have the less to throw away."

"Then don't pay me so much," said Robbie, and he handed back two cents to the gentleman, who had given him ten.

"Well, my little merchant," said the gentleman, "you are too honest. How do you ever expect to make a living, unless you cheat a little now and then?"

Robbie's brown eyes opened very wide, when he heard this question.

"Yes," said he, "I'd rather not live at all, than live by cheating."

"And who taught you this?" asked the gentleman.

"My mother, sir, before she died and went to heaven. And I am sure she would rather have me die, and come to her at last, an honest, upright boy, than live ever so well on money got by cheating."

"You are right, my boy; and you are a noble little fellow to remember such a mother's teachings."

Now it happened that this gentleman, who was a merchant in business, was in want of money, and was just then being tempted to take some, that did not belong to him, in order to help himself out of trouble. But the plain, outspoken honesty of that little pin-pedlar, had such an effect on him, that he resisted the temptation, and, by God's blessing, got honestly out of his trouble.

And, not long after, he sent for little Robbie, the pin-pedlar, and gave him a situation in his office, feeling sure that a boy who was so honest in pins and pennies, would be one to be trusted in more important matters. Robbie was engaged, first as an errand boy; then as a clerk; and at last was taken into the business as a partner.

And thus, we see, that, when we speak by our actions, we speak plainly. And Abel was a model speaker, because by his life, or actions, he was a plain speaker.

But Abel was a model speaker because he spoke by his actions—and this made him—A LOUD—*speaker.*

Sometimes we meet with a person who has a voice that can be heard a long way off. Mr. Whitfield, the celebrated English preacher, had such a voice. When he was in Philadelphia, he preached from a high platform, at the foot of Market street, and, it is said, that while speaking there, the sound of his voice could be heard over in Camden, clear across the river Delaware, and more than a mile away from where he stood. But, when we speak by our actions, we speak louder than we ever can do by our words. There is Abel, speaking by the action he performed when he offered the sacrifice, which God had commanded, It was far away in the heart of Asia, that he spoke by that act; and yet, we hear about it over in this western country. It is nearly six thousand years ago, that Abel spoke by that act, and still, "by it, he being dead, *yet speaketh*." He spoke so loudly by that act, that, all round the world, wherever the Bible has gone, the voice of what he did has been heard. And, if we wish to speak so loudly, that we may be heard for a long time, and to a great distance, we must speak by our actions, by doing what God tells us to do.

Here are some examples of the way in which actions speak.

The Influence of Example. A gentleman met a friend, one Saturday, and invited him to dine with him the next day. "I should be very glad to do so," was the reply, "but to-morrow is the Sabbath, and I never dine out on that day."

Some years afterwards, this same gentleman was traveling in a stage-coach. Directly opposite to him sat a person very attentively reading a book, which he saw was the Bible. When he looked up from his book, they recognized each other, though they had not met before, for a long time. Holding up the Bible he said, "I didn't think much of this blessed book once; but I have to thank you for leading me to examine it, and find out what a treasure it is."

"Indeed?" said the other; "but I don't remember ever doing that."

"Perhaps not," was the answer; "but I once asked you to dine with me on the Sabbath. You declined very kindly, and said you never dined out on the Sabbath. I was angry with you, and thought you were a fool. But your conduct led me to read the Bible. I had not been reading it long before I found out that *I* was the fool, for breaking God's commands. I saw that I was a sinner, and never rested till I found the Saviour, and became a Christian."

That was a little act, but it spoke loudly to that careless man, and proved a blessing to him forever.

A Good Deed Rewarded. Not long ago there was a review of Austrian cavalry, before the Emperor and Empress, in one of the public squares in Vienna. Just as one of the squadrons swept out from the main body of thirty thousand horsemen, a little girl, only four years old, dashed from her mother's side, before the crowd, and ran out on the open field, just in front of the soldiers. The squadron was at full gallop. It was so close that to stop was impossible. It seemed as if the child must be crushed to death. A thrill of horror ran through the crowd, who saw the danger, but were unable to prevent it. The Empress saw it all from her carriage, and uttered a cry of terror, at the thought of the little one, about to be trampled to death. But, at the very moment that the squadron reached the child, a brave soldier, swung himself down from the saddle, holding on by the horse's mane, and catching the child as he swept on, lifted it, with himself, safely into the saddle, without slackening his speed, or losing his place in the ranks. *The child was saved.* Ten thousand voices raised a shout of joy. The Empress, and the child's mother, wept tears of grateful thanks. The Emperor summoned the noble soldier into his presence, and taking from his own breast, a richly ornamented diamond cross, hung it round the brave fellow's neck, and thanked him, before the crowd, for what he had done.

That was a little act. It was done in a moment. But it speaks in a voice loud enough to be heard to the ends of the earth.

A Duke Taught by the Act of a Boy. The Duke of St. Albans had long held an office, under the government of England, which was called a sinecure. This means an office in which he had nothing to do, but for which he yet received a salary. He was led to give up this office by the honest act of a little farmer boy, who worked for him. The Duke was a great breeder of geese. He had a number of men and boys, whose duty it was to take care of these geese. On one occasion, the Duke was present, at the close of the week, when these persons were to receive their wages. Among the rest was a little boy, about ten years old. He had the charge of a flock of geese, and his wages, for taking care of them, were eighteen pence a week. But, when called up on this occasion, he refused to take his wages.

When asked why he would not take them, he said: "Why ye see on Monday morning all the geese flied away; and how can I take money for looking arter birds when there was no birds to look arter?"

This was a little act, but it spoke so loudly to the

Duke, that it made him feel that it was a wrong for him to take money, for work, which he did not have to do; and so he resigned his office.

A Sailor's Act, and How Loudly it Spoke. A good many years ago an English man-of-war called the "Melville Castle" was commanded by a captain, whose name was James A. Haldane. On one occasion this vessel was fighting with a French frigate. In the course of the battle, the French vessel poured a broadside into the "Melville Castle," which swept away all the men from the guns. The captain ordered a fresh supply of men from below. As the men came on deck, and saw the mangled limbs, and bleeding bodies of their comrades, they shrank back for a moment, as if frightened. This made the captain very angry. He swore terrible oaths at them, and wished them all in the bad place.

The brave English tars sprang to their guns, and soon gained the victory over their enemy. When the fight was over, one of the sailors, who was a pious man, and had been greatly shocked at the captain's oaths, went up to him, and taking off his cap, and making a bow, said very respectfully: "Please, sir, if God had heard your prayer a little while ago, where should we all be now?"

That was a little act, and a simple question connected with it. But it spoke in tones louder than thunder, to Captain Haldane. It roused his conscience. It led him to repentance. He became a Christian. He resigned his office in the navy, and became a minister, and, for more than fifty years, he was an earnest, faithful, and successful preacher of the gospel. Abel was a model speaker because his life, and action made him a loud speaker.

And then again Abel was a model speaker, because, the action, by which he spoke, made him—AN EFFECTUAL *speaker*.

The action of Abel, in offering his sacrifice, spoke very effectually to the apostle Paul. We see this clearly enough, from what he says about it in connection with the words of our text. This was one thing that made him so earnest, in going all over the world, to preach the gospel. And, it was because he felt, so deeply, the importance of what Abel taught, when he offered his sacrifice, that he was determined not to "know anything among men, save Jesus Christ, and him crucified." And nothing that Abel could have said, by words, about the sacrifice of Christ, would have had so much effect, in making people feel the importance of that sacrifice, as his quiet action, in standing by his altar, and presenting on it, the sacrifice which God had commanded to be offered. And, if we wish to speak effectually to those about us, we must speak by our actions. It is true, as a good minister in England once said, that—"we can do more good by *being* good, than in any other way."

How Actions Speak. The president of one of the principal banks, in the city of Philadelphia, once asked a young man, who was one of his clerks, to come, and write letters for him, all day on Sunday.

The young man said he would gladly sit up all night, and do anything else in his power, to oblige him; but to work on Sunday was what he could not do, without breaking God's law, and therefore he begged to be excused from doing this.

The president was angry with the young man, and dismissed him from the bank. With an aged mother, depending on him for support, he was thus thrown out of employment, rather than do what he felt was wrong. A few days after this, that president was asked to recommend an honest, and reliable man to be the cashier in another bank. He recommended this very young man. He mentioned this incident, in proof of his faithfulness. "*I know you can trust him*," he added: "*for he gave up his situation rather than work for me on Sunday*, because he thought it was wrong."

No words, which that young man could have spoken, would have had such an effect on the president, as this action, in showing his regard for God's law.

How Example Speaks. A good clergyman, in England, had a careless, idle son. He left his father's house, shipped on board a vessel, and sailed on a long voyage through the Pacific Ocean. His distressed parents grieved over him, and followed him with their prayers, and with good counsels in their letters.

The ship, on which their boy was sailing, anchored, in the course of her voyage, in the harbor of one of the beautiful islands of the Pacific. They lay there, for some days, taking in cargo. In coming back from the island, one day, the sailors brought on board the ship, a little native boy, who could play some curious kinds of music. He amused them very much, for a long time. At last he asked them to please take him ashore again. The sailors said he must not go yet.

"Oh! indeed I cannot stay any longer," said he, "and I'll tell you why. A good Christian missionary has come to the village where I live. From him I have learned all I know about Jesus Christ, in whom I wish now to believe. This is the hour when he meets us, under the shade of a tree, to tell us more about Jesus; and I want to go and hear him."

The sailors were quite touched with the earnestness of the boy, and at once rowed him ashore. But that thoughtless son, of the good minister, was particularly struck, by the conduct of this heathen boy. He could not get over it. It had a voice to him, that was more effectual, than any words he had ever listened to. "Here am I," he said to himself, "the son of a minister in England, knowing far more about Jesus Christ than this poor boy, and yet caring less about him! This little fellow is now earnestly listening to the Word of Life, while I am quite neglecting it."

He went to his hammock that night, in great distress of mind. He wept bitter tears over his sins, and prayed to be forgiven. His prayer was heard, and answered. He soon became a Christian, and great was the joy in his English home, when the good news reached there, that their son who had been dead was alive again, and he who had been lost was found. How effectually that little South Sea islander spoke, to this minister's son, by his earnest conduct, in not letting anything keep him away from the meeting, where the gospel was to be preached! We speak effectually, when we speak by our actions.

The Effect of a Boy's Conduct. An orphan boy, about twelve years old, was shipped as a cabin boy, on board a vessel sailing from Liverpool. It was in the winter time, when this took place. On board of this vessel the old custom prevailed of giving out grog to the sailors. Then the men would get together, and have what they called "a jolly time," over their liquor. On one of those occasions, Jimmy, the cabin boy, was sent forward to the forecastle, on an errand. The men invited him to drink with them, but he declined. Then they began to laugh, and shout, and swear at him. They made so much noise that the captain, who was a drinking man himself, went forward to see what was the matter. When he found out how things stood, he said: "Youngster, you must obey orders on board this ship. Take some of that grog."

"Please excuse me, sir, but I can't drink liquor."

"Jack," said the captain, "take hold of that rope's end, and lay it on this obstinate chap, as hard as you can. I'll teach him that a sailor must learn to obey."

Jack did as the captain told him. The little fellow bore it like a hero. When the flogging was over, the captain pointed again to the liquor, and said, "Now, drink that."

"Please excuse me, sir, but I can't drink liquor," said Jimmy. This made the captain very angry: "Well, now," said he, "go up to the foretop, and stay there all night, without any supper. No one can disobey my orders on board this ship."

Jimmy paused a moment, at the foot of the rigging. It looked dark, and dangerous up there, and he was not used to climbing. But up he went with a brave heart.

When the captain was gone below, the first mate, who was fond of Jimmy, and was afraid he would perish from cold and hunger, took him up a blanket, and some biscuits, and spoke a few kind words to him.

Early next morning the captain came on deck. He went forward, and sung out, "Halloo! there, young chap, come down this minute."

But no one stirred, or answered. A sailor was sent up. He found the poor boy so overcome with cold, that he could neither stir, nor speak. He lifted him up in his arms, and took him down on deck. Then he was carried into the cabin, and laid down by the stove, that its warmth might bring him to. In the meantime the captain poured out a glass of wine, and set it down on the table. As soon as Jimmy was able to stand up, the captain pointed to the glass of wine and said:

"Now, sir, drink that down this moment."

"Please sir," exclaimed the boy, "I'd rather die than drink it. Oh, don't be angry with me sir, and I'll tell you why I can't do it. I was the only child of my parents. We used to live in a nice little cottage, and were very happy together. But, my father took to drinking, and soon everything changed. The furniture was sold for drink. The cottage was given up, and we had to live in a garret. My father died in a drunken spree. This broke my mother's heart. Before she died she called me to her bedside, and said to me:

"'Jimmy, my boy, you know what drink has done for your poor father, and for me. Now, I want you, before I die, as you hope to meet me in heaven, to promise me solemnly, here, before God, that, as long as you live, you will never learn to drink intoxicating liquors.'

"Then I lifted up my hand to God, and solemnly promised never to do it. And now, sir, would you have me break the promise that I made to my poor dying mother?"

This was too much for the captain. He wept like a child, and taking the boy up in his arms, said: "No, no, my little hero. Keep your promise, and God bless you in doing so. And if any body ever says a word to you, about drinking, on board this ship, let me know, and they won't do it the second time."

That brave boy was speaking effectually by his conduct, in carrying out the promise he had made to his dying mother.

And this was the way in which Abel spoke when he offered up his sacrifice. He was a model speaker in *the matter* of his speaking; and in *the manner* of it. The matter of his speaking was the sacrifice of Christ; the only thing that can make us *good*, and *happy*, and *safe*. In the manner of his speaking he was *a plain* speaker, *a loud* speaker, and *an effectual* speaker.

Let us all follow the example of Abel. Let us learn to love and serve the blessed Saviour. Then we shall be model speakers too. By our lives and actions we shall be speaking for Jesus. This will make us, like Abel, to be *plain* speakers—*loud* speakers—*effectual* speakers.

ENOCH, THE MODEL WALKER.

"And Enoch walked with God."—GENESIS V : 22.

THIS is a short account to give of a life that was three hundred years long; but it is a very satisfactory account.

We hear a great deal, in these days, about walking, and walkers. Men, and women too, spend days, and weeks, in walking matches. A sum of money is offered as a prize, and the one who proves the best walker gets the prize. I have no wish to join company with these walkers. But here, in our text, we have a grand old walker spoken of. I should like to join company with him; yes, and I should like all my young friends to unite with me, in trying to take the walk which Enoch took.

Enoch comes next, in our course of "Bible Models." He stands before us as "The Model Walker." What we are told about him is that—"Enoch walked with God." And the question we have to try and answer is this:—*what sort of a walk is a walk with God?*

And in answering this question there are *four* things, about this walk, of which we wish to speak.

In the first place, if we walk with God, we shall find that we have—A SAFE—*walk.*

There are many places, in which people walk, that are very dangerous; but if we are walking with God, as Enoch was, He will guard us from danger, and make the path in which we are walking—safe. Look, for a moment, at some of the things told us in the Bible, to show how safe we are, when we are walking with God.

There was a time, in the life of the patriarch Abraham, when he thought himself in great danger. And no doubt this was true. He had done something which gave great offence to several very powerful kings, who lived near him. He had every reason to expect that they would raise a mighty army, and come against him, to destroy him. God knew just how Abraham was feeling, and He gave him this sweet promise for his comfort;—

"Fear not Abram, I am thy shield." Gen. xv: 1. This must have been very cheering to Abraham. It was just what he needed. It was enough to take away all his fears.

Before gun powder, and cannons were invented, shields were important, for those who engaged in warfare. A shield was a good protection, from the stroke of a sword, or from the wound that an arrow would give. With a shield on his left arm, and a sword in his right hand, the soldier was ready for battle. But, even while holding his shield before him, he was not always safe. Over the top of his shield, or under the bottom of it, an arrow might reach him. Or it might strike him in the back, which the shield did not cover.

But, when we have God for our shield, we are perfectly safe. He will cover head, and feet, and face, and back, all at the same time.

But sometimes an arrow would be sent with such force, as to go right through the shield, and wound severely the soldier behind it. This, however, can never happen, when God is our shield. He is a shield that never can be penetrated.

Satan, our great enemy, tried this in the case of Job. He wanted to injure him in some way. But he could not do it. He found that God was such a shield to Job, that he could not get *over* it; nor *under* it; nor *through* it. Satan compared God's protection of Job to a hedge. He said God had put a hedge about Job, and about his house, and about everything he had. There are many hedges which it is very easy to jump over, or to push through. But, when God makes a hedge about those who walk with Him, it is so high, that no one can get over it, and so thick that no one can get through it. We are perfectly safe behind this hedge. No one can touch us here, unless God shall give permission, as He did in Job's case, when He allowed Satan to bring troubles on Job, which were wisely overruled for good.

In another place we find it said, of those who walk with God—that—"The eternal God is thy refuge, and underneath are the everlasting arms." Deut. xxxiii: 27. How safe they are who have the eternal God for their refuge!

In several sweet passages of Scripture God says He will uphold his people, and save them by his right hand. And in one place He promises to keep them "as the apple of his eye." No part of the body is so carefully protected as the eye. And this gives us a good illustration of the safety of those who walk with God.

A Safe Walk. During a sudden freshet, a laboring man and his child, living in a cottage that stood by itself, were obliged to walk at midnight, for more than a mile through water reaching to the little boy's waist, before they could reach a place of safety.

After they had changed their clothes, and were feeling comfortable, the friend, in whose cottage they had found shelter, said to the little boy: "And wasn't you afraid Jack, while walking through the water?"

"No, not at all," said the little fellow, who was but seven years old: "I was walking along with father, you know. And I knew he wouldn't let the water drown me." This was very sweet. And, if, like Enoch, we are walking with God, let us remember that we are walking with our heavenly Father. And He promises us expressly, "When thou passest through the waters, they shall not overflow thee." Isaiah xliii: 2.

Here is a good illustration of the safety of those who are walking with God.

Hidden and Safe. One morning a teacher found many empty seats, in her school-room. Two little scholars lay dead at their homes, and others were sick. The few children present gathered around her, and said, "Oh! what shall we do?" Do you think we shall be sick, and die too?"

The teacher gently touched the bell, and said, "Children, you are all afraid of this disease. You grieve for the death of your little friends, and you fear that you also may be taken. I only know of one thing for us to do, and that is to hide. Listen while I read to you about a hiding place. Then she read the 91st Psalm; which begins thus: "He that dwelleth in the secret place of the Most High, shall abide under the shadow of the Almighty." They were all hushed by the sweet words, and then the morning lesson went on as usual.

At recess, a dear little girl came up to the desk, and said, "Teacher aren't you afraid of the diptheria?"

"No, my child," she answered.

"Well, wouldn't you be, if you thought you would be sick, and die?"

"No, dear, I trust not."

The child gazed wonderingly at her for a moment; and then, her face lightened up as she said, "Oh! I know! You are hidden under God's wings. What a nice safe place that is to hide in!"

Walking with God is a *safe* walk. *But in the second place,—walking with God is*—A USEFUL—*walk.*

Suppose that you and I were taking a walk through the wards of a hospital. It is full of people, who are suffering from accidents, and diseases of different kinds. There are some people there with broken limbs. Some are blind,—others are deaf; and some are sick with various fevers, and consumption. And suppose, that like our blessed Lord, we had the power, as we went from one bed to another, to heal the sick, and suffering people, in that hospital. Here is a lame man. We make his limbs straight, and strong so that he can walk. Here is a blind man. We touch his eyes with our fingers; they open, and he can see. We speak to those who are suffering from diseases of different kinds, and make them well. Then we might well say, that our walk through that hospital was a useful walk.

But, we have no such power as this, to cure the diseases from which the bodies of men are suffering. Yet this may afford us a good illustration of what we can do for the souls that are suffering around us, when we become Christians, and walk with God. This world is like a hospital. It is full of souls suffering, in various ways, from the evils which sin has brought upon them. The truth of the gospel is God's great cure for all these evils. David teaches us this when he says that—"He sent his *word* and *healed* them." Ps. 107 : 20. And Jesus was referring to this when he said: "As Moses lifted up the serpent in the wilderness, even so must the Son of Man be lifted up, that whosoever believeth in Him should not perish, but have everlasting life." John iii : 14, 15. Moses never did a more useful thing, in all his life, that when he lifted up that serpent of brass, upon the pole, so that all the people, who had been bitten by those fiery serpents, and who were suffering, and dying from the bite, might look to that up-lifted serpent, and live. And when we walk with God, as his loving children, and servants, by our words, as well by our actions, we are helping to "lift up the Son of Man," or to make Jesus known to those around us. This is the only thing that can heal the souls that have been bitten by the serpent sin, and make them well and happy. And if we can do anything like this, by walking with God, it must make that a very useful walk. Let us look at some of the ways in which this may be done.

Bless and Curse Not. A little girl about seven years old was trying to be a Christian, and walk with God. She used to commit a verse of Scripture to memory every morning, and come and repeat it to her mother, before she went to school. Her father was a very wicked man. One morning he was swearing dreadfully, at his wife, when little Sallie came in, and said—"Mamma, I know my text. Please let me say it, and go to school."

"What is the text, my dear?" said the mother, wishing to keep the child from hearing the terrible oaths from her father.

"Bless, and curse not," were the words of the text. As she spoke them, she put up her little rosy lips to her father for a kiss.

The tears came into his eyes, as the little darling turned away from him. But he could not forget the words he had heard. Wherever he went,—"Bless and curse not," rang in his ears. He became a changed man. Words of cursing were no longer heard from his lips. That little girl was trying to walk with God, and we see how useful her walk was.

A Little Act Useful. Not long ago, a Christian gentleman, who was trying to do good wherever he went, stepped into a passenger car in the city of New York. Before taking his seat, he gave to each passenger, a little illuminated card, on which were printed these words,—"Look to Jesus when tempted—when troubled—when dying."

One of the passengers carefully read the card, and then put it in his pocket. As he left the car he said to the gentleman who had distributed the cards: "Sir, when you gave me this card I was on my way to the ferry, intending to jump from the boat, and drown myself. The death of my wife and son had robbed me of all desire to live. But this card has led me to change my mind. I am going to begin, and try to lead a better life. Good day, and may God bless you." This is a real fact. It happened on board one of the Fulton Ferry cars, in March, 1878.

The gentleman who gave those cards was making his walk with God a useful walk.

The Good Done by Shaking a Finger. I knew a good Christian gentleman, some years ago, who taught a young men's Bible class in Philadelphia. One day, as he was going along, near the corner of Third and Dock street, he saw one of the members of his class, —a young man named George Dawson,—coming out of a drinking saloon. He raised his finger, and shaking it gently at him, said in a kind and loving way,— "Take care, George! Take care!"

Not long after George left his home, and settled out in the West. Years passed away, and the teacher had forgotten all about him. One day, in walking down Chestnut street, a good looking gentleman came up, and taking him warmly by the hand, said: "How do you do, Mr. P.? Don't you remember one of your old class?"

"Indeed, sir, I can't remember you?"

"Don't you remember shaking your finger, at George Dawson, a member of your class, as you saw him, coming out of a drinking saloon, and saying—"Take care, George?"

"Oh! yes; I remember that."

"Well, sir, I am George. And thank you for that kind warning, and that friendly shake of the finger. I was just beginning to learn to drink. But, by God's blessing, that saved me. When I settled out West, I remembered your teaching in the class. That led me to become a Christian. Now I am a successful merchant, a member of church, and the superintendent of a Sabbath School. And, under God, I owe it all to you, sir."

Certainly that gentleman's walk with God, was a *useful* walk.

One other illustration of this point.

Some years ago, a gentleman from England, brought a letter of introduction, to a merchant in this country. The stranger was an intelligent man, with very pleasant manners, but he was an infidel. The gentleman to whom he brought the letter of introduction, and his wife, were earnest Christian people. They invited the stranger to make their house his home, during his stay, and treated him with the greatest possible kindness. On the evening of his arrival, before the hour of retiring, the gentleman of the house, knowing what the views of his guest were, on the subject of religion, told him they were in the habit of having family worship every evening; that they would be happy to have him join with them; or if he preferred he could retire to his room. He said it would give him pleasure to remain. Then a chapter of the Bible was read, and the family knelt in prayer, the stranger with them. After spending a few days, in that pleasant Christian home, the stranger embarked on board a ship, and sailed to a foreign land. In the course of three or four years he returned, and stayed with the same family. But what a change there was in him! His infidelity was all gone. He was now an humble, earnest Christian. In speaking to his friend of this change, he said: "Sir, I owe it all to you. When I knelt down with you, at family prayers, on my former visit, it was the first time, for years, that I had ever bowed my knees before God. It brought back to me the memory of my pious mother, now in heaven, and all the teaching she had given me, when a boy. I was so occupied with these thoughts, that I did not hear a word of your prayer. But this led me to give up my infidelity, and seek the blessing of my mother's God. And now, I am as happy as the day is long, in his service."

Here again we see how true it is, that walking with God is a *useful* walk.

In the third place walking with God is—A PLEASANT —*walk.*

When we are taking a walk, there are several things, that will help to make up the pleasure, to be found in that walk. If we have a guide to show us the road; if we have a pleasant companion, to talk with, as we go on our way; if we have plenty of refreshments,— nice things to eat and drink; if there are bright and cheerful prospects, around and before us; and especially, if we are sure of a nice comfortable home, to rest in, when our walk is ended, these will help to make it pleasant,

But when we walk with God, as Enoch did, we have all these things, and more too. And these are sure to make it a pleasant walk. Solomon is speaking of this walk when he says: "Its ways are ways of pleasantness and all its paths are peace." But if you wish to know all about the journey through some particular country, there is no better way of finding this out, than by asking those who have made the journey, what they have to say about it. And this is what we may do here. Let us see what some of those who have walked with God, have to say about the pleasantness of this walk.

Living Alone. "I visited a poor old woman belonging, to my congregation," said a minister. "She was entirely dependent on the church for her support. Her home was a very small cottage. The moment I entered it, I saw how neat and clean everything was. She had just been gathering some sticks, from the lane, with which to cook her evening meal. Her face was one of the sweetest, I ever saw. It was surrounded by the strings of her snow white cap. On the table lay a well-worn copy of the word of God. I looked around for a daughter, or friend, to be her companion, and care-taker; but saw none. I said: "Mother Ansel, you don't live here alone, do you?"

"Live alone! Live alone!" she exclaimed in surprise, and then, as a sweet smile lighted up her face, she added, "No, sir, the blessed Lord lives with me, and *that* makes it pleasant living!" Certainly she found walking with God a pleasant walk.

The Best Sunshine. A Christian lady was visiting among the poor one day. She called, among others, on a little sick girl. Her home was a dreary looking one. The room she occupied was on the north side of the house. There was nothing bright, or pleasant about it. Everything looked dark and cheerless.

"I am sorry you have no sun on this side of the house," said the lady. "Not a ray of sunshine gets in here. This is a misfortune, for sunshine is everything."

"Oh, ma'am, you are mistaken," said the sick girl, as a sweet smile lighted up her pale face. "My sun pours in at every window, and through all the cracks."

"But how can the sun get round on this side of the house?" asked the visitor.

"It is Jesus, 'the Sun of Righteousness' that shines in here," was the reply, "and *He makes the best sunshine.*"

That sick girl found walking with God a pleasant walk.

Strong Faith, or Light in Darkness. A young minister, in the South, tells this story, which beautifully illustrates the point now before us.

Among the negroes on one of the plantations, in my parish, was a woman whom we used to call Aunt Dossy. She was a good Christian, who walked with God, and had the most simple, child-like faith, that I ever met with in any one. She had a husband, and a family of six sons, of whom she was very proud. Several were old enough to help their father in the cotton field, and she was never tired of talking about her boys.

A fatal disease broke out among the negroes, and in one short week Aunt Dossy lost her husband, and all her six children. Her heart was bound up in her boys, and I expected that this heavy stroke would be too much for her. One day, not long after this, I thought I would walk around to her cabin, and try to comfort her.

I found her sitting on the door-step, holding in her hand something that had belonged to one of her boys. She gazed at it earnestly, swaying backwards and forwards, as she kept saying to herself, "Nebber mind, honey, de Lord'll make it all straight."

Wishing to try her faith I said, "Aunt Dossy are you *sure* of that?"

She looked up, with her poor old eyes full of tears, and said: "Yes, massa, just so suah as dat de dead are gone."

"What makes you so sure?" I asked.

"De good Lord himself says so in de book dey reads at meetin, ebery day."

"But how do you know the book is true?

This seemed to stagger her for a moment; but suddenly she exclaimed:—

"Don't de Lord tell it outside him book too? Don't de grass, de flowers, and de birds, and de bees talk it? And fardermore me feels it in *yar*"—smiting her breast. "Ah! massa, you's got heaps o' larnin; you knows heaps moren' poor old Dossy—but Dossy *knows* de Lord's on her side, and He's gwine to help her bear it. He ain't a gwine to leab her now, when de troubles come upon her."

Then she went on again talking to herself, as she

was doing before—"Neber mind, honey, de Lord'll make it all straight."

How beautiful this simple faith was in that poor afflicted widow! She was feeling the truth of what David meant, when he said:—

"Yea, though I walk through the valley of the shadow of death, I will fear no evil, for thou art with me." And if walking with God brings such help and comfort in trouble, as this old negro had, we may well say it is a pleasant walk.

And here let me quote some sweet lines called— "A Little Talk with Jesus," which show us how it is that walking with God is made so pleasant:

"A little talk with Jesus, how it smooths the rugged road:
How it seems to help me onward, when I sink beneath my load;
When my head is bowed with sorrow, and my eyes with tears are dim,
There's nought can yield me comfort like a little talk with Him.

"I tell Him I am weary, and fain would be at rest,
That I'm daily, hourly longing for a home upon His breast;
And He answers me so sweetly, in tones of tenderest love,
'I'm coming soon to take thee, to thy happy home above.'

"Ah! this is what I'm wanting, His loving face to see,
And (I'm not afraid to say it), I know He's wanting me;
He gave His life a ransom, to make me all His own,
And I can't forget His promise, to me His purchased one.

"I know the way is dreary, to yonder far off clime,
But a little talk with Jesus, will while away the time;
And yet the more I know Him, and all His grace explore,
It only sets me longing to know Him more and more.

"I cannot live without Him, nor would I if I could;
He is my daily portion, my medicine and my food;
He's altogether lovely, none can with Him compare,
The chief among ten thousand, the fairest of the fair.

"So I'll wait a little longer, till His appointed time,
And glory in the knowledge, that such a hope is mine;
Then in my Father's dwelling, where 'many mansions be,'
I'll sweetly talk with Jesus, and He will talk with me."

Walking with God is a pleasant walk.

But in the fourth place, walking with God is—A PROFITABLE—*walk.*

We see a good deal of walking done without much profit. But sometimes we hear of people who are able to make their walking pay. There was a walking match in New York not long ago. A number of persons were engaged in it, and the man who won the prize secured twenty-five thousand dollars. That was profitable walking, so far as money was concerned, but, walking with God, is more profitable than this.

Suppose there was a Savings Bank, half a mile from your house, and you are told that if you walked to that bank every week, and put a penny in the treasury; for every penny you put in, you would get a dollar, at the end of the year. A penny a week would make fifty-two pennies by the end of the year, and if for these fifty-two pennies you were to receive fifty-two dollars, that would make your walk to the bank profitable walking. It would be getting what we call a hundred-fold for the money invested there.

There is no such Savings Bank as this. But, when we learn to walk with God, we find that serving Him, is just like putting money in such a bank. Jesus says that if we give a cup of cold water to one of His disciples; or if we suffer for Him, or do any work for Him; we "shall receive a manifold more, in this present time, and in the world to come, life everlasting."

And if such rewards are given, to those who walk with Him, then, we may well say, that *that* is profitable walking.

Here are some examples, of the profit found in walking with God.

Two Strings. An infidel was one day laughing, at a plain farmer, because he believed the Bible. The farmer surprised him by saying, "Well, you see we plain country people, like to have two strings to our bow."

"And pray what do you mean by that?" asked the infidel.

"Only this," was the farmer's answer, "that believing the Bible, and acting up to it, is like having two strings to one's bow; for, if the Bible is not true, still, I shall be a better and happier man, for living according to its teachings, and so it will be profitable for me in this life; this is one string to my bow, and a good one too. And, if the Bible *should* prove true, as *I know it will*, it will be profitable for me, in the next world, and that is another string, and a pretty strong one too. But, sir, if you do not believe the Bible, and do not live as it requires, you have no string to your bow in this world. And, oh! sir, if the tremendous threatenings of the Bible prove true, *as they surely will*,—you will have no string to your bow, for the next world, and what will become of you then?"

This shows us that walking with God, is profitable walking.

Please Help Me. Little Johnny was only four years old, but he was trying to be a Christian, and walk with God, and he found profit in it. One day he was busy in the sunny corner of the nursery, trying to build up a castle, with his blocks. Just as the last block was being put to the tower, to finish it, it all came tumbling down, with a crash. Johnny gazed a moment at the ruins, with a look of disappointment, and then folding his little hands, devoutly said, "Dear Lord, please help me." Then he went to building his castle again. But as he was finishing it, down it tumbled, the second time. Hot tears came into Johnny's eyes; but quickly dashing them away with the back of his hand, he kneeled down, over the ruins of his fallen building, and lifting up his eyes to heaven quietly said, "Please, Lord, help me to build, so it won't tumble down; and please don't let me get mad, for Jesus' sake, Amen." Then he went to work again, and built his castle so that it didn't tumble down. That little Johnny is now a big "John." He is going through college, and he finds help now, just as he did then. He is walking in a way that helps him to conquer difficulties, and, above all, helps him to conquer himself, and this is a profitable way to walk in.

The Profit of Giving. Some years ago, a Christian gentleman, who was walking with God, and was very well off, made up his mind that he would give as much money as he could every year to the Bible Society. The first year he gave a hundred dollars. The year after, he gave a thousand dollars. He went on increasing his gift, every year, until it amounted to twenty thousand dollars a year. When some one asked him how he could afford to give so much, his answer was—"I am richer now, than when I first began to give. I don't know how it is, but I find that the more I give, the more I get."

This is just what the Bible teaches us, when it says: "Give, and it shall be given unto you." This shows us that walking with God is a profitable walk.

The Power of Example. In a town in Bavaria there was a little old-fashioned church. Among those who were in the habit of worshipping there, was a certain duke, living in the neighborhood. He was a good Christian man, who was humbly walking with God. On coming out of church, he was in the habit of talking, in a friendly way, with any of the peasants he might happen to meet with.

One day, he met an old man. They talked together, about different things. The duke felt interested in the old man, and before parting from him, asked if he could do anything for him.

"Noble sir," said the peasant, "you cannot do anything better for me than you have already done."

"How is that?" asked the duke. "I didn't know that I ever did anything for you."

"But I know it," said the old man, "and never can forget it, for you saved my son. He had got to be a very bad young fellow. For a long time he had given up reading his Bible, or going to church. Every day he was getting worse and worse. It almost broke my heart to think of him. One day, in passing by this dear old church, he saw you going in. He said to himself,—'I should like to see what the duke does there.' He went quietly in, and sat down to watch you. But when he saw you praying so earnestly, and devoutly, it made a deep impression on him. It led him to pray himself. He broke off from his evil ways; and now, he is the comfort and joy of my life. I thank you, sir, for this. And this is what I meant when I said you never can do me a greater favor than you have done for me already."

That good duke was walking with God, and when we think how much good he was doing, by the quiet influence of his example, we see what profit there is in this walk.

We Have God Too. Some time ago, a young minister took charge of a small church, in a country town, in the State of New York.

On going round, to visit the members of his congregation, he was asked to call and see an aged widow woman, who was a member of the church. She was both poor and blind. On stopping at the door of her humble cottage, one day, he heard some one speaking within, in a low voice. He found it was the voice of prayer. He waited till the prayer was ended. Then he went in, and made himself known to the blind widow. "How are you, my good friend?" was his first inquiry.

With tears of gratitude streaming from her blind eyes, she said, "Thank God I am very well."

After talking with her for sometime, he asked if there was anything he could do for her. She said if he could send her a loaf of bread, she would feel very much obliged to him, for she added, "we have not had a morsel of solid food in the house for three days."

"Why, my friend," asked the astonished minister, "how is it that you are alive?"

"God is very good to the poor," she said. "The woods are full of huckleberries, and my two little grandchildren gather them. Our cow gives us milk: so we have milk and huckleberries; and *we have God too.*"

This was beautiful. "We have God too!" No matter how little of this world's goods we have, if we can only say: "we have God too;" we are better off than if we had thousands of gold and silver without Him. This was what the good poet Cowper meant, when he looked up to God, and said:

"Give what Thou canst, without Thee, we are poor,
And *with Thee rich*, take what Thou wilt away."

When we are walking with God we can always say this; and it is this which makes such a walk profitable.

Enoch was a model walker, because he "walked with God." Let us all try to follow his example, and we shall find that walking with God, is a *safe* walk;—a *useful* walk;—a *pleasant* walk;—and a *profitable* walk.

NOAH, THE MODEL WORKER.

"Thus did Noah: according to all that God commanded him, so did he."—GENESIS vi: 22.

HEN a young man wants to be a painter, or a sculptor it is very important for him to have the opportunity of studying the best works of the most celebrated artists. And to do this, he will, if it be possible for him, go to Europe and finish his studies there. In London, in Paris, in Florence, in Rome, and other famous cities, there are large galleries, filled with the finest paintings, and pieces of statuary. These are the works of what are called "the old masters." The young artist must study these very carefully, if he wants to be successful as a painter, or a sculptor. He will take these as his models, and try to imitate them.

But God is the greatest, and best of all artists. None can make such splendid pictures, or such forms of beauty as He makes. And the Bible may well be called God's picture gallery. It is filled with the best models, of good characters, that can be found anywhere. In this course of sermons on "Bible Models," we are, as it were, taking a walk through this gallery. We are taking up, one after another, the different examples of piety, and goodness, that are found here. We are setting them before us, that we may carefully study them, and then try to imitate them.

In our present sermon we take up the character of Noah. We may consider him as—"The Model Worker." In our text, what we read of him is thus expressed: "Thus did Noah: according to all that God commanded him, so did he." And in setting his example before us, as a model worker, we may notice *five* things about his way of working, in which we may well try to imitate him.

In the first place Noah was—A READY—*worker*. And in this respect he is a good model to set before us.

It was a very hard thing that Noah was commanded to do. He was told to build an ark, or a ship, that was very remarkable for its size. Nothing like it had ever been heard of before. Its length was to be four hundred and fifty feet; its breadth seventy-five feet, and its height forty-five feet. This was much larger than any of our ordinary ships of war.

But Noah was not a ship-builder himself, neither were his sons. He did not live in a sea-port town, where the people were familiar with the business of building ships. He lived in an inland country, far away from the sea. We do not know that he, or any one else then living in the world, had ever seen a large ship. No doubt they had canoes, and other

NOAH BUILDS THE ARK.

small boats for crossing the rivers. But we have no reason to suppose that any vessels larger than these had ever been built. And this must have made the work that Noah was told to do, very hard indeed. How easy it would have been for him to make excuses when God commanded him to build that huge ark! He might have said, very truthfully: "I do not know anything about the work of building ships. I have no ship carpenters to help me, and know not where to get any."

And if, for reasons like these, he had begged to be excused, from undertaking a work of so much difficulty, it would not have been at all surprising. But Noah did nothing of the kind. He did not make the slightest objection. Instead of this he went out to work at once. No doubt he asked God to help him. And when we get such help as He can give, nothing can be too hard for us. The apostle believed this fully, when he said: "I can do *all things* through Christ which strengtheneth me." And when we remember how readily Noah went to work, to do the hard thing that God had commanded him to do, we may well speak of him as a model worker.

He is a model, worthy of our imitation, because he was—A READY—*worker*.

And it is always pleasant to see those who follow Noah's example, and do the work they have to do in the same ready way. Here is a good illustration of what I mean.

A Sensible Boy. George Harris was a bright, intelligent boy, about thirteen years of age. One day he was sitting on the porch, in front of his house, reading one of those yellow-covered novels, that do so much harm to all who read them. His father came up at that moment, and was sorry to see how George was occupied.

"What are you reading, George?" he asked.

The little fellow felt ashamed, as he looked up; but he gave the name of the book. "I am sorry to see you reading such a book," said Mr. Harris. "I have known many persons injured by reading books of that kind; but I never knew any one benefitted by them."

This was all he said; and then he went into the house. Not long after he saw a light in the next room to that in which he was sitting.

Going to the door of the room he saw George tearing up, and burning a book.

"What are you doing, my son?" he asked.

"I am burning up the book you told me not to read."

"And what are you doing that for?"

"Because I am sure you know better than I do, about it."

George was following the example of Noah, as a ready worker.

Here are some simple lines, which come in very nicely, to wind up this point of our subject. They are headed—*Just Obey*.

> "Do as you are told to do
> By those wiser far than you;
> Do not say,
> 'What the use of this may be
> I am sure I cannot see:'
> Just obey!

> "Do not sulk, and do not sigh,
> Though it seem in vain to try;
> Work away!
> All the ends you cannot see:
> Do your duty faithfully—
> Just obey!
>
> "When at length you come to know
> Why 'twas ordered thus and so,
> You will say,
> 'Glad am I that when to me
> All was dark as dark could be,
> I could trust, and cheerfully,'
> Just obey."

Noah was a model worker because he was a *ready* worker.

*But, in the second place, Noah was a model worker, because he was—*A PERSEVERING—*worker.*

If we have anything hard to do, or anything that will take a long time in which to do it, we never can succeed in doing it without perseverance. The meaning of this word, perseverance, is to keep on trying with a thing until we get through. And no one ever had so much need of perseverance as Noah had, in the work he was told to do. From the day when God first spoke to him, about building the ark, until it was finished,—one hundred and twenty years passed away. All that time he was engaged in the work. And he knew, at the beginning, how long it would take him.

We often begin to do things without knowing at all how long it will take us to get through with them. But God told Noah distinctly how long it would be, from the time when he began to build the ark, until the flood should come, which was to destroy the earth.

We see this in Genesis vi : 3, when it says—man's "days shall be an hundred and twenty years."

How strangely Noah must have felt when he laid the first piece of timber in the keel of the ark, and knew how many years were to pass away before that great vessel would be completed!

We read of men who have become famous, by the discoveries, or inventions they have made, such as the art of printing, the use of steam-engines, and other things. Some of these men were working away for seven, or ten, or fifteen, or twenty years, before they finished their work. And when we read about the difficulties they had to overcome, before they succeeded in what they were trying to do, and how they persevered in overcoming these difficulties, we cannot but wonder at them. And yet, how short the time was in which they did their work, compared with the hundred and twenty years, through which Noah had to go on laboring! His perseverance was the most wonderful ever heard of in the history of our world.

How much trouble he must have had, in getting the right kind of wood, with which to build the ark! And when the wood was found, how much trouble he must have had in getting the right sort of workmen, to carry on the building! And how many other difficulties he must have had, of which no account is given! But, notwithstanding all these difficulties, he went patiently on, for a hundred and twenty years, till his work was done. How well we may speak of Noah as a model of perseverance!

Let us study this model, till we learn to persevere,

NOAH, THE MODEL WORKER. 53

in all the work we try to do, for God, or for our fellow men.

Here are some other illustrations of perseverance, that may help us in trying to learn this lesson.

The Shovel and the Snow-Drift. After a great snow-storm, a little fellow, about seven or eight years old, was trying to make a path through a large snow-bank, which had drifted before his grandmother's door. A gentleman, who was passing by, was struck with the earnestness with which he was doing his work. He stopped to look at him for a moment, and then said:

"My little man, how do you ever expect to get through that great snow-bank?"

In a cheerful tone, and without stopping at all in his work, the little fellow's reply was:

"*By keeping at it*, sir. That's how."

"By keeping at it," Noah was able to get through with the great work he had to do. And it is only— "By keeping at it," that we can expect to succeed in any good work in which we may be engaged.

Here is a story of a soldier's perseverance, and of the good that came from it. We may call it— *Perseverance in Prayer*.

A soldier, who was led to become a Christian, by what he saw of the example of a fellow soldier, gives his account of it thus:

"A new man had joined our company. He was to occupy one of the cots, in the same room with me in the barracks. The first night he was there, before going to bed, he kneeled down by his bedside to pray. And such a scene as then took place! While he was on his knees, some of the men threw their belts at him; some laughed, some whistled, some swore. One man leaped over a bed, and came and shouted in his ears; but still the new comer went on till he was through with his prayers. On the second night all the men were on the look out, to see whether he would kneel down again. But he did kneel, as on the previous night. The moment he did this, the noise and confusion were worse than before. The men shouted, and screamed, and made the most horrible noises. But the man of persevering piety went on with his prayers. On the third night when he began to pray there was less noise than on the second night. On the fourth and fifth nights, as he persevered in his prayers, the noise grew less and less. On the sixth night as soon as he had kneeled down, one of the men, who had been the most active in the disturbance, cried out to his companions: 'I say, boys, he's genuine; he stands fire. We'll let him alone.'

"After that he had no more trouble. The men respected him; and some of them, who never had courage to do so before, followed his example and kneeled down to say their prayers."

Stroke on Stroke. James Barker was a farmer's boy about twelve years old. One day his father gave him an axe, and told him to cut down an old tree, which stood in front of their house. He went to work on the tree, but his blows made little impression on it. By and by he got discouraged, and sat down on a log to rest. "It's no use," said he in a doleful sort of way.

"What's no use?" asked an old wood-chopper, who was just then passing by.

"Why for me to try to cut down this tree."

"Nonsense! my boy, you can do it. Just keep at it. Stroke on stroke will cut down the biggest tree that ever grew. Don't expect to cut it down with one blow. Remember stroke on stroke."

This is an important lesson to learn. It was by "stroke on stroke" that Noah built the ark. With God's blessing we shall always succeed by "stroke on stroke."

LITTLE BY LITTLE.

> "Little by little the time goes by—
> Short if you sing through it, long if you sigh;
> Little by little—an hour, a day,
> Gone with the years that have vanished away;
> Little by little the race is run,
> Trouble, and waiting, and toil are done!
>
> "Little by little the skies grow clear;
> Little by little the sun comes near;
> Little by little the days smile out,
> Gladder and brighter with pain and doubt;
> Little by little the seed we sow
> Into a plentiful harvest will grow."

Noah was a model worker because he was a *persevering* worker.

But, in the third place, Noah was a model worker, because he was—A THOROUGH—*worker*.

We see this in our text, when it tells us—"Thus did Noah; according *to* ALL that God commanded him, so did he."

Some people are willing to obey God just so long as He tells them to do what they like to do. But if He commands them to do anything that is disagreeable, they are not willing to obey Him. But this was not the way in which Noah obeyed God. We cannot doubt, for a moment, but that in the great work of building the ark, there were many things he had to do, which were very disagreeable to him. But this made no difference with Noah. The question with him was not, is this, or that, or the other thing, which I am doing, pleasant to me? is it what I like to do? No; but it was—is this what God has told me to do? If it was—he did it. "*All* that God commanded him he did."

And it is very important for us to follow the example of Noah in this respect, because this is the only kind of service that God will accept. It was what David taught us when he said, "Then shall I not be ashamed, when I have respect unto *all* thy commandments." And this was what Jesus taught us when he said: "Ye are my friends if ye do *whatsoever* I command you."

And it is always pleasant to meet with persons who are trying to serve God as thoroughly as Noah did.

Whole-Hearted Christians. A religious meeting was once held among some working-men. One after another of them rose up to speak of their experience on the subject of religion. This was the way in which one of them spoke about himself: "I used to be an odd-job Christian; but now, thank God, I'm working on full time."

This was very expressive. There are a great many "odd-job Christians." They work for Jesus just when it suits them. For the rest of their time they are pleasing themselves. But Noah was not one of this kind. He was on full time. He was a *thorough* worker. He was always trying to do everything that God commanded him to do.

The Faithful Fisherman. There is a fishing village on the coast of Cornwall, in England, where the people are poor, but pious and intelligent. One year they were very much tried. The winds were contrary for nearly a month together, so that the men had not been able to go out fishing. At last, one Sunday morning, the wind changed, and came out fresh and fair. Some of the men whose faith was weak, and who had not learned to be thorough workers, went down to the beach, and were on the point of getting their boats ready to go a fishing, notwithstanding it was the Lord's day.

"I'm sorry it's Sunday"—said one of them—"*but—if* we were only not so poor."

There was one man among them who had learned, like Noah, to be a thorough worker for God. He spoke out thus:

"*But, if;* what do you mean by this, my friend? Surely you are not going to break God's law with your 'buts,' and 'ifs!'"

The people gathered round him, and he went on to say, "Mine's a religion for all weathers, fair wind or foul. 'Remember the Sabbath day to keep it holy.' That's the law, my friends. Who can afford to break it? True, we are poor; but what of that? Better to be poor and have God's blessing, than rich, and have His curse. Let those go a fishing to-day, who can afford to break God's law; but I never knew any good to come of a religion that changed with the wind."

No boat was launched that Sunday. The men all stayed at home, and went to church. And in the evening, just when they would have been coming home, a terrible storm arose which lasted all through the night. It was a storm which no fishing boat could have lived through; and then the men felt thankful that they had not broken God's law on that day. And they thanked their friend for his good advice which had kept them from doing so.

Obeying Orders. An English farmer was one day at work in the fields, when he saw a party of huntsmen riding about his farm. He had one field which he was especially anxious they should not ride over, as the horses' hoofs would greatly injure the crop. So he sent one of his boys, and told him to shut the gate, and keep watch there, and on no account to let any one go through it.

The boy went; and had scarcely taken his post there, before the huntsmen came up and ordered him to open the gate. He declined to do so; telling them what his orders were, and that he meant to obey them. They threatened him; but he did not mind their threats. They offered him money; but he refused to receive it. At last one of them came up to him, and said in commanding tones:

"My boy, you do not know me. But I am the Duke of Wellington. I am not accustomed to be disobeyed; and now, I command you to open that gate, that I and my friends may pass through."

The boy lifted his cap, and stood uncovered before

the man whom all England delighted to honor; and then answered firmly: "I am sure that the Duke of Wellington would not wish me to disobey orders. I must keep this gate shut; no one can pass through it, but by my master's express permission."

The brave old warrior was greatly pleased with this. Then he took off his own hat, and said, "I honor the man, or the boy, who can neither be bribed, nor frightened into disobeying his orders. With an army of such soldiers I could conquer not the French only, but the world." Then handing the boy a sovereign, he put spurs to his horse and galloped away.

The boy went back to his work, shouting out, as he did so, "Hurrah! hurrah! I've done what Napoleon couldn't do,—I've kept out the Duke of Wellington."

That boy was following the example of Noah, and was learning like him to be a thorough worker.

But, in the fourth place, Noah was a model worker, because he was—A COURAGEOUS—*worker.*

If we had a history of all that took place while Noah was building the ark, how interesting it would be! It was such a strange work that he was engaged in! Nothing like it had ever been heard of in that country. People would come from all quarters. They would look on in wonder. They would ask Noah why he was building such a great vessel as that, where there was no water within reach, for it to sail in? And when he told them, as no doubt he did, that God was going to send a flood of water to drown the world for its wickedness, and that when the flood came, he and his family would be saved in this ark that he was building, then, we can easily imagine how they would laugh at him. They would say he was crazy. They would call him an old fool, and make all sorts of fun of him. And this is something which it is always very hard to bear. Many men who have courage enough to go boldly into battle, and face the glittering swords, or roaring cannon of their enemies, have not courage enough to go on doing a thing when men laugh at them, and ridicule them for doing it. But Noah did not mind this at all. He let them laugh as much as they pleased, while he went quietly on, with the work that God had given him to do. And so we may well say that he was a courageous worker.

And we must imitate the example of Noah in this respect, if we wish to serve God acceptably. We must be brave enough to do what we know to be right, no matter what others may say or do. And it is always pleasant to see those who have courage to do what is right, as Noah did.

A Noble Boy. A poor boy who had a patch on his knee, was attending school. One of his schoolmates nicknamed him "Old Patch." "Why don't you fight him?" asked another of the boys. "I'd give it to him, if he called me such a name."

"Oh!" answered the boy, "you don't suppose I'm ashamed of my patch, do you? For my part I'm thankful for a good mother to keep me out of rags. I honor my patch for her sake." That was the right kind of courage.

A Real Hero. There was a little girl named Constance. Her father was dead, and her mother quite poor. Constance went to a school which was also attended by the children of several rich families in the neighborhood. These children used to make great fun about poor Constance, because she was not as finely dressed as they were.

One day they were going home from school. Constance was walking a little way before them. One of the girls pointed at her, and said, "See how many patches she has in her dress! One, two, three, four." Then the boys all laughed at her. Poor little Constance! She burst into tears, and tried to run home.

"Cry-baby! cry-baby," shouted the boys.

"I don't want her to sit by me," said Ella Gray. "What right has she to come to *our* school?" asked proud Lily Gross.

There was only one boy, in that school, who was brave enough to do what was right, under these circumstances. His name was Douglass Stewart. He felt sorry for poor Constance, and breaking away from the rude boys and girls, he ran up to her to try and comfort her.

"Never mind what they say. Let me carry your books. Cheer up! it's only a little way to your home, isn't it?"

Constance looked up through her tears to see the bravest boy in the school by her side.

"I live in the little house under the hill," said Constance. "It isn't like your grand house."

"No matter for that. It has pretty vines, and climbing roses, and it's a very nice house to live in," said Douglass, smiling. "I dare say you are very happy there."

"Yes, but I don't want come to their school any more," said Constance, softly.

"Oh, things will be all right in a day or two," said the boy, kindly. "Never mind them just now."

And it turned out as Douglass said. There was no one in the school who had more influence with the scholars than he had. And when they saw how bravely he took the part of poor Constance, they all felt ashamed of themselves; and after that no one in the school ever spoke an unkind word to her. This was truly noble in that boy. He was acting like a real hero.

Here are some simple lines with which we may close this part of our subject. They show us some of the different ways in which true courage will lead us to act.

> "Dare to think, though others frown,
>   Dare your words in thoughts express;
>   Dare to rise, though oft cast down;
>   Dare the wronged, and scorned to bless.
>
> "Dare from custom to depart;
>   Dare the priceless pearl possess;
>   Dare to wear it next your heart;
>   Dare, when others cease to bless,
>
> "Dare forsake what you deem wrong;
>   Dare to walk in wisdom's way;
>   Dare to give where gifts belong;
>   Dare God's precepts to obey.
>
> "Do what conscience says is right;
>   Do what reason says is best;
>   Do with all your mind and might;
>   Do your duty and be blest."

Noah was a model worker because he was a courageous worker.

And then in the last place, Noah was a model worker, because he was—A SUCCESSFUL—*worker*.

He labored on through all those long years until the ark was finished. And then, when the flood came, he was saved himself, and his family was saved, while all the rest of the world was swept away in its wickedness. And who can tell how much good Noah did by his successful work on the ark? That good has extended to all who have lived since then. You and I owe a debt of gratitude to Noah for his successful work. If it had not been for the way in which he did that work, we never should have lived in this world, and never have had the opportunity of doing any good here. And when we think of all the good that has been done in the world, we see that Noah has had a part in it; for unless he had worked as he did, till the ark was finished, none of this good could ever have been done. And this is a thought that may well encourage us in working for God. We never can tell how successful our work may be, and what great good may follow from it.

Praying over Lessons. "There," said a little boy, "I've learned my lessons sooner than ever I did before. I do believe it did me good to pray over my books."

He was asked what he meant by saying that. "Well, you see, when I came home from school, and looked over my lessons, they seemed very hard. At first I said to myself, 'I never can learn them in the little time I have to give to them.' But then, I remembered what my Sunday-school teacher had told me, about Daniel and his three friends; so I thought if prayer helped them, it might help me. Then I prayed over my lessons, asking God to help me, and give me a good memory, and then I learned my lessons in half the time it generally took me."

Here was a successful worker. And we shall find prayer a great help to success in all the work we have to do.

The Left-Hand Letter. A young man left home to go to college. His mother was an earnest Christian. She was very anxious that her son should be a Christian also. Before leaving home she begged him, with the tenderest love, not to put off this important matter. But he could only think about his studies, and about what he was going to do, when he got through college. In all her letters to him, his mother had some kind and loving words to say, on the subject of religion.

There was a revival of religion in college, while he was there, and many of his class became Christians. His mother wrote to him, earnestly urging him to improve the opportunity, and to give himself to the service of God. But he would not listen to her. Then many days passed by without hearing from his mother, whom he greatly loved as he ought to do. He was afraid that something had happened to her, and the thought distressed him greatly. And he was right, in what he feared.

His mother had lost the use of her right hand. This unfitted her from attending to many of her duties. The hardest thing connected with this accident, to her, was the thought she could no longer write to her son, and speak to him about the blessed Saviour.

But she resolved to try and write him a letter with her left hand. This was hard work; and when finished the writing was so crooked, and miserable-looking, that she could hardly keep back her tears on seeing it. But it was the best that she could do. Before sending it, she kneeled down, and asked God to bless it, and make it the means of doing good to her dear boy.

Then the letter was sent. On taking it out of the post-office, her son looked at it with great anxiety. "What can it mean?" he said to himself. "I am expecting a letter from mother. This is from home; but it is not my mother's writing. Has anything happened to her? Can it be that my darling mother has died, and I not yet a Christian?"

Then he hastened to his room. With trembling hand he tore open the letter. It was signed by his mother. She told him of the accident that had happened to her, and of her effort to write this with her left hand. The crooked words were hard to read. It took him a long while to get through with them. But, after just briefly mentioning the accident to her hand, the rest of the letter was all about one thing—namely, her earnest desire that he should become a Christian. And every word that he read seemed to go right to his heart. As he finished the letter and folded it up, he said to himself: "Well, if my salvation makes my mother so anxious, that she can't wait till her hand gets well, but must write about it with her left hand,

I am sure it is time for me to attend to it at once, and by God's help I will."

He went to church that evening with some of his class-mates, and never rested till he had found a hope in Jesus, and had given himself up to his service.

This good mother was a successful worker. And, if, like her, we ask God's help in our work, we shall be successful too.

And thus we have looked at the five things about Noah, which made him a model worker. He was a model worker. He was a *ready* worker;—a *persevering* worker;—a *thorough* worker;—a *courageous* worker;—and a *successful* worker. And it will help to make us useful, and happy in serving God, if we take Noah as our model, and try to follow his example in all these respects.

The Collect for All Saint's Day is a very suitable one to use after studying such a subject as this: "O Almighty God, who hast knit together thine elect in one communion and fellowship, in the mystical body of thy Son Christ Jesus our Lord: Grant us grace to follow thy blessed saints in all virtuous and godly living, that we may come to those unspeakable joys, which thou hast prepared for those who unfeignedly love thee; through Jesus Christ our Lord. Amen."

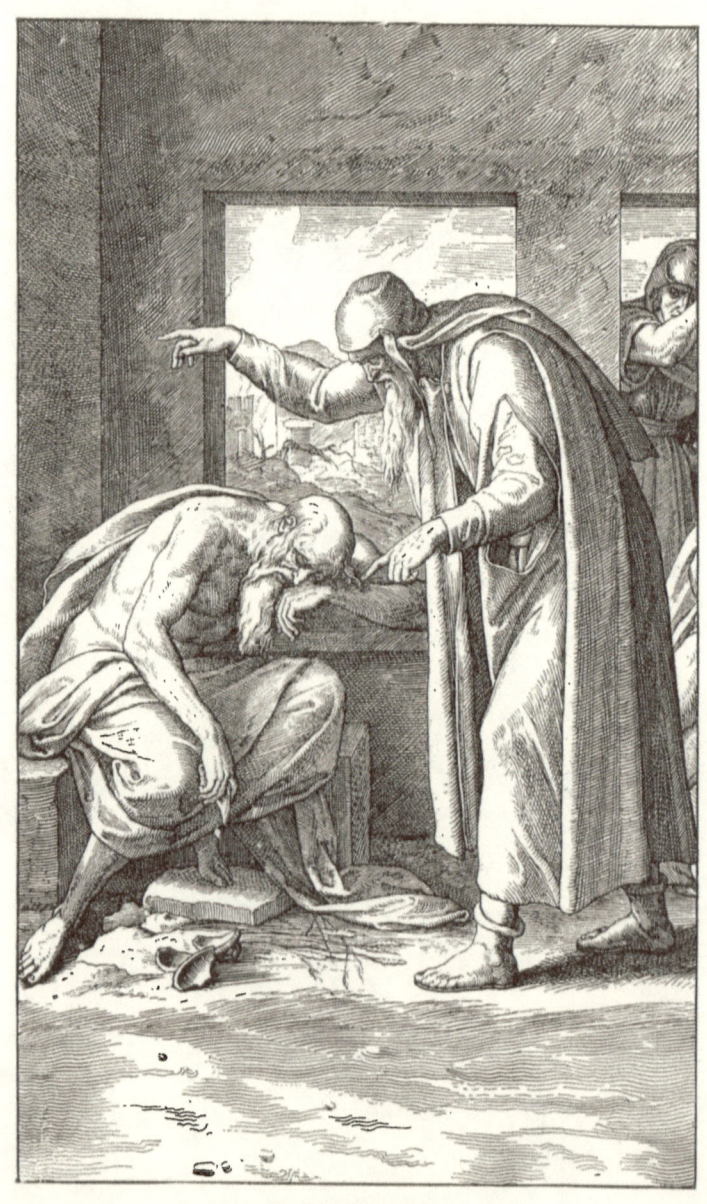

JOB IN AFFLICTION.

JOB, THE MODEL OF PIETY.

"Job—was—one that feared God."—JOB i: 1.

HE history of Job is very interesting. We find the book that bears his name placed next to the book of Psalms in the Bible, but we must not suppose from this that Job lived about the time of David. This was not the case. Job must have lived not very long after the deluge. Somewhere between the time of Noah and of Abraham is about the place to which he belonged.

The book of Job is probably the oldest book in the Bible, or in the world. It is a wonderful book on many accounts. And one of the most wonderful things about it, is the amount of knowledge it contains in reference to astronomy, and natural history, and geography and such like subjects. But more wonderful still than this is the knowledge that we find in the book of Job about God, and the nature of his service—and the right way of worshipping Him. And so, when we come to speak of Job as one of the Bible models, perhaps the best thing to do will be to consider him as the *model of piety*.

This is just the view of his character which the words of our text would lead us to take. "Job—was one that feared God."

And when we come to study this model, we find that there are *five* things about it, which we should remember, and try to imitate.

In the first place Job was a model of—HOME PIETY.

The apostle Paul tells us that we should "learn first to show piety at home." 1 Tim. v: 4. This is the right place in which piety should be shown. Some persons are particular about going regularly to church. They pretend to be very good, and pious, when among strangers; but they are not careful how they act at home. This is not right. If we are really trying to be good Christians, and to love and serve God, then *home* is the place in which we should let our religion be seen. It should make us more respectful and obedient to our parents, and more kind, and loving, and gentle to our brothers and sisters, and to all about us, at home, than those are who do not profess to be Christians.

This was what Job's piety did for him. He had seven sons and three daughters. He was in the habit of having family worship with them. They had grown up to be good men and women, under the influence of their father's home piety. His sons were settled near their father, in houses of their own. They were in the habit of having social gatherings at each others houses. Their sisters, and all the members of their large family, were always invited to be present on these occasions. And when the feasting was over, their father was accustomed to gather them all together, for special religious services, when he prayed that God would forgive them, if any of them had said, or thought, or felt, or done, anything that was wrong while the feasting was going on. And it was in this way that Job was a model of piety at home. And we should all try to follow his example here. For, while real piety is a beautiful thing to see anywhere, it is always most beautiful when seen at home. Here are some illustrations of this statement.

The Power of Example. A young man who was about to be ordained to the ministry, in talking with a friend, about what led him to become a Christian, said:

"I was once very near becoming an infidel, but there was one argument in favor of the religion of Christ, which I could never answer, and that was the beautifully consistent life of my father. *This* was the only thing that kept me from becoming an infidel. My father's beautiful home piety, was what saved me."

The Influence of Home Piety. A gentleman was speaking to a young friend, who was going to join the church. "Under whose preaching were you converted?" was his inquiry.

"It was nobody's *preaching*, but it was Aunt Mary's *practising*, which led me to become a Christian," was the answer given.

A young man who had been living a very careless, and ungodly life became a Christian. The change in his conduct and character was very great. All his friends noticed it. One of them asked him, what it was that led to this change.

"Well," said he, "you know what a good Christian John Yates is. It was living in the same house with him that led to this change."

"Did John talk to you on the subject of religion?"

"No; he never opened his lips on the subject, till I went and talked to him about it. But then his life was speaking to me all the time. There was such a sweetness in his temper; he was so bright and cheerful, and there was so much beauty in the way he acted, that I felt dissatisfied with myself every time I saw him. I felt sure that he had a power, and a peace, and a comfort, of which I knew nothing at all. So at last I went to his room to ask him about it. He talked so sweetly to me, and prayed so earnestly for me, that I never rested till I became a Christian." This was home piety producing its proper effect.

How Children may Show Piety at Home. An old lady was sitting in her arm-chair by the fire. To a friend, who came in to see her, she said: "Look at my little grand-daughter there, she is feet, and hands, and eyes, and everything to me."

"How so?" asked her friend.

"Why, you see, she runs about so nimbly to do the work of the house; she fetches me so willingly whatever I want; and when she has done, she sits down and reads so nicely to me a chapter in the Bible. She is like a little angel to me." That dear child had learned to "show piety at home;" and this is the best thing for us all to learn.

Job was a model of home piety. Let us all try to follow his example in this respect.

But, in the second place, Job was a model of—INTELLIGENT—*piety.*

Job lived so long ago that we could hardly have expected to find he had very clear views about the character of God, and the way to serve Him. But he had. Indeed it is wonderful how much he knew about these things. Let us take a single passage from the book of Job to illustrate this point. In the 19th chapt., vs. 25, 26, we find him speaking thus: "I know that my Redeemer liveth; and that he shall stand at the latter day upon the earth; and though after my skin worms destroy this body, yet in my flesh shall I see God." These words are used in our burial service. We repeat them beside the open graves in which we bury our friends when they die. They are very beautiful words. They point us to Jesus. They show us that Job knew about the Saviour, who was to come into the world, in the fulness of time; and who was to secure to his people the resurrection from the dead.

Job lived before any part of the Bible had been written. But he got his knowledge about these things from the God of the Bible. And when we remember this, we do not wonder so much to find how clear his views were about God and his service. He went to God for his knowledge, and it was this which made him a model of intelligent piety.

And if we wish to imitate Job, in this respect, we must get our views of what true piety is, from the Bible. All knowledge is valuable—but the knowledge of God, and the right way of serving Him, which we get from the Bible, is the most valuable of all. St. Paul said this knowledge was so excellent that he would consider the loss of everything he had, a gain, if he might secure it in this way.

And if we come to the Bible to find out what true piety is, and how we are to serve God, we shall understand this matter as Job did, and our piety, like his, will be intelligent piety.

It Says so in the Book. Two men were standing on the deck of a ship, which was on the stocks, ready to be launched. One of them was the foreman, and the other was one of the carpenters, engaged in building the vessel. "Well, David," said the foreman, "I've been thinking I would like to have a little talk with you. I hear you are one of those who say they are sure of being saved. Is that so?"

"Certainly," said David.

"But how do you know it?"

"Can you tell me how wide that gutter for water is, that runs round the deck?"

"Why, it's just fourteen inches all the way round," said the foreman. "I'm sure of that."

"But what makes you so sure?" asked David.

"Because it says so in the book; and I go by the book." As he said this he took a memorandum book out of his pocket, in which were marked the exact size, and position of everything on the deck.

"I'm sure it's just fourteen inches, for here it is written down in the book, and I got this book from headquarters."

"Oh! I see," said David. "Now, please look here.

That is exactly how I know that I am saved. '*It says so in the book; and I go by the book.*'" And as he said this he pulled a New Testament out of his pocket. "This book came from headquarters. Just see what is written in it. 'God so loved the world, that he gave his only begotten Son, that whosoever believeth in him should not perish, but have everlasting life.' John iii : 16. 'Believe on the Lord Jesus Christ, and thou shalt be saved.' Acts xvi : 31. 'He that believeth on the Son *hath* everlasting life.' John iii : 36. Now I know that I believe; and the book tells me I am saved. In this way I am sure of it."

That man knew what he was about. "He went by the book." That made his piety like Job's, an intelligent piety.

A Cure for Anger. Two little sisters, one seven, and the other five years old, were playing together, when a dispute arose between them. Lucy, the elder, feeling that her anger was rising, said:

"I am getting angry; I had better go out of the room for a few minutes."

She went out, and going to her own room kneeled down, and asked God to help her not to get angry. Then she went to her sister, and as it always takes two to make a quarrel, there was no quarrel between those sisters, because Lucy would have nothing to do with it.

She had not read the Bible in vain. She understood the meaning of such sweet promises as these, "Fear not, for I will help thee." Isaiah xli : 10. "Ask, and it shall be given you." St. Matt. vii : 7. And this knowledge was a great help to her. Her piety was an intelligent piety.

True Comfort. An aged Christian was once reduced to great poverty, and yet he never murmured. A kind-hearted neighbor met him in the street one day, and said to him, "You must be badly off, I cannot tell how you manage to maintain yourself and your wife; and yet you are always cheerful."

"Oh, no," said the old Christian, "we are not badly off. We have a rich Father, and he does not suffer us to want."

"Is it possible that your father is not dead yet? Why he must be very old indeed."

"My Father never dies. Of course I mean my Father in heaven. He always takes care of me." This old man understood the meaning of God's promises, and he believed them. This made him happy. And this is enough to make any one happy. This poor man shows us how we may imitate the model Job sets before us, of—intelligent piety.

In the third place, Job was a model of—PRACTICAL—*piety*.

His piety did not show itself in what he said only, but also, and mainly, in what he did. And while he showed his piety at home, he did not confine it there. He carried his religion with him, wherever he went. In the 29th chapter of the book which bears Job's name, we have a beautiful word-picture of the practical piety of this good man. In showing us how he made his piety practical, this is what he says: "When the ear heard me, then it blessed me; and when the eye saw me, it gave witness to me; because I delivered the poor that cried, and the fatherless, and him that had none to help him. The blessing of him that was ready to perish came upon me; and I caused the widow's heart to sing for joy." "I was eyes to the blind, and feet was I to the lame. I was a father to the poor; and the cause which I knew not, I searched out." This is a very beautiful picture of practical piety.

We have some examples of good Christian men and women who are like Job in this respect. But there ought to be many more of the same kind. Indeed every Christian ought to imitate the model of practical piety that we find in Job. And if we really love Jesus, there is no better way in which we can show our love to him than by trying to be like Job, in this respect.

And if, from the example of Job, we look up to the example of Jesus we shall find them both, very much alike in this respect. When Jesus "went about doing good" He was making His piety practical. And if we wish to be His true and faithful followers, we must learn to "tread in the blessed steps of His most holy life." Let us look at some illustrations of the way in which we may do this.

Bessie and Her Mission. Pansie Merl was a little girl about seven years old. She was trying to be a Christian. During a long spell of sickness, which Pansie had, her dear mother made her a doll. They called the doll Bessie. The good mother cut out a lot of underclothes for the doll, with dresses, and aprons, and sacques, and then she helped Pansie to make them all up. After that, during all her sickness,

Pansie spent a great deal of time in dressing and undressing her doll, and in folding up her clothes and putting them away in a nice little set of drawers which her father had given her. And in doing this the dear child found the greatest possible delight and comfort.

When she got well she continued to feel a great interest in the doll, and never forgot the comfort she had found in it during her sickness. And while thinking about it, one day, the idea came into her mind that she might make her dolly a sort of missionary. She made up her mind that when she heard of a sick child in their neighborhood, too poor to have any playthings, she would take her dolly, and the little trunk containing its clothes, and lend it to the poor child to amuse and comfort her, until she got well again. Then when dolly came back, she had her mended. Her clothes also were mended, and washed, so as to be ready for another mission of mercy. That was Bessie's mission. And many a poor sick child was made happy in this way. Surely that little girl, in her own simple way, was following the example of practical piety, which the patriarch Job left us so long ago!

A Beautiful Example, or *Lady Stanley*. There is a good story told of Lady Stanley, the wife of the late well-known Dean Stanley, of Westminster Abbey, which illustrates very nicely this part of our subject.

There is a hospital in London near the famous Abbey of Westminster. Lady Stanley was in the habit of spending a good deal of time in this hospital —talking with the sick and suffering people there, and trying to cheer and comfort them. Among these was a poor woman, suffering from a painful, and dangerous disease. Lady Stanley's kind words had been a great comfort to her, on her sick bed. The doctors said that her life could only be saved by her having to go through a very painful operation. When it was first mentioned to her she felt quite unwilling to submit to the operation. They told her that she must certainly die unless the operation were performed. "I think I could bear it," she said, "if Lady Stanley could be with me while it was being done." Lady Stanley was sent for. When the messenger arrived at her home, he found her dressed in the splendid robes which ladies wear when called upon to attend on Queen Victoria. She had been thus summoned, and was just about starting for the Queen's palace. She received the message from the hospital. There was no time to change her dress; so she threw a cloak over her, and hastened to the hospital. She spoke some encouraging words to the poor woman, and stood by her side till the operation was over, and the poor suffering patient was made comfortable. Then the noble Lady hastened to the palace. She apologized to the Queen for her delay in coming, and told her what had caused the delay. The good Queen praised her for kindly waiting on one of her suffering subjects, before coming to wait on her. This was noble both in the Queen, and in Lady Stanley. And here we have a beautiful illustration of that practical piety of which we have so excellent a model in Job.

In the fourth place, we have in Job a model of— PATIENT—*piety.*

The apostle James says: "Ye have heard of the *patience* of Job." And this is the first thought that comes to us when the name of Job is mentioned. He was indeed, a wonderful model of patient piety. Job was a very rich man, with a large family of seven sons and three daughters. In the short space of one sad day, he heard of the loss of all his property, and of the death of all his children. Only think what a terrible calamity that was! It was enough to overcome the patience of any one. Suppose we try to put ourselves in Job's place, and think how we should have felt under such a trial as that! We should have been tempted to say some very bitter things against the providence of God for permitting so great, and heart-crushing an affliction to come upon us.

But Job said nothing of the kind. He listened quietly to the messengers, as they came in, one after another, till the whole sad story was told. Then we read that "Job arose, and rent his mantle, and shaved his head." This was the way, in which people in that eastern country were accustomed to express their feelings when in great sorrow. And then—"he fell upon the ground and worshipped, and said—The Lord gave, and the Lord hath taken away; blessed be the name of the Lord. In all this Job sinned not, nor charged God foolishly."

This was wonderful. What a model of patient piety Job was!

Not long after this, another great trial came upon this patient man. All at once his health was taken away from him, and his body was covered, from head to foot, with painful, and offensive sores and boils. This must have made him most loathsome to himself, and to all about him. The patience of his wife quite gave out now. She lost all control of herself. And in her anger she said to him reproachfully—"Dost thou still retain thine integrity? Curse God, and die. But he said unto her—what! shall we receive good at the hand of the Lord, and shall we not receive evil? In all this Job did not sin with his lips."

This was wonderful indeed! Well may we speak of Job as a model of patient piety! It is always pleasant to see piety of this kind. But we need not go outside of the Bible, for our illustrations on this point of our subject. One other illustration will be enough. We find this in the New Testament. Jesus will be our example here. And thus we shall have Job as the model of patient piety from the Old Testament, and Jesus as our model of the same from the New Testament.

We have seen what a wonderful model of patience we have in Job; but, we have a still more wonderful model of the same in Jesus. The patience of Job was beautiful indeed, at the beginning; but it did not last. When he found that his trials continued longer than he expected, he got discouraged, and said some very impatient things. He failed in his patience before he got through with his trials. And so it is, with all the examples of piety and patience, that we find among our fellow creatures. They fail, like Job, sooner or later. If we examine them closely, we shall be sure to find a blot about them somewhere. But it is different with Jesus, our blessed Saviour. His example is the only really perfect one that was ever seen in this world. His example is perfect in everything. But it is especially so in his patience.

The trials of his life were many and great, and yet, under them all, he was never known to speak one cross, or angry word, or to do one unkind, or impatient act. But the trials connected with his death were greater far, than those he had to bear in his life, and here too his patience was perfect. See, there is the divine Sufferer, hanging on the cross. The crown of thorns is still racking his sacred brow with anguish. The rough, cruel nails in his hands and feet are sending untold tortures all through his quivering frame. No tongue can tell the agony he is suffering. His unfeeling enemies are standing by, unmoved by the sight of the nameless pangs, and torments he is enduring. Not one of them sheds a tear, or heaves a sigh, or speaks a word of sympathy. Instead of this they mock him in his misery, and say all sorts of unkind, and cruel things about him. This would seem too much for the patience of any one to bear. But, did the patience of Jesus fail here? No. Mark! He is speaking now. And what is he saying? He is praying for his enemies. And what is he praying for? Listen; these are his words: "Father, forgive them; for they know not what they do!" This is wonderful indeed. Here is patience, such as was never seen, or heard of, before or since. And if we try to be like him, in this respect, then we shall indeed be examples of patient piety.

In the Collect appointed for us to use on the Sunday before Easter, we are taught to pray—"that we may *follow the example of his patience.*" And if we offer this prayer aright, and seek the grace that will enable us to be, what we are here taught to pray for, then, like Job in the Old Testament, and like Jesus in the New Testament, we shall learn to be models of patient piety.

But then there is one other point for us to notice, in the model of piety which we have in Job, and *that is, he was a model, or example of*—REWARDED—*piety.*

When Satan was trying to get permission to tempt Job, one of the questions that he asked was—"Does Job serve God for nought?" He meant to say that Job was selfish in his religion; and only served God for the pay or profit he expected from it. But he was mistaken here. Job was not selfish in his religion. He knew very well that there was a reward to be found in the service of God. But this was not the only thing he thought of in that service. When God gives us promises, as his servants, He means that we should think about them, and be influenced by them.

Remember how it was with Moses. When he refused "to be called the Son of Pharaoh's daughter," and turned his back on all the treasures of Egypt, we are told that "he had respect unto the recompense of the reward." This means that his eye was fixed on that reward. He was thinking about it, and resolving by the help of God to gain it. And this is just what God wants us to do. The service of God is the most profitable service that any one can engage in. In the end, it pays better than any other. This was what Solomon meant when he said: "The merchandise of it is better than the merchandise of silver, and the gain thereof than fine gold." And this was what David meant when he said: "In keeping God's commandments there is *great reward.*" And this was one of the thoughts that comforted Job, in the midst of his great trials. And it was this thought which led him to say—"When He hath tried me, I shall come forth as gold." And so he did. For when his trials were over, we read that God gave him as many children as he had before, and twice as much property. What his reward in heaven has been we do not know; but we shall know when we get there. And then we shall see how true it is that Job is an example, or model, of rewarded piety. And all who serve God, as faithfully as Job did, will find themselves richly rewarded. Here are some illustrations of the way in which true piety is rewarded.

Profitable Living. A collecting agent for the American Bible Society, called on a plain farmer for his contribution to the Bible cause. He was not by any means a wealthy man—but worked his own farm. He looked over his books for a few moments, and then said—"My contribution this year will be seventy dollars."

"Why, this is a wonderfully large contribution," said the collector. "How can you afford to give so much?"

"I will tell you," said the farmer. "Six years ago, I felt that I was not giving as much as I ought to give. So I made up my mind, that I would try to give, in proportion to what the Lord was giving to me. This was the plan which I concluded to adopt. I said to myself, I will lay aside for the Lord's use five cents, on every bushel of wheat I raise; three cents on every bushel of oats or barley; and ten cents out of every dollar made by the wool and butter, and other things that I sell from my farm. At the close of the first year, after adopting this plan, I found that I had twenty dollars to give away. The second year I had thirty-five dollars; the third year, forty-seven; the fourth, forty-nine; the fifth, fifty-nine; and this year I have seventy dollars to give away. My own experience proves the truth of Solomon's words, when he says, in one place, '*There is that scattereth, and yet increaseth:*' and in another place—'*The liberal soul shall be made fat.*'"

We see the piety of this good man, in the liberal way in which he made use of his money, for doing good with it. And we see how his piety was rewarded in the gradual increase of his income. This is one of the ways in which God rewards those who show their piety by giving freely to his cause.

The Price Paid. The Chinese, as a people, are very fond of money. They will do almost anything to get it. And whatever they see people doing they think that it is always for the purpose of getting money. When they see some of their people being baptized, and joining the church, after hearing the missionaries preach, they think it is because the missionaries have paid them money, for doing this. "One of our new converts," said a Chinese missionary, "recently had a talk with a neighbor on this subject, when the following conversation took place:"

"How much did these foreigners give you for joining their church? Twenty dollars?"

"More than that."

"A hundred dollars?"

"More than that."

"A thousand dollars?"

"More than that."

"Then, pray, how much?"

"More than the value of the weight of this mountain, in gold and silver."

"In the name of Boohha! do tell me, then, what they gave you?"

"They gave me *this* PRECIOUS BOOK," said the Christian Chinaman, holding up his Bible. "This tells me of God, of Christ, of Calvary, of Salvation, and everlasting life in heaven; and this is worth more than all the world to me."

Here was piety rewarded indeed! The promises of God's blessed book are the reward of all who learn to love and serve Him. And the value of this reward is so great, that there are no figures by which we can express it.

I have just one other illustration of this part of our subject. We may call it—Piety Rewarded—or Telling the Truth.

A young man, who was a member of the church, and an earnest Christian, had a situation in a large commission-house in New York. On one occasion a large quantity of beans that had been damaged, was sent to this firm, for them to sell.

When these damaged beans were received, a lot of beans of the first quality was purchased. Then they went to work to put up the beans in barrels. At the bottom and the top of each barrel, a lot of the good beans was put, so that whichever end of any barrel might be opened, the good beans would be seen, though the rest of each barrel was filled up with the bad beans. When the barrels were all closed up, the head of the firm went to work and marked them thus: "Beans A—No. I." On seeing this, the clerk said to his employer, "Do you think it right, sir, to mark those beans—'A—No. I?'"

"Hold your tongue, sir! it's none of your business!" was the sharp reply.

The clerk said no more. The beans were all barreled, and marked—"A—No. I," and stowed away in the upper part of the warehouse. A sample of beans of the first quality, was kept in the office for examination.

One day, a gentleman came into the office, who wished to buy a large quantity of beans. He examined the sample there, and liked them very much. "Can I see the beans in the barrels?" he asked. "Certainly, sir," said the head of the firm, and he told the clerk already spoken of, to take the gentleman upstairs. A barrel was opened. He looked at them carefully. They were just like the sample he had seen below. Then he said to the clerk: "Young man, the sample of beans shown me in the office, and these at the top of the barrel, are of the first quality. I can't get such beans anywhere for so low a price. But answer me honestly one question—are the beans in these barrels of the same quality all the way through?"

The clerk hesitated for a moment. He knew his employer would expect him to say—yes, but his conscience told him he ought to say no. He resolved to be true to his conscience. So he answered—"No, sir, they are not."

"Then, I don't want them," said the gentleman, and left.

The young man returned to the office.

"Did you sell that man those beans?" asked his employer.

"No, sir," said he.

"Why not?"

"Well, sir, the man asked me to tell him honestly, if the beans were of the same quality all through the barrel, as they were at the top. I told him they were not. Then he said he didn't want them, and left."

"Well, sir, you can go to the cashier and get your wages," said the employer. "We don't want you here any longer."

So the young man lost his situation. You may be ready to say—"Well, this was rather a poor reward for his piety." But this was not the end of it. A few days after he received a note from his late employers, asking him to call on them. He went to see them.

"We have a place of great importance to be filled," said the head of the firm. "We need for it a person in whose truthfulness and honesty, we can have the most entire confidence. The salary is three hundred dollars a year more than you received in your former position. Will you accept it?"

"I will sir, with thankfulness."

"Very well, then it is yours."

That young man's piety led him to run the risk of losing his situation rather than tell a lie. But he had the reward of his piety in the much better situation which it secured to him.

Thus we have considered Job as a model of piety.

He was a model of *home* piety; of *intelligent* piety; of *practical* piety; of *patient* piety; and of *rewarded* piety. Let us pray God to give us grace to follow his example, in these five different ways—and then, wherever we go, we shall be models of piety too!

ABRAHAM, THE MODEL OF FAITH.

"Abraham believed God."—ROMANS iv : 3.

HEN we hear, or read of the good men, whose histories are written in the Bible, we generally connect with each of them, the thought of some one particular thing, for which he was especially remarkable. And it is in these things that they come before us as our models. Thus we have spoken of Abel as the *model speaker* because he taught us how to speak by our *actions;* and of Enoch as the *model walker*, because it was said of him that—"he walked with God." We spoke of Noah as the *model worker*, because—"*all* that God commanded him—he did."

And when Abraham comes before us, we always think of him as the man who was remarkable, above all others, for *his faith in God*. "Abraham believed God"—says St. Paul in our text. And the same thing is said of him over and over again in the Bible. And for this reason, he is spoken of as "the father of the faithful." And so, when we come to consider the character of Abraham as one of "the

Bible models"—we may well speak of him as—*the model of faith*.

And there are *four* things about the faith of Abraham, in which we may take him as our model, and try to have the same kind of faith.

In the first place, the faith of Abraham was—a SIMPLE—*faith;* and in this respect it is a good model for us to follow. And in speaking of Abraham's faith, as a simple faith, I mean that it was a faith which asked for nothing but the word of God to rest upon. Sometimes people are not willing to take God at his word, and let their faith rest on that alone. They are not willing to believe what God says, just because *He* says it. They want to have arguments, or signs, or wonders given them, to prove that God's word is true.

We have examples of this kind of faith in the Bible. We have one of these examples in the case of Hezekiah, the king of Israel. He had a very severe spell of sickness at one time. While he was suffering under this sickness, God sent him word, by the prophet Isaiah, to prepare for death, as this was to be his last sickness. This distressed him very much, for he did not wish to die then. He wept, and prayed earnestly, that God would spare him, and let him live a little longer. God heard his prayer, and sent him word by the prophet, that He would make him well again, and let him live for fifteen years longer.

But Hezekiah's faith was *not* a *simple* faith, like that of Abraham. He was not ready to take God at His word. He asked the prophet to give him a sign, by which he might know that what God had promised him was true. Abraham believed God, without asking for any sign. Abraham's faith was a *simple* faith; but Hezekiah's faith was not of this kind. If you wish to know about the sign which God gave to Hezekiah, you will find it in the 20th chapter of II. Kings.

And then we have another illustration, of the same kind, in the New Testament. Before John the Baptist was born, God sent the angel Gabriel, down from heaven, to tell his father Zacharias about it. Zacharias was a priest. And one day, as he was standing by the altar, in the temple at Jerusalem, conducting the worship of God, the angel came and stood by his side. He told him that though he was an old man, and had never had a son, yet God was going to visit him in mercy, and that before long he would have a son born in his house. He told him by what name he was to be called, what a great and good man he would grow up to be, and that he was to be the forerunner of Christ—the long promised Saviour of the world.

Now, if the faith of Zacharias had been like that of Abraham—he would have taken God at his word, and the message of the angel, would at once, have filled him with gladness. But it was not so. Instead of believing what the angel had told him, and rejoicing in it, he said—"whereby shall I *know*" that this is all true? And he asked for a sign. You can read about it in the first chapter of St. Luke.

Now let us look at some illustrations of simple faith, like that which Abraham had.

Here is a story of a good Christian mother, who believed God, just as Abraham did.

She had a large family of children, and as they grew up they all became Christians, and joined the church. One day, the minister of the church to which she belonged, called to visit her. In the course of his conversation with her, he said: "My good friend, Mrs. Jones, what a happy woman you must be, to know that all your children have joined the church, and are trying to serve God!"

"Yes," she replied, "I am very happy to think that all my children are Christians. And if I had a hundred, it would be the same with them all."

"But how do you know that?" asked the minister.

"I know it because of God's promise. The promise which God made to Abraham was—'*I will be a God to* THEE.' God made the same promise to me when I became a Christian. And He makes that promise to all His people. I believed God, just as Abraham did. And He has never failed to be a God to me. But then God promised at the same time, to be a God to Abraham's children, or seed, as well as to himself. And God has made the same promise to me. I believe His promise, and He has fulfilled it by making my children all Christians."

This good woman took God at His word. She had *simple* faith in Him, as Abraham had.

Faith in Mother. Two little children, brother and sister, were going down-stairs to breakfast, one morning. As they went slowly down, they were full of eager talk about what their mother had said to them. They were both under six years of age. The boy's name was Gershom, and his sister's name was Phœbe.

Gershom had been out walking with his mother the evening before. "Phœbe," said he, "only think; mother promised me last night, that if I'm a good boy till summer comes, she'll give me a nice big ship to sail on real water. Won't that be jolly?"

"Yes, it will," said Phœbe. "And do you know Ma promised me, the other day, that if I be real good, for a month, and don't cry, when I am put to bed at night, she'll give me a nice, new wax doll, with clothes to dress it in. Won't that be splendid?"

These dear children had simple faith in their mother. They never thought for a moment that she would not keep her promises. Now it happened so, that though they did not see their mother at this time, she was near enough to hear what they said. As she listened to them she said to herself—"What faith these dear children have in my promises to them! I must be very careful to keep those promises! And if *they* have such faith in *me*, what faith should I have in *God?*"

And then she lifted up her heart in prayer, and said: "O Heavenly Father teach me to have just this simple faith in Thee, and to believe every promise, given in thy holy word, for Jesus' sake, Amen."

How She Knew. A minister of the gospel was having service, every evening for a week, in his church. As he was going out of the church, after one of these services, he stopped to speak to a number of persons, who were waiting in the aisle. In passing from one to another of them, he noticed a dear little girl, about seven years of age, who sat at the end of one of the pews, waiting for her mother, who was in another part of the church. She was a sweet, interesting-looking child. The minister stopped near this girl, and looking her in the face, said: "Are you a Christian, my child?"

"Yes, sir," she answered, with a smile.

"And how long have you been a Christian?" he asked.

"Since last night, sir. I heard you preach here. What you said, made me feel that I was a great sinner. When I got home, I went up to my room. Then I kneeled down and told the Lord Jesus about my sins. I asked Him to forgive them, and give me a new heart, and save me. And He heard me, and saved me then; and now, I cannot tell you how happy I feel."

"But *how* do you *know* that Jesus heard you, and saved you?" asked the minister.

The little girl seemed puzzled for a moment, and then, as a sweet smile lighted up her face, she said, "I know he did, because he has promised to do it, in the Bible, and I am sure '*he cannot break his promise.*'"

That, was simple faith indeed. It was just like the faith of Abraham. And this is the kind of faith we should try to have. The first model point about Abraham's faith, which we should try to imitate, is—that it was a *simple* faith.

The second thing about the faith of Abraham, which is a good model for us to imitate, is that it was—an OBEDIENT—*faith*. It led him to do whatever God told him to do. And our faith is good for nothing, unless it leads us to be like Abraham in this respect.

Some of the things that God told Abraham to do were very hard, and yet his faith led him to go straight on and do them. One of the hard things that God told Abraham to do, was to leave his own country, and his father's house, to go and live among strangers, in a country that was far away from all his friends and relations. God did not tell Abraham to do this just on purpose that he might have something that was hard to do. This is not God's way of dealing with His people. When He tells us to do anything, He always has a good reason for it. And so it was here. God had a very good reason for telling Abraham to go out from his own country, and to leave forever all his friends and relations. And this was the reason; it was *to keep Abraham and his family from becoming idolators*. The fact was, that all the people then living in that part of the world, were giving up the worship of the true God, and learning to worship idols. Abraham's relations were doing this also. And God knew that if he stayed there among his own relations, the great danger was that he would follow their example, and become an idolator like them. Now it was very important that there should be at least one family in the world, among which the knowledge of the true God should be kept up, and which should worship Him in the right way. And God had chosen Abraham's family to be the one which should do this. But, if Abraham remained in his own country, and among his relations, who were all becoming idolators, God saw that he would be likely to follow their example and also become an idolator. And *this* was the reason why God told him to leave his home, and friends, and

ABRAHAM LEAVES HIS OWN COUNTRY.

go to a strange country. God knew that if Abraham and his family were in another country, among strangers, they would not be influenced as much by their example, as they were by the example of their own relations. And *this* was why God told Abraham to leave his home and friends, and go into a foreign country.

The country that Abraham lived in was called Chaldea. It was far away in the eastern part of the world. The country to which God wanted him to go and live in, was Canaan—the land where his descendants the Jews, afterwards lived. The journey from Chaldea to Canaan was very long. It was a difficult—a dangerous—and an expensive journey. But when God told Abraham to take it he did so. Neither the length of the journey, nor its difficulties, its dangers, nor its expense, had any influence in keeping him back from doing what God told him to do. Abraham's faith was an *obedient* faith. It led him to *do*, at once, what God told him to do. And we should try to imitate Abraham's faith, in this respect. Our faith will be good for nothing unless it leads us to *obey* God—and do whatever He tells us to do. Let us look at some examples of this kind of faith, that we may try to have faith just like it.

Obedient Faith. It was a beautiful definition of this kind of faith which a little Sunday-school girl once gave. She was asked the question What is faith? and this was her answer—"*It is doing what God tells us to do, and asking no questions.*" That was a beautiful answer.

General Havelock's Faith. General Havelock was

one of the bravest soldiers in the English army; and he was as pious as he was brave. One time he was away from home, and engaged in some very difficult work. Some one asked his wife—where the General was, and what he was doing. Her answer was: "I don't know just where he is, or how he is employed; but *this I know, perfectly well:* wherever he is—*he is trusting in God and doing his duty.*" He had a faith like that of Abraham. It was an *obedient* faith.

A Child's Faith in her Father. The children of a Sunday-school were about to engage in the exercises of their anniversary. One part of these exercises was that each scholar was to take up a bouquet of flowers which was to be presented as a floral offering. In one of the classes, one of the bouquets had been lost. Of course there was one scholar in that class, who had no flowers to take up. It was too late to get another bouquet. The teacher went to the superintendent to ask what she had better do about it.

Now, it happened, that the superintendent had two little girls of his own, in that class, named Jane and Carrie. After thinking over it for a moment, he said to the teacher, "Suppose you ask my Carrie to give up her bouquet, for the scholar who has none, and she and her sister can take up one between them." The teacher went back to her class, and asked Carrie to give up her bouquet for the scholar who had none. For a moment she felt disappointed at the thought of having no flowers of her own to take up. But looking up to her teacher, she asked: "Did father say that I was to do this?" "Yes, my child," replied her teacher, "that is what your father said."

ABRAHAM, THE MODEL OF FAITH. 97

In a moment the flowers were given up. Here was Carrie's faith in her father showing itself to be an obedient faith.

The Faith of the Fireman's Daughter. Some time ago, the cry of fire was raised in one of our public schools. Of course this was very alarming. The children were greatly frightened. They cried, and screamed in their terror, and rushed eagerly to the stairway, each one struggling to reach the door, and get out. In the crowd and pressure thus occasioned, several of the scholars had limbs broken, and were otherwise seriously injured. But, after awhile, it was found to be only a false alarm. There was really no fire. But amidst all this noise and confusion, there was one little girl, who never cried, or screamed, but remained quietly in her seat.

When the alarm had passed away, and the wounded girls had been carried to their homes, and the exercises of the school had begun again; the teacher, who had been greatly surprised at the conduct of this girl, said to her, "Mary, my child, tell me how it was that you were so still and quiet, and acted so differently from the rest of the girls, while the alarm of fire prevailed?" *This* was Mary's answer; and you will see how nicely it illustrates the point of the subject now before us.

"Why, you see, Miss," said Mary, "my father is a fireman; and he has often told me, that if ever there should be a cry of fire in the school, the best thing for me to do was to remain quiet in my seat; for I should be safer there than anywhere else.

"I was dreadfully frightened when I heard the cry of fire. I wanted very much to scream, and run to the stairway, as the other girls did. But I remembered what my father had said about it. I knew he understood what was safe better than I did. I had faith in my father; and it was minding him that kept me quiet, when all the school was in an uproar." This is a very good illustration. It shows us that Mary's faith in her father was an obedient faith, like that of Abraham. It led her to remember what he had told her to do; and when the right time came it led her to do it. And we see how her obedient faith proved a blessing to her. And if we have this kind of faith it will always have the same effect upon us.

*The third thing, about Abraham's faith, which is a model that we should try to imitate, is this—it was—*A CONQUERING—*faith.*

I mean by this that it was a faith which helped him to overcome the greatest difficulties. There was one great trial in Abraham's life, and the way in which he met it shows the conquering character of his faith. I refer here to the command which God gave him about offering his son Isaac as a sacrifice.

This son had been promised to him, many years, before he was born. He was the son of his old age. God had promised him that Isaac's children should be very numerous, and become a great nation; and that the Saviour of the world, and its greatest blessing, would be one of his descendants. We cannot wonder therefore, that, knowing all these things Abraham must have been very fond of Isaac. He must have loved him as few fathers ever loved a son. His heart was, as we say, "*wrapped up*" in Isaac. That any evil should happen to him; and especially that he should die, while he was yet young, was a thought that never could have entered Abraham's mind. And yet God spoke to him, one day, and told him to take his son Isaac, whom he loved, and go to the land of Moriah, and offer him for a burnt sacrifice, on one of the mountains which He would show him! How terrible this must have seemed to Abraham! For a father to kill his own son,—and that son one about whom God had given so many promises—why there was something dreadful, in the very thought of it. There never was a command given to any one, that was harder to obey, than this, which God gave to Abraham. If he had stopped to *reason* about it, he never could have done it in the world. But he did not stop to reason about it. No, "Abraham *believed* God." He felt sure that it was right to do anything that God told him to do. His faith conquered all the difficulties in his way, and he made up his mind, at once, just to do what God had told him to do. And rising up early the next morning, and taking Isaac, and two servants with him, he started to go to the mountain which God was to show him, there to offer up his darling Isaac as a burnt sacrifice.

The apostle Paul tells us that in going on to do this, Abraham expected that God would raise Isaac from the dead, after he had been offered up as a sacrifice.

It took him three days to reach the mountain where this sacrifice was to be offered. That must have been a sorrowful journey to Abraham. When they reached the place, Abraham left the two young men, his servants, at the foot of the mountain, while he and Isaac went up to the top of the mountain by themselves. It may be he was afraid that the young men would have tried to prevent him from offering up Isaac, as a sacrifice. When he reached the top of the mountain, with Isaac, he built an altar, and laid the wood in order, upon it. Then he had to tell Isaac what God had sent him there to do. What a surprise it must have been to him! If Isaac had not been willing to let his father do, what he said God had told him to do, he could easily have prevented him; for he must have been a young man of sixteen or eighteen years of age, while his father was a feeble old man. But he made no 'opposition. He let his father tie his hands, and lay him on the altar. Then Abraham took the knife to slay his son. But just then God called to him out of heaven, and told him to stop. He only wished to see if he was willing to obey such a command as He had given him. Then God gave him some blessed promises, about the coming Saviour of the world, as a reward for his conquering faith. Isaac was taken down from the altar. His bound limbs were loosed; and a ram, that was caught by its horns, in a thicket near by, was offered up as a sacrifice in the place of Isaac. And here we see what a conquering faith it was that Abraham had!

We find persons still with this same kind of faith, and those who have it are always able to do great things. Here are some examples of what I mean.

A Sailor's Conquering Faith. Some time ago, on board of one of our great ships of war, there was one sailor who was a Christian, and who was not ashamed to let it be known that he was so. Every evening he used to go by himself, behind one of the big guns, and read the Bible, and then kneel down and pray. The other sailors laughed at him, and made fun of him. But still he went on. One evening, just as he was beginning to read his Bible, another sailor came quietly up to him, and asked if he might pray with him. This made the Christian sailor very glad. Then there were *two* instead of *one*, to read and pray every night. The other sailors continued to laugh at them, but they went steadily on. At last the captain of the ship heard of these two men. He sent for them to his cabin. He told them how glad he was to hear of the way in which they were trying to serve God, and encouraged them to go on. "I'll have a place curtained off for you, my lads, on the gun deck, where you can be entirely private; and I'll give strict orders that none of the men shall disturb you, while you are reading and praying." He did so. And after this nobody disturbed those praying men; but, one after another joined their company, till finally as many as *thirty* used to meet every evening, to hear God's word read, and to join in the prayer that followed it.

The good captain who did this was a Roman Catholic. I wish I knew what his name was, that I might tell it out to his honor. Such a man deserves to be honored. And the brave sailor, who led on in this good work, was a man who had the same sort of conquering faith that Abraham had.

A Child's Faith. Willie was a little boy, about seven years old. His father was a drunkard, and his mother had a very hard time to get along. One day, in winter, Willie said—"Mother, can't I have a pair of new boots? my toes are all out of these. The snow gets in, and I feel awful cold."

The tears came into his mother's eyes, as she said: "Well, Willie dear, I hope soon to be able to get you a new pair." After waiting for some days, Willie said: "Oh, mother, it's too bad! Can't I get some boots, somehow?" He stood thinking a moment, and then said: "Oh! I know what to do. I'll ask God to get them for me. Why didn't I think of that before?" Then he went up to his own little room, and knelt down by his bed, and covering his face with his hands, he said: "O God, father drinks; mother has no money; my feet get cold and wet; I want some new boots. Please, Lord, get me a pair, for Jesus' sake. Amen."

He said this prayer every day, and was waiting for an answer. Shortly after this, a kind Christian lady, who lived near them, called in one day and asked Willie to take a walk with her. Willie went. Pretty soon the lady saw Willie's toes coming out of his boots. She said: "Why, Willie, dear, look at your feet. They'll freeze. Why didn't you put on a better pair of boots?" "These are all I have, ma'am." "All you have! but why don't you get a new pair?" "Mother has no money, to get them with. But I've asked God to get me a new pair, and I'm waiting till He sends them." Tears filled the lady's eyes, as she led him into a shoemaker's shop, and had him fitted with a nice new pair of boots. This made Willie very glad, and he thanked the good lady for her kindness. As soon as he returned home, he went to his mother, and showing his new boots, said, "Look, mother, God has sent my boots. Mrs. Gray's money bought them, but God heard me ask for them, and I suppose He told Mrs. Gray to get them for me." Then he kneeled down by his mother, and said, "O God I thank thee for these nice, new boots. Make me a good boy; and take care of mother, for Jesus' sake. Amen." Willie's faith was a conquering faith, like that of Abraham.

The Tolling Bell—or Susie's Faith. Little Susie belonged to a Sunday-school in a town in New England. She loved the school very much, and she took a special interest in the missionary meetings, which were often held during the week, in connection with the school.

Some time ago, at the close of the school, one Sunday, the superintendent gave notice that there was to be a missionary meeting, on the afternoon of the next Wednesday, when a native missionary from Nestoria would be present, and give an interesting account of the country from which he came, and of the missionary work that was going on there, and he hoped that as many of the scholars as could do so, would attend this meeting. Susie made up her mind that she would certainly go, if she could. There was an "if" in the case, and she was not certain that she would be able to go. It seems that Susie's own mother was dead, and she had a step-mother, who was not always as kind to her, or as willing to oblige her, as her own mother would have been. Susie didn't know whether she would be allowed to go to this meeting. But she prayed, each day, that God would order things so that she might go.

On Wednesday afternoon the church-bell began to ring for the meeting, at a quarter before two o'clock. As soon as Susie heard the bell she went to her mother and asked if she might go to the missionary meeting. The answer she got to this question was not a very pleasant one. It was this: "No; you'll do no such thing; but stay at home, and mind your work."

Susie didn't pout, or cry, or tease. She knew that would do no good. But what was much better, she went up to her room, and kneeling down she prayed that, "if it were best for her to go to the meeting, God would cause the bell to keep on ringing till her mother was willing to let her go." That was a strange prayer to offer. Then Susie went about her work. It was a quarter before two when the bell began to ring. Two o'clock came and it went on ringing—ding—dong, ding, dong. A quarter past two came, and it went on ringing. Half past two came—and then a quarter of three, and it went on ding, dong still. Susie began to wonder what it could mean. She had never heard it ring so long at one time before. Just as she was thinking this, her mother came into the room, and said, "It seems to me that bell is never going to stop ringing. Susie, if you think you can get ready in time, you might as well go to the meeting." "Oh, thank you, thank you," said Susie. She did get ready, and had a real good time at the meeting. But what was the meaning of the bell ringing so long? Simply this. The sexton made a mistake about the time of the meeting. He thought it was to be at two o'clock, and so he began to ring the bell at a quarter of two. And when he had once begun to ring, he couldn't stop, but had to go on ringing till the meeting began. The apostle Paul tells us that "God makes *all things work together* for good" to His people. And here we see how He overrules even the mistakes of men to answer the prayers, and reward the faith of those who are trying to serve Him. Susie had a conquering faith, like that of Abraham.

But there was one other thing about the faith of Abraham, in which he was a model for us to imitate. *Abraham's faith was*—A COMFORTING—*faith*.

When our Saviour was on earth, in speaking to the Jews, one day, he said: "Your father Abraham desired to see my day, and he saw it, and was glad." I suppose he referred here, to the promises that God gave him, after he had shown that he was quite willing to have offered up his son Isaac as a sacrifice, if God had not told him to stop. Then, as Abraham stood beside that altar, God told him about the great Saviour of the world, who was to be one of the descendants of Isaac. He told him what a blessing to the world that Saviour would be, when He came. Abraham believed what God told him, and this faith gave him comfort, or made him glad. His faith was to him *like eyesight*. This was what Jesus meant—when he said—"Abraham desired to *see* my day, and he *saw* it, and was glad." And it always makes people glad when they have faith in Jesus, or when they see Him as their Saviour. It is like the joy which God's people have in heaven. It is true, as the hymn says, that:—

> "A bleeding Saviour *seen* by faith,
> Gives joy like that above."

This was what David meant, when he said: "Thou hast put gladness in my heart more than"—(the men of the world have)—"when their corn, and oil, and wine increase." It always has been true, it is true now, and it always will be true—that faith in Jesus, like that which Abraham had, is a comforting thing. It gives us the purest, and most satisfying joy which we can ever know in this world. Let us look at some illustrations of the comfort which this faith gives.

Hold of Papa's Hand. A little girl about six years old, was very fond of going to her father's office, and walking home with him at the close of the day. She came running in, one day, saying with a glad voice—"Papa, I've come to 'scort you home." "Very well, darling," said her father, "I'm very glad to have the pleasure of your company." She took my hand, he said, and we were soon on our way. "Now, Papa," she said, "let's play I was a poor blind girl. You must let me take tight hold of your hand, while you lead me along, and tell me how to go, and when to stop."

So the merry blue eyes were shut tight, and I led her along saying—"Now, step up, and now step down." And pretty soon we reached home, and then throwing her arms around my neck, she said: "Wasn't that nice, Papa? and I never slipped once."

"But," said her Mamma, "didn't you feel afraid, to go on in the dark, my darling?"

A look of trusting love lighted up her face, as she replied—"Oh, no, Mamma! I had tight hold of Papa's hand, and *I knew he would take me safely over the hard places.*"

This is a beautiful illustration of what faith in God is, and of the comfort which it gives.

The Prayer of Faith. Two little girls, named Annie,

and Bessie, about six years old, were one day walking along the road in the country, when they saw, at some distance off, a number of cows, coming down the same road—"Annie," said Bessie, "I'm very much afraid of cows." "So am I," said Annie. "But, if we ask our Heavenly Father, to keep the cows from hurting us, He can do it, and then we needn't feel afraid. Let us kneel right down and ask Him." So they knelt down by the side of the road, and asked God to keep the cows from hurting them. Then they walked home in comfort. On reaching there they told their mother about it, and said that "God did keep the cows away, for they went by on the other side of the road, and did not come near us."

The father of these little girls was not a Christian, and when he heard them telling their mother about it, the thought of their simple faith, and the comfort it gave them, brought the tears into his eyes, and led him to pray God to give him just the same kind of faith that these darling children had.

A Wife's Comforting Faith. Some years ago, Major M., a distinguished officer of the army, and a man very much esteemed by all who knew him, had a long, and severe attack of sickness. He got so low at last, that his physician gave him up. His friends all expected him to die, and were greatly distressed at the thought of losing him. But while others were mourning over his expected death, his wife remained calm and even cheerful. A particular friend was astonished at her calmness, and said to her: "Mrs. M., how is it that you can be so composed, when your husband is so near the end of his life?" "My husband will not die now," was her quiet answer. "But everybody thinks he will; and the doctor has given him up. Why do you think he is not going to die?" "*My faith in God makes me think so.* God has said, 'Ask, and ye shall receive.' Now, I have asked God that he will not take my husband away, till he becomes a Christian, and gives evidence that he is ready to die. He has not yet given that evidence. And so I do not think he is going to die now."

And it turned out just as she said. A change came over her husband's symptoms. He began to get better. He was restored to good health. He became an earnest Christian, and lived for years a useful, happy life. Now, what a comfort that good wife's faith in God was, at a time when nothing else in the world, could have been a comfort to her!

I have just one other illustration of the comfort which true faith gives in time of danger.

A ship was once tossing on the stormy sea. The violence of the storm had been so great that the ship had sprung a leak, and was filling with water. The only hope for those on board was to get into the life-boats which the ship carried with her. These were hoisted over into the angry sea. They seemed like tiny things to look to for safety, in the midst of such a fearful storm.

Among the first to venture into one of those little boats was a Christian mother. She had a child in her arms, and a little boy sitting by her side, and clinging to her dress. She did not cry or scream. The child in her arms was asleep, notwithstanding the storm; and the little boy at her side was quiet.

A gentleman, one of the passengers, was surprised to see the little fellow so quiet, and said: "Are you not afraid of the storm, my boy?" "I don't like the storm a bit," said the boy; "but mother is here, and I never feel afraid where she is." Thus his faith in his mother gave him comfort. And then looking at the mother, the gentleman asked, "And are you not afraid, my friend?" She shook her head; and then pointing upwards, she said: "God is ruling this storm, sir. He is my Father. He will not let the storm hurt me; and so I do not feel afraid." Her voice, as she spoke, could hardly be heard, amidst the howling of the winds, the roaring of the waves. But the gentleman was very much struck with the faith of the child in his mother, and the faith of the mother in her God. He was not a Christian, and had no such faith as this in God. But he saw how much comfort this good woman found from her child-like faith in God. He never forgot that Christian mother's faith. The boats reached land in safety. And he was led to pray for the grace that would make him a Christian, and help him to exercise the same comforting faith in God.

Let us remember the four model points in Abraham's faith, of which we have spoken. It was a *simple* faith—an *obedient* faith—a *conquering* faith—and a *comforting* faith. Let us pray earnestly that God may give us the same kind of faith that Abraham had; for, if we have this, it will be sure to make us useful and happy Christians.

MOSES, THE MODEL OF FAITHFULNESS.

"Moses was faithful."—HEBREWS iii : 2.

E are told that Moses was the meekest man on earth. (Numbers xii : 3.) We might have taken him as the model of meekness. That would have made a good subject. I was uncertain at first which of these two models to take. But I think the one chosen, is the more important of the two. This includes the other; but the other does not necessarily include this. Moses might have been meek, without being faithful; but he could not have been faithful without being meek. And so I thought it was best on the whole, to take Moses as the model of faithfulness. And we may speak of four ways in which he was faithful.

*In the first place, he was—*FAITHFUL TO GOD.

This is the right place for faithfulness to begin. It is impossible for us to be faithful to ourselves, or to others, till we are faithful to God. If the mainspring of your watch is broken, it is impossible for it to keep time. You may wind it up, ever so often, but it will

MOSES HEARS A VOICE OUT OF THE BURNING BUSH.

run down, at once, and then stand still. The watch is of no use until you get a new mainspring in it. Now, if we compare ourselves to watches, we are like watches with the mainspring broken. The only thing to do, in such a case, is to get a new mainspring. And this is what Jesus came into the world to do for us. Sinful hearts are like broken mainsprings. And when Jesus gives us new hearts, it is like putting new mainsprings into the broken watches. And when this is done the first effect it will have upon us will be to make us like Moses, faithful to God.

We see this illustrated in the apostle Paul, when his heart was changed by the vision which he had of Jesus, on the way to Damascus. Then a new mainspring was put in the broken watch of his sinful soul. And it began to work in just the way of which we are speaking, by making him faithful to God. The first question that he asked, after this great change had taken place, was, "Lord, what wilt *Thou* have me to do?" This was the case with Moses. There he is at the burning bush, near Mount Sinai, in the wilderness. God appears to him, in the flames of that bush. He tells him that He wants him to go back to Egypt. When he gets there he must go into the presence of King Pharaoh, and demand of him that he shall let the children of Israel go out from their bondage in Egypt. And then He told Moses, that He wanted him to lead the Israelites through the wilderness, to the land of Canaan, which He had promised to them. Now, this was the hardest work that ever a man was called upon to do. Moses knew how hard it would be. We need not wonder therefore to find, that at first, he tried to get excused from engaging in this work. But when he found that this was really what God wanted him to do, he stopped making excuses, and went bravely on to do just what God told him to do. In *this*, he showed his faithfulness to God. And then, for forty long years, he went on, through scenes of the greatest difficulty and trial, doing the work that God had given him to do, and thus showing himself as a model of faithfulness to God. And this is the model that we must try to follow.

If we learn to love the Saviour, and become Christians, this is the first thing that we shall seek to do. We shall strive, above all things, to be faithful to God, as Moses was.

Here are some illustrations of the way in which this kind of faithfulness will show itself.

A Worthy Example. We have all heard of Jenny Lind, the famous Swedish singer. Here is a good story, which shows her faithfulness to God. On one occasion, when she was in Stockholm, the capital of Sweden, the King was going to have a musical festival at his palace on the Sabbath day. He sent an invitation to this great singer to come and take part in these exercises. But she declined the invitation. Then the King waited on her in person, and *commanded* her to come to his entertainment. This was a very high honor, for a king to show to one of his subjects. Most persons would have gone, under these circumstances. But Jenny Lind still begged to be excused. And when the King asked for her objections she said:

"Please your majesty, I have a greater king in

heaven to whom I must be faithful. I cannot do what your majesty desires, without breaking the commandment of my Heavenly King, and offending Him. So please excuse me for declining to do what your majesty wishes."

That was noble. Few persons would have had the courage to show their faithfulness to God under such circumstances, as brave Jenny Lind did.

The Conscientious Hair-Dresser. In the city of Bath, England, during the last century, lived a hair-dresser, who was not a religious man, and who was in the habit of keeping his shop open on Sunday. But in the course of time a change came over him, and he became a Christian. Then he was greatly troubled at the thought of breaking the fourth commandment by working on Sunday. He went and talked with his minister about it. He urged him to give up the practice, as he could not expect God's blessing to follow him while he continued to do this. The man said he was sure his trade would be ruined if he gave up his Sunday work. But finding that he could have no peace or comfort, while he went on in this way, he finally made up his mind to do his duty, and be faithful to God, whatever the result might be.

He gave up his Sunday work, and went regularly to church. The result was just as he feared. His genteel customers left him, and his business fell off, so that he was obliged to give up his fashionable shop, and finally he had to take a cellar, under the market-house, and shave people of the poorest class.

One Saturday evening, about dark, a gentleman

from one of the stage coaches, in which the travelling was done, before the days of railways, asked for a hair-dresser, and was directed by the hostlers to the cellar opposite. Coming in hastily, he asked to be shaved quickly, while they were changing the horses, as he did not like to break the Sabbath day. This touched the poor barber in a tender spot, and he burst into tears, as he asked the stranger to lend him a penny to buy a candle with, as it was too dark to shave him with safety, and he had not a penny in the world.

He gave him the penny, wondering to himself how poor the man must be! When he was shaved he said to the barber, "There must be something strange in your history, which I should like to hear, when I come back. But I have no time now. Here is half a crown for you. What is your name?"

"My name," said the astonished barber, "is William Read."

"William Read," said the stranger; "and what part of England are you from?"

"From Kingston, near Taunton."

"What was your father's name?"

"Thomas Read."

"Had he any brothers?"

"Yes, sir, one, after whom I was named; but he went to the East Indies, and as we have never heard from him, we suppose he must be dead."

"Come along with me," said the stranger; "your uncle is dead, and has left a large fortune, which I will put in your possession, as soon as you prove the truth of what you have just said."

He was able to give the proof required, and then his uncle's large fortune came into his possession.

Now see how strangely God's providence worked, to bring about this result! It was this man's faithfulness to God, which brought him into the way of the lawyer, who had charge of this fortune. If he had not been so poor, that he had not a penny with which to buy a candle, he might never have heard of, or received that fortune. But he was faithful to God, and God blessed him for his faithfulness; and this is what He will always do.

Moses was faithful to God. This is the first point in the model he has left us. We should try to follow his example here.

The *second* point to notice in this model is,—*that Moses was*—FAITHFUL TO HIMSELF.

He refused to be called the son of Pharaoh's daughter. He chose rather to suffer affliction with the people of Christ, than to enjoy the pleasures of sin for a season. He considered the reproach he bore for Christ, greater riches than the treasures of Egypt. He looked away from Egypt, with its wealth, its honors and its pleasures, and desired to secure a share in the riches and honors of God's heavenly kingdom. And these two things, faithfulness to God, and faithfulness to ourselves, always go together. We cannot be faithful to ourselves, till we are faithful to God. If we refuse to become Christians, we are doing ourselves the greatest harm. This is what God means when he says: "All they that *hate me, love death.*" Prov. viii : 36. But when we begin to be faithful to God, and to ourselves, then we are putting ourselves in the way of all good. God says to us, "*From this day will I bless you.*" Haggai ii : 19.

Let us look at some examples of this kind of faithfulness, and of the blessing that follows it.

Brave Ben. "A Boy Wanted"—was the notice put up in the window of a nice-looking country hotel. A boy named Ben, read it, and said to himself, "I wonder if I would do for that place? I must do something to earn money, or how will poor mother be able to live? I guess I'll step in, and ask about it."

So Ben went in. It was the first time he had ever been in a bar-room. The place looked neat and clean, and there were no drunken men about. But the smell of the place was sickening, and Ben's heart sank within him, at the thought of living in such a place. The keeper of the house was a good-natured, pleasant-looking German. In payment for his services, he offered Ben his board, and such sums of money as he could make by holding the horses of travelers, who stopped to get a drink, and by doing little jobs for them. And then in return for these privileges, he was to make himself generally useful about the place, and in the absence of the master, he was to pour out drinks from the glittering bottles, to any poor wretches who could pay for them.

"Well, now," said the proprietor, after giving Ben this account of what he expected of him, "you have heard what I want you to do; are you ready to begin work?"

"Give me a few minutes to think over it," said Ben, "and I'll make up my mind one way or the other."

"Well, you may think about it, but I get plenty more

boys, if you not like it," said the German, a little angry, and speaking somewhat brokenly, as he always did at such times.

Ben said nothing more, but went out to the pump to get a drink; and then he sat down on a grassy bank to think the matter over.

"What would mother think of my having a place in a bar-room? I dare say I could make a good deal of money; but would she be willing to use money made in this way? Then," continued Ben, "what would God think of it? Is there not somewhere in the Bible, a curse pronounced on him who putteth the bottle to his neighbor's lips? And if I get used to selling liquor to others, might it not end in my learning to drink myself? No, I can't think of taking such a place as this," said Ben to himself. Then he returned to the tavern.

The proprietor stood on the porch.

"Well, boy, what you think of my offer?" he inquired. "I think I can't take the place," said Ben, boldly. "I want work very much, but there are three reasons why I am not willing to do this sort of work. One is, that God would not like it. Another is, my mother would not like it. And then I don't like it myself. I am afraid it might end in my becoming a drunkard. Good morning, sir."

Ben walked away, leaving the German much puzzled to make out what the boy meant. But there was another person present, who understood him perfectly. A gentleman had driven up in a buggy, to inquire the way to the next town. He was much pleased with Ben's answer to the tavern-keeper. He overtook him, and invited him to take a ride in his buggy, as he wished to have a talk with him.

Ben got in, and the gentleman said: "My boy, I honor you for refusing to work in a bar-room; and on that account you will be just the boy for me. I want a clerk that I can trust, and a boy who is faithful to God, faithful to his mother, and faithful to his own conscience, is the kind of boy that I want."

Then he named a very generous sum, that he was willing to give, and Ben went home to his mother that day about as happy as a boy could be.

I Can't Afford It. "Just come and work awhile in my garden, on Sunday mornings, will you, Jim?" said a working-man, with his pick-axe over his shoulder, to an old hedger, who was working on a thick hedge.

Jim took off his cap and made a bow to the speaker, and then said: "No, master, I can't afford it."

"Oh! I don't want you to do it for nothing. I'll pay you well for the work."

"Thank you, master, but I can't afford it."

"Why, man, it will put something in your pocket, and I don't think you are too well off."

"That's true; and that's the reason why I say I can't afford it."

"Can't afford it! Why, surely, you don't understand me."

"Yes, I do; but I'm not quick of speech. Please don't snap me up, and I'll tell you what I mean. It's very true, as you say, that I'm not well off in this world. But I've a blessed hope of being better off, in the world to come. My Lord and Saviour has said, 'I go to prepare a place for you, that where I am there ye may be also.' I learned that text more than twenty years ago, and it has been a great comfort to me."

"Well, but what's that got to do with your saying in answer to my offer—'I can't afford it?'"

"Why, no offence to you, sir, but it's got all to do with it. If I lose my hope in that better land, I lose everything. My Saviour says I must keep the Sabbath day holy. If I break His command I shall not be prepared for the place He is preparing for me. And then all my hope is gone. And this is what I mean by saying, 'I can't afford it.'" That was noble in the poor hedger. It showed that he was trying to be faithful to his God, and faithful to himself.

Moses was a model of faithfulness—he was *faithful to himself.* Let us try to imitate the model he has set in this respect.

But in the third place, Moses was—FAITHFUL TO HIS FAMILY. And here he was a good model for us to follow.

It was through the influence of Moses that his brother Aaron became the high priest of the Jewish Church, and his sister Miriam led the people in the praises of God. We have one of the hymns she taught the people to sing, when the Egyptians were drowned in the Red Sea, and the Israelites were wonderfully delivered. We read (Exod. xv : 20, 21), "And Miriam the prophetess, the sister of Aaron, took a timbrel in her hand; and all the women went after her with timbrels and dances. And Miriam answered them, Sing ye to the LORD, for he hath triumphed gloriously; the horse and his rider hath he thrown into the sea."

Moses was not satisfied to go to heaven himself, but he tried to get all his family to go with him. Hobab, his father-in-law, lived in the wilderness, near Mount Sinai; and when the Israelites came to that part of the country, on their journey to the promised land, he came to visit his son-in-law. Moses took advantage of that opportunity to persuade Hobab to go with them. He said to him—"We are journeying unto the place of which the Lord said, I will give it you; come thou with us, and we will do thee good." Numb. x : 29. And so he persuaded him to go along with them. Here we see what a model he was of faithfulness to his family. And if we try to imitate this point of the model he has left us, we shall be blessings to our families, as he was to his. Here are some illustrations of the way in which this may be done.

A Faithful Aunt. A Sunday-school teacher was talking to one of her scholars, who had joined the church. "Nellie," she said, "tell me whose preaching it was that led you to become a Christian."

"It was nobody's preaching," was the pleasant, smiling reply; "but it was *Aunt Mary's practising.*" The life that faithful aunt had led before her, was the means of leading her to the Saviour. It was not what the aunt had *said*—but what she had *done*—her faithfulness to her family—her consistent example, which had been the means of her niece's conversion.

A Faithful Mother. The Bishop of Manchester, in England, was giving the prizes one day to the scholars, in a school with which he is connected. A large number of the parents and friends of the scholars were present. They all knew and loved the Bishop, as a good, and learned, and very useful man. In the midst of their exercises, as he stood surrounded by the scholars, the good Bishop was led to speak of his mother.

"She was a widow," said he, "with some children to support and educate. God helped her to be faithful. She sacrificed her own ease and comfort for the good of her children. Her home was a poor one. She had to struggle hard for our support. But she managed to make that home the brightest and the happiest place to us. Her children, through her faithful efforts, have since risen to positions of honor and usefulness, where they are helping to make the world better. She is now," said the Bishop, and here his voice was broken with deep feeling—"She is now living in my house, paralyzed, speechless, helpless, but every time I look at her dear face, I thank God for giving me such a mother. All that I am, and all that I have I owe to her."

There was hardly a dry eye in that assembly, while the Bishop was uttering these touching words. That was a faithful mother, indeed.

Minding Orders. Frederic II., King of Prussia, used to rise very early in the morning. He gave strict orders to his servants to wake him at four o'clock in the morning, and not on any account to let him sleep later than that. He had a new servant once, who had been told all this about waking up the king in the morning, and not letting him sleep any longer. The king wished to find out if this man would be faithful in minding the orders that had been given him.

So the next morning at the appointed hour, this new servant came to the king's bed, and awoke him, and telling him that it was time to get up.

"Let me sleep a little longer," said the king, "for I am still very tired."

"Your majesty gave me positive orders to wake you at just this hour," said the servant.

"Very well," said the king, "but just let me sleep a quarter of an hour more."

"Not another minute," said the servant; "it has struck four o'clock. You ordered me to insist on your majesty's rising at this hour; and I must mind my orders."

"Very well," said the king, "now I know that you are a faithful servant. If you had not minded your orders I should have dismissed you, at once, from my service. But now I feel that I can rely upon you. And so long as you continue faithful you may be sure of your situation."

The Faithful Servant. George and Harry were neighbors, and worked in the same shop. But summer season had come when work was slack. And Mr. Wilson, their employer, as he paid them their wages one Saturday night, told them that he should only have work for one of them at present. He said they might both come on Monday morning, and he would make up his mind in the mean time, which of them should have the work.

On their way home Harry counted over the wages paid him, and then said to his friend, "Why, George, Mr. Wilson has paid me a quarter of a dollar more than I am entitled to." Then George looked over his

MOSES, THE MODEL OF FAITHFULNESS. 123

money, and found that he also had a quarter too much.

"I wonder what it means," said Harry.

"That question is easily answered," replied George. "Mr. Wilson was very busy when he settled with us, and in his hurry he just gave us a little too much."

"Well, I mean to go right straight back and return my quarter to him."

"You'll be very foolish if you do any such thing," said George. "What's such a trifle as a quarter to a rich man like Mr. Wilson? And I'm sure you have worked hard enough for all the money you've got, and more too. You can do as you please; but I'm going to keep my extra quarter."

"I remember one place in the Bible," answered Harry, "where it says: 'He that is faithful in that which is least, is faithful also in much; and he that is unjust in the least, is unjust also in much.' (Luke xvi: 10.) I want to be faithful," said Harry, "and I'll take it back at once." He did so; while George put his quarter in his pocket and went home.

Mr. Wilson was very much pleased with Harry for bringing back the extra quarter, and thanked him warmly for it. Now it happened that this matter of the extra quarters given to these boys, was not an oversight, or mistake. Mr. Wilson wished to try the honesty, or faithfulness of these two boys; and he took this way of doing it. When the two boys came to him on the next Monday morning, he had no difficulty in deciding which of them to keep in his employ. He chose Harry, because he was sure that he was faithful. He entrusted the shop to his care for several months, while he was away on business, and was so well pleased with his management, that when the busy season came on in the fall, he made him superintendent of his shop. And, in the course of time, Harry became Mr. Wilson's partner, while George worked on in the same shop, but only as a common laborer. A character for faithfulness is one of the surest elements of success in any position. And there is no telling how much good we may do, by setting the example of faithfulness before us, and following it.

And then, there is one other thing about this model to speak of. Moses was not only faithful to God—to himself—and to his family;—*but he was faithful*—IN ALL THINGS.

It says, in connection with our text, that he—"was faithful in all his house." This does not mean only his own family, but the whole house of Israel. Moses was, as it were, the head, and father of the Jewish Church and nation. And he was faithful to them all. He tried, by all the means in his power, to teach them, and guide them, and do them good. We have an account of his faithfulness to his people in the 18th chapter of Exodus. There we read how he used to spend his whole time, from morning till night, in listening to their complaints; in settling their disputes; and in trying to do them good. When his father-in-law came to visit him, in the wilderness, he was frightened when he saw how much work Moses was doing. He told him that he would kill himself, if he kept on working at that rate. And then he persuaded him not to work so hard, but to get some of the people to help him in this work. But this shows us how faithful he was to all about him. And we should try to imitate the model that Moses sets us here. We should be faithful to everybody. Let us look at some illustrations of this kind of faithfulness.

Faithfulness and its Reward. Fred Harris was a boot-black boy in the city of London. His mother was a widow, and they lived in a garret up a dirty alley. Mr. Harris, her husband was a merchant, very well off, when she married him. But he afterwards became intemperate, and failed in business. When he died he left his family in utter poverty. They had to struggle very hard for a living. Mrs. Harris took in sewing, and Fred went out every day with blacking-brushes, and in this way they tried their best to support themselves.

One day Fred was standing at the corner of the street, looking out for a job. "Black your boots, sir?" he cried out to a gentleman, who was passing along the busy street. "Well, yes, you may," said the gentleman, as he stopped and placed his foot on the box.

When Fred had finished his work, the gentleman gave him sixpence, which was more than the regular price, and told him he might keep the change. "Thank you, sir," said Fred, taking off his cap, and making a polite bow. Then he put away his brushes, and just as he had done this, he saw a pocket-book lying on the ground, near where the gentleman had stood. Feeling sure that he had dropped it, while getting his boots blacked, he picked it up and ran off in the direction in which the gentleman had gone, in the hope of overtaking him, and of giving him back his pocket-book. But it was too late; he could see nothing of him. All that day he was thinking of this pocket-book, and kept a sharp lookout for the owner, that he might return it to him. But he never came in sight. When Fred reached home that night, he told his mother about the pocket-book he had found, and handed it to her. She opened it, and found the name of the owner in it—"Mr. J. Erskine, Merchant, 52 Queen Street." And on looking further, she found a fifty pound note. That was about two hundred and fifty dollars of our money.

"Why, Fred," she exclaimed, "here's a fifty pound note. We must return it at once to the gentleman whose name is here. It's too late to go to-night, and we shall have to put it off till the morning."

Fred was up next morning bright and early. He put on his best clothes, and after breakfast started with his mother, for the gentleman's place of business in Queen Street. On arriving there they asked for Mr. Erskine, and were shown into a room to wait for him, as he was then engaged. In a little while he came in, and Fred recognized him in a moment, as the gentleman whose shoes he had blackened the day before. Going up to Mrs. Harris he said:

"Well, ma'am, what can I do for you?"

"I came sir, to return your lost pocket-book, which my son found yesterday."

"Have you got it with you?"

"Yes, sir," replied Mrs. Harris, handing the book to him. He opened it and found the note inside, and everything in its place. This satisfied him that the mother and her son were honest and faithful. Looking at Fred, he said, "Surely I have seen you before, my man?" "Yes, sir," he replied, "I brushed your boots, yesterday morning. I found the pocket-book, just after you left, and ran after you to return it, but you were out of sight."

Mr. Erskine asked Fred if he would not like a place in his office. He said he would, very much. Then he gave Mrs. Harris money enough to get Fred a nice new suit of clothes, and told her to send him to his office early the next morning. Fred got his new clothes, and was at the office in good time the next morning. He was industrious and faithful. This ensured his success. He was soon able to get a nice comfortable home for his mother, and to support her by his own wages. He afterwards became the head clerk to Mr. Erskine; and when he died he left his business in Fred's hands, and he got to be a rich man. This was all the result of God's blessing on his faithfulness.

Here is a good story about a boy who was faithful in all things. He was a little Scotch boy, who came over to this country to live with his uncle, Mr. Lee. His name was Willie Grant. Willie found two cousins in his uncle's family, Robert and Johnnie Lee, about his own age. They soon became very fond of their Scotch cousin. He was little, but bright and full of fun. He could tell curious stories about his home in Scotland, and his voyage across the ocean. He was just about as far advanced in his studies as his cousins were, and the first day he went to school with them, they thought him a remarkably good scholar. He wasted no time in play, when he ought to be studying, and he recited finely. At night, before the school closed, the teacher called a roll, and every boy who could say that he had not whispered in school during the day, when his name was called would answer—"ten"—and that would be his mark for the day. When Willie's name was called, he was asked if he had whispered during the day? "I have," he replied.

"How often?" asked the teacher.

"Some eight or ten times," was the answer.

"Then I must mark you zero," said the teacher, sternly, "and that is considered a great disgrace."

When they were going home, his cousin Johnnie said to him, "Why, Willie, I didn't see you whisper."

"Well, I did," said Willie; "I saw others doing it, and so I asked to borrow a book; then I lent a slate-pencil, and asked a boy for a knife, and did several such things. I supposed that was allowed."

"Oh! we all do that," said Robbie, blushing. "There isn't any sense in the old rule. Nobody *can* keep it, and nobody *does*." "Well, I will for one," said Willie, "or else I'll say so. Do you suppose that I'm going to tell half a dozen lies, all in a heap?"

"Oh! we don't call them lies," said Johnnie. "None of us would have had a good mark to-night, if we had been as particular as you are."

"Well, what of that, if you had all told the truth?" laughed Willie, bravely.

In a short time the boys in the school all got to understand little Willie Grant. And they all loved him. He studied hard; he played with all his might in playtime; and yet, because he was so faithful in telling the

MOSES, THE MODEL OF FAITHFULNESS.

truth, he got fewer good marks than any of them. He never preached to the boys, or told tales about them; but it often made them feel ashamed, when they saw how faithful he was in always telling the truth himself, whether he got good marks or not. They often talked about him; they all loved him, and because he was so firm in telling the truth, they nicknamed him—"*Little Scotch Granite.*"

Well, at the close of the session, when the list of marks was read over, Willie's was so low, that he could hardly keep from crying, for he was very sensitive, and he wanted to stand high on the list.

After reading the list over, the teacher made a short speech. "Boys," said he, "I have a little gold medal to give, before we break up. And I wish to give it, not to the boy who has the largest number of good marks on my list, but to the one among you who has been the most faithful in all his duties, and the most truthful in telling about them. And I want you to let me know who ought to have this medal?"

In a moment, more than forty boys cried out—"Little Scotch Granite! Little Scotch Granite!"

Willie got the medal, and went home feeling very happy that day. He had been faithful all through the session, and he had his reward, not only in the gold medal that hung round his neck, but in the good opinion of his fellow scholars, and in the respect, and confidence of his teacher.

Now, we have spoken of *four* good points in the model that Moses has left us. He was *faithful to God; faithful to himself; faithful to his family;* and *faithful in all things.* Let us try to follow this model.

Then we shall be faithful, and God will bless us, and make us blessings to all about us.

I will close this sermon with some simple lines. The heading to them is—"The best that I can do."

And if we try to follow them they will lead us, like Moses, to be faithful in all things.

These are the lines :—

THE BEST THAT I CAN DO.

"I cannot do much," said a little star,
  "To make the dark world bright!
My silvery beams cannot struggle far,
  Through the folding gloom of night;
But I'm only a part of God's great plan,
And I'll cheerfully do the best I can."

"What is the use," said a fleecy cloud,
  "Of these few drops that I can hold?
They will hardly bend the lily proud
  Though caught in her cup of gold!
But I am a part of God's great plan,
So my treasures I'll give, as well as I can!"

A child went merrily forth to play,
  But a thought, like a silver thread,
Kept winding in and out all day,
  Through the happy golden head;
Mother said, "Darling, do all you can,
For you are a part of God's great plan!"

She knew no more than the glancing star,
  Nor the cloud, with its chalice full,
How, why, and for what, all strange things were—
  She was only a girl at school!
But she thought, "It's a part of God's great plan
That even *I* should do all that I can."

So she helped a younger child along,
   When the road was rough to its feet,
And she sang from her heart a little song
   That we all thought passing sweet,
And her father, a toil-worn, weary man,
Said, "I, too, will do the best that I can!"

Our best! Ah, children, the best of us
   Must hide our faces away,
When the Lord of the vineyard comes to look
   At our tasks at the close of day!
But, for strength from above, 'tis the Master's plan,
We'll pray, and we'll do the best that we can.

JOSEPH, THE MODEL REALIZER OF GOD'S PRESENCE.

"How then can I do this great wickedness, and sin against God?"—GENESIS xxxix: 9.

HESE were the words of Joseph when he was tempted to do what was wrong. He was one of the best, and greatest men of whom we read in the Bible. And one of the chief things that helped to make him so good, and great, was the constant sense he had of God's presence. He not only *believed* it; but he *felt* it. He *realized* it. He acted all the time, as though he saw the eye of God looking at him. And so we may speak of Joseph as—*the model realizer of God's presence*. And if we learn to follow this model, it will prove a great blessing to us.

It is easy to speak of *four* ways in which his sense of God's presence proved a blessing to Joseph. And if we learn to follow the model he thus sets before us, it will be a blessing to us in the same ways.

In the first place, when Joseph realized God's presence—he found in it—COMPANY IN HIS LONELINESS.

JOSEPH IS SOLD TO THE ISHMAELITES BY HIS BROTHERS.

We can easily think of different occasions in Joseph's life when he must have felt very lonely. There was one, for instance, when he came to his brethren, to inquire how they were, as they were feeding their flocks in Dothan. They saw him coming, and made up their minds to kill him. When he came up to them, they seized him roughly, and stripped him of the coat of many colors, which his father had given him. Reuben persuaded them not to kill him. But they cast him into a deep pit, and left him there by himself, all night. How lonely he must have felt then!

And after this, when he was sold as a slave into Egypt, and found himself a stranger, in that strange land, with not a single person in the whole country that he knew, and not one that knew him, how lonely he must have felt!

And then, when on account of the false accusation of his master's wife, he was suddenly cast into prison, how lonely he must have felt! But we are told that "the Lord was with Joseph," in the prison. And the sense he had of God's presence, took away the feeling of loneliness, and made him happy, and contented, even when he was shut up in that lonely cell.

And this sense of God's presence which he had, must have given him a feeling of companionship in all his times of loneliness.

And there are times with us all, when we have to be separated from our friends, and be left alone. But, if we learn to realize God's presence as Joseph did, this will make us feel that we have pleasant company in our most lonely home.

One of the best and holiest men that ever lived, was

Henry Martyn, the English missionary to Persia. In carrying on his work there, he had many long and lonely journeys to take. But, how sweetly he realized God's presence, as giving him company in his loneliness, is seen in these beautiful lines, which were found after his death, written on one of the blank leaves of the Bible, that he carried with him, wherever he went.

> "In desert woods with Thee, my God,
> Where human footsteps never trod,
>   How happy could I be!
> Thou, my repose from care, my light
> Amid the darkness of the night,—
>   *In solitude my company.*"

And how many of God's dear children have realized His presence in just the same way! Here are some illustrations of this.

The Companionship of Jesus. This incident was told by one of our chaplains in the late war.

"I went into a tent connected with the general hospital one day," says he. "There, on one of the beds, lay a beautiful drummer-boy, about sixteen years of age, burning up with fever.

"'Where is your home, my young friend?' I asked.

"'In Massachusetts, sir,' was his reply. 'And do you not feel very lonely here, so far away from your father and mother, and all your friends, and so sick as you are?'

"I never can forget," says the chaplain, "the sweet smile that lighted up his deep blue eyes, and played over his fevered lips, as he said, in answer to my question, 'Oh, no, sir. How can I feel lonely when Jesus is with me?'"

That dear boy was realizing God's presence, in just the way of which we are speaking; and he found company in it.

The Presence of Jesus. In one of the countries of India, where the leprosy prevails, a young Christian girl was taken with this terrible disease. A cell was prepared for her to occupy. She was carried to this cell, and was told that she must remain there, by herself, as long as she lived. None of her friends could be allowed to come and see her, for fear of taking the disease. How dreadful this was! Of course she felt very sad on entering that lonely place. But hear what took place to give her comfort. When she fell asleep, the first night spent in that cell, she had a dream.

In that dream she saw the blessed Saviour come into her cell. He was wearing the crown of thorns on his head, and in his hands and feet she saw the marks of the nails which had fastened him to the cross. He stood by the side of her bed, and laid His hand lovingly on her head, while, in the gentlest possible way He said: "Fear not, my child. I will be with thee, and will never leave thee, or forsake thee!"

She woke in the morning feeling very differently from the way she had felt the night before. She never forgot that dream, and the thought of it lighted up her cell, and took away all its loneliness. It enabled her to realize the presence of Jesus, and in that she found sweet company. Her sufferings were very great. After awhile she lost her eyesight. But, even in her blindness, she felt that Jesus was with her, and the thought of His presence took away her sense of loneliness. She realized the truth of John

Newton's sweet lines, in which, when speaking of the presence of Jesus, he says:—

> "While blest with a sense of His love,
> A palace, a toy would appear;
> And prisons would palaces prove,
> If Jesus would dwell with me there."

The Visits of Jesus. There was an old Christian gentleman, who had been for many years a successful merchant. He was once very well off, and had been surrounded by a happy family. But he had failed in business, and was left very poor. His wife and children had all died. In poverty and loneliness he had to spend the closing years of his life. A Christian friend, who used to call and see him occasionally, was talking with him one day, and said, "Well, I hope Jesus visits you sometimes." "*Visits* me sometimes," said the old man, "why, *he lives with me at* ALL *times!*" And so, in realizing the presence of that blessed Saviour, he found company in his loneliness. And if we follow the model which Joseph sets before us, it will bring this blessing to us; and we shall find company in our loneliness.

In the second place, as he realized God's presence, Joseph found—COMFORT IN TROUBLE.

And we shall find the same, just so far as we follow the model he has left us. Few persons have had such great troubles to bear as Joseph had. And yet he bore them bravely, and cheerfully. And the secret of it was, he felt that God was present with him, all the time, and he found comfort in this thought. This gave Joseph comfort, when nothing else could have done so. And if we follow the model which he left us, and learn to realize God's presence, as he did, we shall find comfort, under all our troubles, in the feeling that He is with us. Let us look at some examples of the way in which this comfort is found.

The Nearness of God. A city missionary in London used often to visit a poor old widow. She lived in a garret alone by herself. All she had to live on was half a crown a week, allowed her from some charity. This was only a little over half a dollar of our money, and was barely enough to keep her alive.

The missionary used to notice, standing on her window-sill, an old broken tea-pot, in which a strawberry plant was growing. He felt interested in watching it, and seeing how it grew. One day he said to the old woman,—"I am glad to see how nicely your plant is growing. You'll soon have some berries ripening on it." "I don't care about the fruit," she said. "It's not *that* which leads me to watch over this little plant. But I am too poor to keep any living creature with me. And I love to have this little plant in my room. I know it can only live and grow by the power of God. And as I look at it, from day to day, and see it growing, it makes me feel that God is here with me, and I find great comfort in that thought."

Don't Worry. During the reign of Oliver Cromwell in England, an English ambassador was going to Sweden, to represent his country there. He was a good Christian man; but things were in such a troubled state in England, that he was sorry to be obliged to leave, and was greatly disturbed on this account.

The last night he spent in England, before sailing

for Sweden, he was so distressed that it was impossible for him to sleep. He had a faithful man-servant, who was an earnest, intelligent Christian. He was grieved to see his master so much distressed. He heard him tossing about on his bed, and sighing and groaning. At last he rose, and went into his master's chamber, and apologizing for disturbing him, at such an hour, he begged to be allowed to ask him two or three questions. Permission was granted. Then he said: "Pray, sir; don't you think that God governed the world very well, before you came into it?"

"I do."

"And pray, sir, don't you think that He will govern it quite as well, when you are gone out of it?"

"Certainly I do."

"Pardon me, sir, but don't you think you might safely leave Him to govern it while you are in it, without being so much troubled?"

This was a view of the matter he had never taken. But he saw it was the right view to take.

He thanked his faithful servant for the suggestion he had made. He resolved to put away the thought which had been troubling him. Then he turned over, and went quietly to sleep. He realized God's presence, and this gave him comfort in his trouble.

The Secret. "Mother," said a little girl, ten years old, "I want to know the secret of your going away into the woods, every morning, and evening." Their cottage was a very little one, and when this good mother wanted to be alone to pray, she had to go into the woods near by, for this purpose. "Why do you ask this question, my dear?" said the mother.

"Because I think you must go there to see somebody you love very much."

"What makes you think so?" asked her mother.

"Because I always notice that when you come back, you seem happier than when you went."

"Well, suppose I do go there to see a friend that I love very much, and that after meeting him, and talking with him, I feel happier than before, why should you wish to know anything more about it?"

"Because I should like to go with you, and perhaps it will make me happier too." "Well, my child, when I leave you in the morning, and the evening, and go into the woods, I go to meet my blessed Saviour, and pray to Him. And when I come away I feel that He is with me; and the thought of His presence is a help and a comfort to me all day."

"Oh! that's the secret of it, is it?" said the child; "then please always let me go with you, when you go, and then perhaps the blessed Saviour will be with me too, to help and comfort me." Yes! that is just what He will do for us all, if we follow the model Joseph has left us, and learn to realize His presence, wherever we are.

I have one more story to tell in connection with this part of our subject. It is about a storm at sea, and the comfort that was found from realizing God's presence. We may call it—

The Mind Stayed on God. A ship was tossed at sea in a tremendous storm. Day after day the storm raged, and lashed the ocean into foam and fury. The captain, who had followed the sea for many years, said *that* was the severest storm he had ever met with. The wild winds whistled fearfully through the rigging; and wave after wave broke over the ship, with a force that threatened its destruction.

There was a precious treasure on board that ship. She was carrying two young missionaries out to India, to preach the gospel of Jesus, to the benighted heathen. And with them were two noble-hearted Christian ladies. They had "forsaken houses, and brethren, and sisters, and father, and mother," and all the comforts of home to be helpers to those Christian men, in the great work to which their lives were devoted. One of them lay helpless in her berth, utterly prostrated by sea-sickness. The captain had just come down from the deck, into the cabin, looking very sad and sorrowful. "The ship must go down. They had better all prepare for death," he said. Then he covered his face with his hands, and wept, as much in sympathy for his passengers, as from a sense of his own danger.

One of the ladies asked her husband if it would not be well for them to have prayers? He said the confusion was too great to engage in any formal service. She asked if they could not sing a hymn?

"Sing, my dear, by all means, if you can. I can't sing under these sad circumstances." The lady struck up, all alone, in a clear, though trembling voice, the words of that beautiful hymn,

> "How firm a foundation, ye saints of the Lord,
> Is laid for your faith in His excellent word!
> What more can He say, than to you He hath said,
> You who unto Jesus for refuge have fled.

'In ev'ry condition—in sickness, in health,
In poverty's vale, or abounding in wealth,
At home and abroad, on the land on the sea,
As thy day may demand, so thy succor shall be.

"Fear not, I am with thee! Oh, be not dismayed!
For I am thy God, and will still give thee aid;
I'll strengthen thee, help thee, and cause thee to stand,
Upheld by my righteous, omnipotent hand.

"When through the deep waters I cause thee to go,
The rivers of woe shall not thee overflow;
For I will be with thee thy troubles to bless,
And sanctify to thee thy deepest distress.

"When through fiery trials thy pathway shall lie,
My grace, all sufficient, shall be thy supply;
The flame shall not hurt thee; I only design,
Thy dross to consume, and thy gold to refine.

"The soul that to Jesus hath fled for repose,
He will not,—He will not, desert to his foes;
That soul though all hell shall endeavor to shake,
He'll never, no never, no never, forsake."

As the lady went on singing this sweet hymn, her voice gained in strength, and the gentlemen joined with her, their confidence in God increasing as they went on. The sick lady, though a staid Presbyterian, and not a Methodist, sat up in her bed, clapped her hands and shouted "Glory to God!" The captain wiped away his tears, rose up, and said, "I'll make one more effort to save the ship," and then went up on deck. On reaching the deck he found that the thick black clouds had parted; the wind had died away; and the sun shone out upon them with its cheering rays. Jesus had said to the roaring winds—"Peace, be still." The storm had passed away; and they went on their voyage comforted and rejoicing. What a beautiful illustration this was of that sweet promise—"Thou wilt keep him in perfect peace, whose mind is stayed on thee—*because he trusteth in thee!*"

That good Christian lady had a realizing sense of God's presence, and *that* brought comfort to herself, and her companions, in the great trouble that was overwhelming them. And in all the cases I have mentioned, we see what comfort was found in trouble, by those who followed the model, Joseph has set us, of realizing God's presence.

In the third place, Joseph found—STRENGTH FOR DUTY—*in realizing God's presence; and if we follow the model he has set us, we shall find the same.*

When his father told him to take that long journey, from Beersheba, where he lived, to Shechem, where his other sons were feeding their flocks, that he might see his brethren, and inquire how they were, Joseph obeyed his father, without a moment's hesitation. He knew very well that his brethren did not love him. They hated him because of his dreams; and because their father had unwisely let it be seen, that he loved Joseph more than he did any of his other sons. Joseph had reason therefore to fear that his brethren would not be kind to him. But, of course, he could have had no idea of the cruel way in which they were going to treat him. Still he obeyed his father at once. He felt sure that God would be with him, and this thought gave him strength to do his duty.

The same feeling gave him strength to do his duty

in the house of Potiphar; and very soon he rose to the highest place in that household.

And when he was cast into prison, he did his duty there so faithfully, that the keeper of the prison, soon had so much confidence in him, that he left the whole management of it in his hands. And it was the constant feeling of God's presence, which Joseph had, that gave him strength to do his duty, in all those trying circumstances. And if we follow the model Joseph has left us, of realizing God's presence, it will have just the same effect on us. It will always give us strength for duty, whatever that duty may be.

Let us look at some illustrations of this point. We may begin with a story about:—

A Brave Sailor Boy. He was a cabin-boy on board an English man-of-war. He had a pious mother, and was trying to be a Christian; and the story shows how the sense he had of God's presence strengthened him for duty, under very trying circumstances, and made him eminently useful to his shipmates, and to his country. The sailors called this boy "Cloudy." The incident, to which I refer, took place in the midst of a terrible naval battle between the English and the Dutch. The flagship of the English fleet was commanded by the brave Admiral Narborough. His vessel, had got separated somehow, from the rest of his fleet, and was drawn into the thickest of the fight. Two of its masts had just been shot away, and had fallen with a fearful crash upon the deck. The Admiral saw that all would soon be lost unless he could bring up the rest of his ships to help him. He summoned a lot of his men upon the quarter deck.

He could not send a boat, but he asked if any of them would volunteer to swim through the fight, and take an order for the rest of the fleet to come up, at once to his help. A dozen men offered to go; and little Cloudy made the same offer. The Admiral smiled, when he looked at him, and said: "Why, Cloudy, what can you do?"

"I can swim, sir, as well as any of them. You can't spare these men from the guns, sir. It won't make much matter if I am killed. But I'm sure that God will take care of me. Please, sir, let me go." "Go, my brave lad," said the Admiral, "and may God bless you!"

He thanked the Admiral, and running to the side of the ship, sprang over into the sea, and struck out bravely towards the ships, which he was to order up. The men cheered him, and then went back to their guns.

The fight went on; but the Dutch were getting the best of it. The Admiral was feeling very sadly. He did not see how he could hold out much longer. He said to himself—"I have never hauled down the flag of old England yet. I'd rather die than do it now. But how can I help it?"

Just then he heard a firing to the right. Looking through the clouds of smoke, that surrounded him, he saw that the brave boy had got through his long and dangerous swim. He had delivered the order entrusted to him; and the expected ships were coming, crowding down upon the enemy. This turned the tide of battle. The Dutch were soon beaten, and the flag of old England was not hauled down that day.

In the evening the Admiral called his men on deck, to thank them for their brave conduct. And then, turning to Cloudy, who was also present, he said:

"And I want especially to thank you, my brave lad, for your noble conduct. *We owe this victory to you.* I hope to live to see you have a flagship of your own, some day."

And it turned out just so. That cabin-boy went on, realizing God's presence; and this gave him strength for duty, till he was knighted by the king, and known in the English navy as—Admiral Sir Cloudsly Shovell.

The Thought of God's Presence. A boy, about fifteen years of age, attended a mission chapel in China. He had become a Christian, and was trying to serve the Lord Jesus. His father was dead, and his mother and brothers were still heathens. They did not want him to be a Christian. They treated him very unkindly, and did all they could to keep him from going to hear about Jesus; but still he went. One Sunday his mother sent two of his elder brothers to bring him away from the mission service. She had his hands tied behind him and beat him severely. Then she told him to go and work in the garden, all the rest of the day, and said that if he did not do as he was told, she would whip him to death.

He told his mother that since he had learned about Jesus, he loved her better than he had ever done before. He said he wanted to do what was right, and be a good son to her. He was willing to work hard all the week; but that the Sabbath was God's day, on which He had said we must not work. "Jesus is watching me all the time, mother. He will see me if I work to-day, and it will displease Him. He is so great, and so good, that I dare not disobey His command. If you are determined to whip me to death for not working on the Lord's day, I will pray to Jesus to forgive you, because you do not know what you are doing. But I would rather be whipped to death, than do what I know will offend the Lord Jesus Christ. We must all die once, and since I have found Jesus I am not afraid to die. Death will only take me to heaven, when I shall be happy with Jesus forever." What a noble speech that was for a boy to make! He was realizing the presence of Jesus, and that gave him strength to do his duty. The brave boy's speech had such an effect on his mother that she untied his hands, and gave up the idea of whipping him any more. She let him go to the missionary meetings. She began to attend the meetings with him, and before long she learned to love the Saviour too, and became a Christian.

And if we follow the model that Joseph has left us, we shall find that realizing the presence of God will be sure to give us strength for duty.

And then, when Joseph realized the presence of God, he found that it gave him—VICTORY OVER TEMPTATION. And if we follow the model he has left us, we shall find that it will do the same for us.

The wife of his master, Potiphar, was trying to persuade Joseph to do what would have been very wrong. But, the thing that kept him from doing it, was the feeling he had that God was looking at him, all the time. This led him to say, in the words of our text—"How can I do this great wickedness, and sin against God?" It gave him victory over temptation.

But we all have temptations to meet with, wherever we go. And the very best way of meeting these temptations, is to imitate the model Joseph has left us, by trying, as he did, to realize God's presence, and never to forget that his eye is always upon us.

The Thought of God's Eye. Emma Gray was a Sunday-school girl, who was trying to serve the Lord Jesus Christ, and to make herself useful. As she was going to school one day, during the week, she passed a little boy, whose hand was thrust through the railings of a gentleman's front garden, trying to steal some flowers.

"Oh, my little boy," said Emma, kindly, "do you think it's right to take those flowers; without asking leave?"

"I only want two or three," said the boy, "and nobody sees me."

"You are mistaken there, my boy. God is looking at you from yonder blue sky. He says we must not take what does not belong to us, without leave. And if you do it, He will see it, and it will grieve Him."

"Then, if He's looking at me I won't do it," said the little fellow. And so, as he thought of God's eye, or realized God's presence, it gave him the victory over the temptation to steal those flowers.

Spoiling his Trade. A mission Sunday-school was started in a very wicked part of London. A good many boys in that neighborhood got their living by stealing. Some of these boys were persuaded to go to this school. One boy, who was a great thief went there. After he had been going for some time, one of his companions asked him how he liked the school.

"I don't like it at all," said he.

"Why not?" asked his friend.

"Because, you see, they are all the time talking about God seeing you, and the like o' that; and it just makes a fellow feel afeard. It takes all the pluck out o' me, I know.

"Many a time now, when I see a good chance to get a hankercher, or a nice purse of money, just as I'm going to take it, I think of that great eye looking at me. And then I'm afeard, and have to stop. So, you see, it's spoiling my trade. And I'll either have to give up going to the school, or else have to learn another trade, and try and get my living in some other way."

Here, we see, the true effect which must always follow from realizing God's presence. We cannot go on doing what we know to be wrong, when we feel that God is looking at us. It always gives us victory over the temptation to do what we know is wrong. It did this for Joseph, and it will do the same for us.

How many wicked words and acts, children, as well as grown people, might be kept from saying and doing, if they could only be reminded, at the right time, that God is looking at them!

Those Four Words. A gentleman, who is an earnest Christian, and a faithful Sunday-school teacher, tells this story of himself when he was a boy.

My father had a grafted pear tree in his garden. It was a very choice graft, and he watched it with great care. The second year it blossomed, but it only bore one pear. As there would be no more that year, he was very anxious about it. He hoped that no rough wind would blow it off. He looked at it every morning and evening, and was glad to find it safe.

He told all the children, on no account to touch it, for the fruit was tender, and must not be handled. The thought never occurred to him that one of his children would wish to steal it.

Every one, that came to see my father, was taken into the garden to look at that pet pear; and they all said that it was likely to ripen into a first-rate fruit, and that next year the tree would bear many more.

I never touched the pear with my fingers, but my eyes were often fixed upon it, and I longed to taste it. Instead of resisting this temptation, and praying for strength to overcome it, I gave way to it, till I became a slave to it. The desire for that pear got to be my master.

One night, after we children were all in bed, the thought of that pear would not let me sleep. I crept out of bed, and went to the window. My father and mother were not at home, but the back door was left unlocked, for them to get in if they came home late.

I put my head out of the window and saw the tree; after awhile I saw the pear. I said to myself my mouth is parched, and I must have something to moisten it.

I put on my clothes, and crept down the back stairs on my bare feet, went out at the back door, and soon reached the pear tree. As I stood there, the thought came into my mind, "What will father say?" But I answered the question by saying to myself—"He will not know who took it."

So I had made up my mind to take the pear and eat it. I stood there under the tree, and was looking up, with my hand stretched out to take the pear. But just then I saw a star, shining down upon me, through the leaves. All at once it seemed as if I heard some one repeat these four words:

Thou God seest me.

I put my hands before my eyes, and ran, as fast as I could, to the open door, and up the back stairs to bed.

There I stood trembling. I knew that God had seen me, and I thought my father and mother, and the servants and neighbors must know of it, and that everybody would call me a thief.

But I crept into bed, and thanked God for keeping me from stealing that pear. Then I fell asleep, and slept sweetly.

The next day, my father came in from the garden, and said "the pear was ripe, and might be taken down and eaten; but who was to have it?" I cried out, hardly knowing what I did—"God ought to have it."

This was so strange an answer, that my father and mother wondered at it, and father said: "Pray, what put that into your mind?"

I felt my cheeks getting red, and tears came into my eyes. I began to sob. Then I told how near I had come to being a thief, and how God had made use of that star to keep me from it.

My mother cried aloud; father wiped the tears from his eyes, and taking me very tenderly to his breast, said, "Then it shall be as you say; God shall have the pear, and we will give it to Him through one of His dear children."

"Suppose," said he to mother, "we give it to our neighbor's child, poor little Annie, who has been so long on her sick bed. Her lips are often very much parched, and she seldom has anything to moisten them with but cold water."

Mother consented willingly enough. She went with me herself, to carry the pear to the poor sick child. And how she did enjoy it! and how she thanked us for it! It did me more good than if I had had a dozen such pears given me to eat, without any fear or dread.

Here we see how this boy got the victory over temptation by realizing God's presence.

Joseph stands before us as the model realizer of God's presence. It was a blessing to him in four ways.

It gave him *company in his loneliness; comfort in trouble; strength for duty;* and *victory over temptation.* And if we learn to realize that presence as he did, it will be a blessing to us, in just the same way. Remember these four words whenever you think of Joseph: *company—comfort—strength—*and *victory.*

I will close this sermon with some sweet lines, which contain the substance of all I have now been trying to say. They were written for children, and are so plain and simple that even the little ones in the Infant school may understand them. The heading to them is:

NEVER OUT OF SIGHT.

"I know a little saying,
    That is altogether true;
My little boy, my little girl,
    This saying is for you.
'Tis this, O blue and black eyes,
    And gray—so deep and bright—
No child, in all this careless world
    Is ever out of sight.

"No matter whether field or glen,
    Or crowded city's way,
Or pleasure's laugh, or labor's hum,
    Entice your feet to stray;
Some one is always watching you,
    Or whether wrong or right,
No child in all this busy world
    Is ever out of sight.

"Some one is always watching you,
    And marking what you do,
To see if all your words and acts
    Are honest, brave, and true;
And watchful, more than mortal kind,
    God's angels, pure and white,
In gladness, or in sorrowing
    Are keeping you in sight.

"O bear in mind, my little one,
    And let your mark be high!
You do whatever thing you do,
    Beneath some watching eye;
Bear it in mind, my little one,
    And keep your good name bright,
No child in all this great round world
    Is ever out of sight."

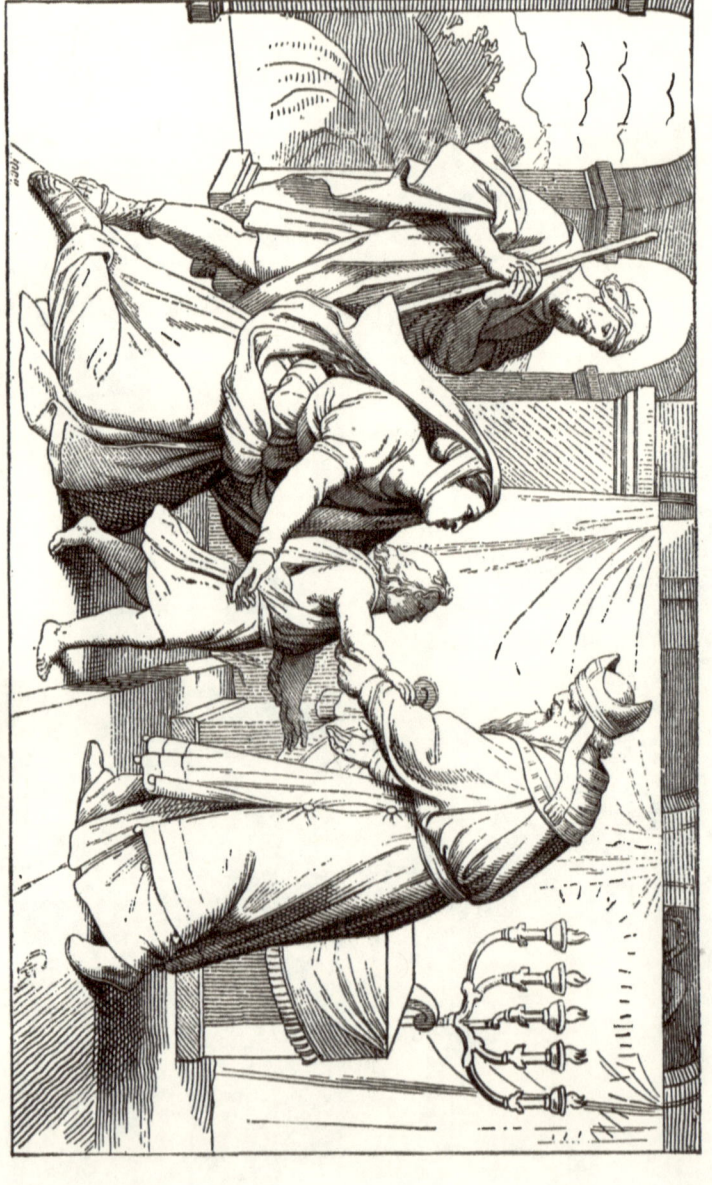

SAMUEL'S MOTHER BRINGS HIM TO ELI THE PRIEST.

SAMUEL, THE MODEL OF EARLY PIETY.

"And the Lord came and called—Samuel, Samuel. Then Samuel answered, Speak; for thy servant heareth."
—1 Samuel iii: 10.

THESE words were first spoken more than three thousand years ago. Samuel, to whom they refer, was then only a little boy. In the first verse of this chapter he is spoken of as—"the *child* Samuel." His mother had been married a good while, but had no children. She wanted very much to have a son. She prayed earnestly to God to give her a son; and she promised the Lord that if He would hear her prayer, and be so kind as to let her have a son, she would "give him unto the Lord all his days." God graciously heard her prayer. A son was born to her. She was filled with gladness, when this event took place, and she called his name Samuel, which means "asked of the Lord." She did not forget her promise, but nursed her son tenderly, and carefully, till he was weaned, and then she took him to the tabernacle of the Lord at Shiloh, and gave him to Eli the Priest, and left him there, that he might make himself useful in the service of God's house. Dear child! he was too young then to do much work. But he could light a candle, or sweep the floor, or hold a dish, or run on an errand, or shut a door; and because he did such little things, to please God, it is said that "*Samuel ministered to the Lord;*" and in this way he was very useful.

One night, Eli, who was an old man, had gone to bed; the service of the day was over; the lamp of God was yet burning in the tabernacle, and Samuel had lain down to sleep. All was still, and quiet as the grave, when suddenly he heard his name called—"Samuel—Samuel." He answered at once,—" Here am I"—and, supposing it was Eli, the aged priest, who wanted him, he rose—"and ran to him, and said, here am I, for thou calledst me. And he said I called not; lie down again. And he went and lay down." This was done three times, and each time Samuel ran to Eli, and asked what he wanted. At last Eli felt sure that it was God who was calling Samuel. Then he told him to go back once more, and if he heard the call again, to say—"Speak, Lord, for thy servant heareth."

The call came again. Samuel answered it. God spake to him, and he became, from that time, the servant and follower of the Lord.

We are not told how old "the child Samuel" was when this took place. We know not what his age was when his mother took him up to Shiloh, and left him there with Eli. And we know not how long he had been there, when God called him. But I suppose we

SAMUEL, THE MODEL OF EARLY PIETY.

may safely say that he was not more than eight or ten years old. And if this was so, then we may take Samuel as—*the model of early piety*.

And when we come to examine this model, we find that there are *four* good points about it; and each of these furnishes a good reason, why every young person should try to imitate the model which Samuel has left us.

In the first place, Samuel's early piety made him— A MODEL OF USEFULNESS.

Samuel became a *prophet* of the Lord, and was very useful in this way. He made known to the people of Israel, what God wanted them to do, and taught them how they were to serve and please Him.

And then he was a *judge*, as well as a prophet. He went out at stated times among the people, and settled their disputes and quarrels, and so he was the means of promoting peace and happiness among them. He did a great deal of good to the people of Israel in this way. And then, though Samuel was not a soldier, yet when the Philistines, their enemies, came against them in battle, he prayed to God for the success of the Israelites, and thus he was the means of obtaining a great victory for them. In addition to all this he was very useful as a teacher. He established schools that were called—"the schools of the prophets." They were places where young men, who were going to serve God as prophets and teachers of the people, might learn about the duties of religion, and be trained, and fitted for their work. And how much good was done to the people of Israel, in this way, no one can tell. And so we see that Samuel's whole life was one of usefulness in many ways. And all this grew out of his early piety.

And if we try to love and serve God, while we are young, as Samuel did, it will make us models of usefulness, as he was. We may not be prophets, or judges, like Samuel, but still it will be sure to make us useful. When we become Christians, and learn to serve God, it will make us useful in a great many ways. Then, as the apostle Paul says, we shall find that "whether we eat, or drink, or whatsoever we do," we shall be able to "do all to the glory of God." No matter how poor we may be, or how young, we shall yet be able to make ourselves useful, and do a great deal of good.

Here are some illustrations of the usefulness of young persons who were trying to serve God.

What a Child Did. In the neighborhood of Belleville, Alabama, was a man who was an infidel. He did not believe in God, and never thought of trying to please or serve Him. He lived in this beautiful world, and daily received God's mercies, but never thought of thanking Him for them. In this man's neighborhood, there lived a little girl who loved and served Jesus. While her father was absent from home, at one time, on business, she was taken very ill. He was sent for to see his child die. When he reached home, he found his neighbor, the infidel, in his sick child's room.

The little girl said to her father, "Papa, I'm going to die, but I am not afraid to die. I know that I am going to the blessed Saviour, and that I shall be happy forever with Him. Oh, papa, I want you to tell all the children about Jesus, and tell them to love and trust in Him."

She went on, for some time speaking of the happiness she had found in Jesus. While the dear child was thus speaking, the infidel looked on, and listened, till the big tears came rolling down his cheeks, and he said to the little girl's father,—"I must give up my infidelity. I know now that there is a God. Your little girl has proved it to me."

Surely that little girl's piety made her useful.

Another Illustration. A little girl named Mary, went with her parents from New England, to a home on one of the Western prairies. She was only ten years old, but she was trying to love and serve the blessed Saviour. When settled in her new home, she began to think what she could do to make herself useful there. She asked her mother, one day, if she might go and call on some of their neighbors' children. Her mother consented, and she went. In the first house at which she called, were two little girls, about her own age, named Susie and Jennie. Children-like they soon became well acquainted with each other, and were talking freely.

"Where do you go to Sunday-school?" asked Mary. "Sunday-school!" exclaimed the children; "what's that? we never saw one. What do they do at Sunday-school?" asked the children. "Come to our house next Sunday, at two o'clock, and I'll show you." The children promised to come. Mary secured the same promise from four other children in the neighborhood. Then she longed for Sunday. It came at last. At two o'clock the six little girls were all on hand. Mary welcomed them, and gave them seats in the parlor. "Now," she said, "I'm going to show you what a Sunday-school is." Then she took her hymn-book, and selected one of the hymns they used to sing in their school at home. She sang it alone; then she read the lesson she was to teach; then she knelt in prayer; then she sang another hymn. "And now," she said, "I'm going to tell you all I can remember, that our teacher told us about this lesson."

She talked on for fifteen or twenty minutes, while the children sat spell-bound with what they were hearing. Then followed another hymn, and the school closed.

"Well, what do you think of the Sunday-school?" asked Mary.

"Oh! it's splendid," they all exclaimed. Then they promised to come again next Sunday, and each to try and bring another scholar.

The next Sunday they had twelve scholars. The Sunday following there were twenty-four. Then the grown-up people in the neighborhood began to feel an interest in the work. A Bible class was formed. The school grew. Little Mary's parlor was too small for it. A school-house was built. Then a congregation was organized, and a church building put up. That church is now one of the strongest in all that part of the country, and *little Mary began all this good work.* How useful she made herself in trying to serve God!

Preaching a Sermon with a Shovel. I read lately about a little boy, who was trying to be a Christian, and of the good he did with his shovel. He was a shop-boy in a large store in Boston. Part of his duty was to keep the pavement, in front of the store, clear of snow and ice during the winter. A gentleman in that neighborhood watched this boy, and was very much pleased with him. He told his children about him, and urged them to follow his example. "No matter how early I go down," said he, "I am sure to find that pavement cleaned off. It does one good just to see it. The boy who keeps that pavement so clean, preaches a sermon with his shovel. It is a sermon on doing our work well, and not shirking it; a sermon on doing things promptly and without delay; a sermon on sticking to things day after day, and not giving up; a sermon on doing our own part, and not waiting for others to do theirs."

And if we are trying to serve God, as that boy was, whether we are working with needles, or brooms, or shovels, or hammers, or saws, or whatever it be, we shall be able to preach sermons, or make ourselves useful with them. Samuel's early piety made him a model of usefulness. And if we follow his example, in trying to serve God, while we are young, it will make us models of usefulness.

But, in the second place, Samuel's early piety made him—A MODEL OF HAPPINESS.

Religion is intended to make us happy. Loving and serving God, is the secret of true happiness. We sometimes see persons who profess to be religious, but who have very long faces, and always look gloomy and sad. They do not understand what religion is. There is some mistake in their views of it. Samuel's piety did not make him sad and sorrowful. Although while he was young he had to live away from home, and only saw his father and mother once a year, when they came up to worship God at the tabernacle, yet he was cheerful and happy. And when he grew up to be a man, he was always happy and cheerful. The people all loved him. They had confidence in him; and when they were in trouble, they would come and tell him of it, and ask his advice about what they had better do.

When our Saviour was on earth, in his conversation with the woman of Samaria, at Jacob's well, as we read in the 4th chapter of St. John, he compared true religion to a well of water, or a well of happiness in our hearts, "springing up unto everlasting life." This is the most beautiful definition of religion that ever was given. Samuel had this well of water in his heart, and no wonder that it made him happy. And if we learn to love and serve God, while we are young, as Samuel did, Jesus will open up this well of water in our hearts; and then, wherever we may be, and whatever may happen to us, we shall always be happy. Religion is intended to make us happy. It is God's great secret of happiness, and no one can be truly happy without it.

Now let us look at some illustrations of this subject.

Many years ago there was a good minister in England whose name was Toplady. He wrote a great deal of very sweet poetry about religion. There is a beautiful hymn of his, written on the words: "My meditation of Him shall be sweet." I will quote part of this hymn, because it illustrates very well this part of our sermon.

"When languor and disease invade
  This trembling house of clay;
'Tis sweet to look beyond our cage,
  And long to fly away;
Sweet to look inward, and attend
  The whispers of His love;
Sweet to look upward to the place
  Where Jesus pleads above.

"Sweet to look back, and see my name
  In life's fair book set down;
Sweet to look forward, and behold
  Eternal joys my own.
Sweet to reflect how grace divine
  My sins on Jesus laid;
Sweet to remember that His blood
  My debt of suffering paid.

"Sweet on His righteousness to stand
  Which saves from second death;
Sweet to experience day by day
  His Spirit's quickening breath,
Sweet on His faithfulness to rest,
  Whose love can never end;
Sweet on His covenant of grace,
  For all things to depend.

"Sweet in the confidence of faith
  To trust His firm decrees;
Sweet to lie passive in His hands
  And know no will but His.
Sweet to rejoice in lively hope,
  That when my change shall come,
Angels shall hover round my bed,
  And waft my spirit home."

Those who feel in this way, cannot help but be very happy; and yet this is the way that every one should feel who really loves Jesus.

For Mamma. A little girl, whose name was Dora, was busy at the ironing table one day smoothing out the towels and stockings. A Christian friend happened to come into the room just then. She looked at the industrious little girl a moment, and asked:

"Isn't this hard work for those little arms?"

A look of sunshine came into Dora's face, as she glanced towards her mother, who was rocking the baby, and softly said:

"It isn't hard work, when I do it for Mamma." She loved her mother, and that made it pleasant to work for her. And so, when we love Jesus, it makes everything pleasant that we do for Him. This is why religion makes us happy.

The Two Sailors. Two shipwrecked sailors were trying to reach the shore in a boat. One of them was a Christian, happy in the love of Jesus; the other was not a Christian. The storm was raging fearfully. After being tossed upon the waves, their boat was finally upset, and they were both seen struggling amidst the foaming billows. They were not far from the shore, and a friendly hand there, had fired out to them a rocket line. The man who was a Christian had caught hold of this line. Then he made his way up to his comrade, who did not know Jesus, and passing the line to him he said, "Take this, and try to save your life, for you are not prepared to die. I am safe in Jesus. Death has no sting for me. Take this rope and get on shore, and then learn to love the Saviour, so that you may be ready to die at any time." Thus they parted, and the drowning man who had so nobly given up his own life to save his companion, was heard, amid the howling of the storm, singing these words:

> "Jesus, lover of my soul,
> Let me to thy bosom fly,
> While the billows——"

But, just as he uttered the word—"billows"—a great wave swept over him, and he was seen no more.

How noble this was! And what a beautiful illustration this is, of the power of religion to make people happy under any circumstances!

Here is another illustration of a similar kind. We may call it,—

The Christian's Triumph. A Christian lady in New England, who was very rich, had just moved into an elegant new home. It was splendidly furnished. The walls were hung with the finest paintings. Here and there might be seen beautiful pieces of marble statuary. All that wealth could purchase, to make a home bright and attractive, had been put in that house. And then this lady had a loving husband, and a charming young daughter. But, shortly after moving into this lovely home, she was taken very sick. Her disease was one which the doctors could not cure. She would soon have to die, and leave her beautiful new home. Yet she shed no tears, and uttered no complaints.

A friend came in to see her one day. She expected to find her very sad and sorrowful, and had been trying to think of something she could say to comfort her. But she found her calm and cheerful. After talking with her a while, she looked around on the elegant things, and said to her friend: "Does it not make you feel sad, to think of leaving this sweet home? You have everything to live for."

"Very true," said the noble Christian, "but then you must remember, my friend, that I have everything to die for."

That was true. Yes, and it is true in reference to all who love the blessed Saviour. The home that is prepared for them, with Him, is better, far better, than anything this world contains. And if we are loving and serving Jesus, we may well say, with this good Christian lady, that we "*have everything to die for.*" And those who know this, may well feel very happy.

I will finish this part of our sermon, by quoting some lines which give a beautiful description of the Christian's feeling in this world, and show the secret of his happiness.

They are headed—*Trust in Jesus*. And this is the way in which they speak of a Christian:

"Happy, Saviour, must I be,
As I learn to trust in Thee;
Trust Thy wisdom me to guide,
Trust Thy goodness to provide;
Trust Thy saving love and power,
Trust Thee every day and hour;
Trust Thee as the only light
In the darkest hour of night;
Trust in sickness, trust in health,
Trust in poverty, and wealth;
Trust in joy, and trust in grief,
Trust Thy promise for relief;
Trust Thy blood to cleanse my soul,
Trust Thy grace to make me whole;

> Trust Thee living, dying too,
> Trust Thee all my journey through;
> Trust Thee till my feet shall be
> Planted on the crystal sea;
> Trust Thee, ever blessed Lamb,
> Till I wear the victor's palm;
> Trust Thee till my soul shall be
> Wholly swallowed up in Thee."

This is just the way in which true Christians will learn to trust in Jesus. It was trusting in this way, that made Samuel a model of happiness. And if we learn to follow his example, it will make us models of happiness too. The second thing about Samuel, is that his early piety made him a model of happiness.

In the third place, Samuel's early piety made him— A MODEL OF PERSEVERANCE.

To persevere means to keep on doing, whatever we begin to do, without giving up. One reason why some people never succeed in what they begin to do, is that they do not persevere. They soon get tired, and give it up. But this was not the way with Samuel. When he began to serve God, he persevered in it. He kept on trying without getting tired. He never gave it up, but went steadily on with it. From that memorable night—"When little Samuel woke, and heard his Maker's voice," until the day of his death, he persevered in serving God. He went steadily on, trying always to do God's will, and to please Him in all things. And it was a long time in which he thus persevered. We have seen that Samuel was only eight or ten years old when he began to serve God. We are not told how old he was when he died. But it is probable that he was not less than ninety years of age at the time of his death. Then he must have gone on serving God for eighty years. That was a long time. And when we think of Samuel, during all those years, as continually trying to serve God, and never getting tired, or giving up, we may well speak of him as—"*a model of perseverance.*" And if we try to serve God when we are young, as Samuel did, we shall be able to follow his example in this respect, and like him, we too, shall become models of perseverance.

But some may be ready to ask, "How can we be sure of this?" I answer, "Easily enough." It was the grace of God, which made Samuel pious when he was young; and which enabled him to persevere in serving God through all the years of his long life. And what the grace of God did for Samuel, it is able to do for you and me. That grace, like God himself, is Almighty. Whatever we have to do, we can do easily with the help of that grace. St. Paul said, "I can do all things through Christ strengthening me." He meant that he could do this by the help of God's grace. And this is just as true now, as it was eighteen hundred years ago, when St. Paul was here on earth.

The grace of God makes hard things easy, and crooked things straight. It enables us to go on in serving God as long as we live. It will make us like Samuel, models of perseverance. And it is the boys and girls who begin to serve God, when they are young, and learn to persevere, who become the most useful.

Let us look at some examples of perseverance, that may encourage us in trying to learn this very important lesson.

The Persevering Boy. A good many years ago, there was a poor boy in England, who was learning to be a shoemaker. Before he got through with his trade, he became a Christian. Then he made up his mind that whatever he attempted to do, he would keep on, and persevere till he got through with it. Afterwards he determined to study for the ministry. He began his studies, and went on perseveringly with them till he got through.

After he was ordained he went out as a missionary to India. And he became one of the most useful missionaries that the church ever had. He learned the language of the people among whom he preached. Then he made a grammar of that language. After this he made a dictionary. This dictionary filled up three large, heavy volumes. Then he translated the New Testament, and different parts of the Old Testament, into that language. This opened up the knowledge of Jesus, and his salvation, to millions of people in that country. The missionary of whom I am speaking was the celebrated *William Carey.*

Somebody asked Mr. Carey one day, how he managed to get through with so much work? The answer he gave to this question is one that we should all remember. He said: "I did it by plodding." To plod, means to keep on with anything we are doing, till we get through with it. To plod is the same as to persevere. And so Carey the missionary, in the great work he did in India, stands before us as—*a model of perseverance.*

The Story of a Bootblack. More than a hundred years ago, there lived a boy in the city of Oxford, in

England, whose name was George. He was so poor that he used to clean the boots of the students at the University, as the only means he had of getting a living. He was a Christian boy. He was very obliging and pleasant in his manners. He was warm-hearted, and generous, to all. The young men, whose boots he blacked, learned to love him. After awhile when they found out that George wanted to become a student, they agreed to help him along. They found him very quick to learn, and very persevering in his studies. He never lost a moment of time, but learned his lessons with the utmost diligence. He soon got to be one of the best students in the college. In this way he went on perseveringly, till he got through. Then he studied theology, and became a minister. Some of those who had helped him on, when he began his studies, made fun of him, and persecuted him, when they saw what an earnest Christian he was. But this did not move him. He was firm as a rock. Nothing could change him. He went steadily on, till he had finished his studies. Then he began to preach, and soon became one of the most eloquent, and successful ministers in the country. So many people flocked to hear him, that no church could hold them. Then he preached out of doors, in the open fields, and sometimes there would be as many as twenty thousand people at one time, listening to his preaching. He went about all over England, and all through this country, preaching the Gospel of Christ, and doing an amount of good, that never will be known till the last great day. This bootblack boy became the famous *George Whitfield*—the greatest preacher that the church has known, since the days of the apostle Paul. George Whitfield was a model of perseverance.

I will finish this part of our sermon, with a story of *two persevering bishops.*

The first of these was Bishop Doane, formerly Bishop of New Jersey. On one occasion he was in New York, trying to raise money for St. Mary's College at Burlington, where he lived.

He stayed there till the close of the week, intending to return home by the last train on Saturday evening. It was very important for him to reach home that evening, for he had an engagement to preach, and hold confirmation the next day. A little while before it was time for him to start for the train, a gentleman called to see him, who had some money to give him for the college. The Bishop was very uneasy, for he was afraid he might miss the train. As soon as he could do so, he excused himself to the gentleman, and hurried away to the railway station. But, when he arrived there, he found to his sorrow, that the train had left about ten minutes before! The Bishop was greatly troubled. He could not bear to think of not being in his place the next day. Many a man would have said: "Well, it's not my fault. I did the best I could. I can't help it. I am very sorry not to be able to keep my engagement for to-morrow. But I must give it up."

But Bishop Doane did not think, nor feel, in this way about it. He was a persevering man, and he resolved, if it was possible, to try and get home before Sunday morning. So he went to the agent and said: "My friend, is there no other train that goes through Burlington to-night?"

"No, sir," was the reply; "no passenger train. There is a freight train that leaves here in about half an hour."

"Very good," said the Bishop, "suppose you give me a ticket on that train. I can sit on the engine, or on the platform, in front of one of the cars. I have a very important engagement in Burlington to-morrow; and I must be there, if possible."

"I would gladly do so," said the agent, "if I could. But it is against the positive rules of our company, to take passengers on a freight train."

"Well," replied the Bishop, "I wouldn't on any account, tempt you to break the rules of the company. But have you room for any more freight in this train?"

"Yes, sir, plenty."

"Then put me on the scales, and see how much I weigh."

The agent weighed him, and said, "A hundred and seventy-five pounds."

"What do you charge," asked the Bishop, "for carrying that much freight?"

The agent told him. The Bishop gave him the money, and then said, "Now put me in one of the cars, and *carry me to Burlington as freight.*"

This was done, and the Bishop reached home, in time for his engagement on Sunday.

The other persevering Bishop, was Bishop Randall, the first missionary Bishop of Colorado, in the far-off West. He was spending a winter in the East, one year, trying to raise money for the college he had started at Denver. On one occasion, he was engaged to preach in a village a few miles from New York, where they had promised to give him a collection for his college. But the day proved to be very stormy. It had snowed steadily all night, and was snowing, and blowing furiously in the morning. The snow lay in great drifts along the road. The church was a long distance off. It was impossible to ride. If he went, he would have to plod his way through the piles of snow; and the Bishop wondered if it would be worth while to go, as there would be no congregation, and, of course no collection. But he was a persevering Bishop, and so he determined that *he* would be at the church, whether any one else was there or not. So he started; and battling manfully with the storm, he finally reached the church. When the time for service came, there was nobody there but himself and the sexton. After waiting a while, three or four gentlemen came in, and then they went on with the service. The Bishop talked about his college, with as much earnestness as though the church had been full.

At the close of the service, one of the gentlemen came up, and said, "Bishop, I have been very much interested, in what you have said about your college. I wish you would call at my office, in New York, tomorrow, and tell me some more about it." Then he told him where his office was, and the Bishop promised to call.

He called accordingly the next day. The gentleman asked him various questions about the college. The Bishop talked on awhile. Then the gentleman said, "Excuse me for a moment, sir." He turned to his desk; took out his check book, and drew the

Bishop a check for a thousand dollars. Then he went on asking questions, and the Bishop went on talking. Presently the gentleman said: "Please hand me back that check." Then he tore it up, and gave the Bishop one for fifteen hundred dollars. The Bishop talked on awhile longer. The gentleman's interest seemed to increase; and finally he took the check back again, and gave the Bishop one for *two thousand dollars.* And so, the persevering Bishop got his reward.

And if we learn to serve God early, as Samuel did, we shall become models of perseverance, like him.

And then, in the fourth place, Samuel's early piety made him—A MODEL OF HONOR.

The Bible speaks of two kinds of honor. One is "the honor that cometh from man," and the other, "the honor that cometh from God." The first of these is not worth much. It does not help to make us good or happy. It is only an empty name. In England, for example, when the Queen wishes to give a man what is called "the honor of knighthood," she allows him to have the title of Sir, written before his name. Thus, if his name was known as John Smith, he will, after this, always be spoken of as—*Sir* John Smith. This is considered a great honor, and men feel very proud of it. But, when Sir John Smith dies, this honor will all pass away. He will not be able to carry it with him, into the other world. It is like writing a man's name on the sand by the sea-shore. When the next tide rolls over it, it will be all swept away.

But "the honor that cometh from God" is very different from this. It is not a mere name. It is not the honor of what we *are called*, but of what we *are made to be*. It is something that will help to make us good, and great, and happy. And it is something that will last forever. When the angel Gabriel wanted to give Zacharias, the father of John the Baptist, an idea of the honor which belonged to him, he said: "I am Gabriel, that stand in the presence of God." St. Luke i : 19. He had the honor of standing close by the throne of God in heaven. He had this honor eighteen hundred years ago. He has this honor still, and he will have it forever.

And so it was with Samuel. He had the honor of being the servant of God. He had the honor of speaking, and working for God, when he was here on earth, more than three thousand years ago. And he has this honor still. God says, "Them that honor me, I will honor." Samuel honored God by beginning to serve Him while he was young. And God honored him by making him good, and great, and useful; and by causing him to be known, wherever the Bible is read, as "the friend of God." What an honor this was! We may well say that Samuel's early piety made him "a model of honor."

And, in the same way God will honor all those who serve Him, and especially those who learn to serve Him while they are young. God honors his servants by teaching them to do honorable things. Here are some illustrations of what I mean.

The True Gentleman. Harry Edmon was a Christian boy. One day while playing with some other boys in the street, he stumbled against an old man, and knocked his cane out of his hand.

In a moment, he ran and picked up the cane, and handing it respectfully to the old man, he said:

"Pardon me, sir, we were playing too roughly. I hope I did not hurt you."

"Oh, not a bit!" said the old man, very pleasantly. "Boys will be boys, and it's best they should be. Go on with your play, my lad."

Harry took off his cap, and made a polite bow, and then turned to his companions. One of the boys said to him, "Harry, why did you take off your cap so politely to that old fellow? He's no gentleman. He's only Giles the huckster."

"That makes no difference," said Harry; "the question is not whether he is a gentleman, but whether *I* am one." That was honorable in Harry.

Here are some sweet, simple lines about a poor little boy, who was trying to be a Christian, and how he made himself a model of honor. They are headed

JAMIE THE GENTLEMAN.

There's a dear little ten-year-old down the street,
   With eye so merry, and smile so sweet;
I love to stay him whenever we meet,
   And I call him Jamie the gentleman.

His home is of poverty, gloomy and bare,
   His mother is old with want and care—
There's little to eat, and little to wear
   In the home of Jamie the gentleman.

He never complains—though his clothes be old,
   No dismal whinings at hunger or cold;
For a cheerful heart, that is better than gold,
   Has brave little Jamie the gentleman.

His standing at school is always ten—
"For diligent boys make wise, great men,
And I am bound to be famous some day, and then—"
Proudly says Jamie the gentleman—

"My mother shall rest on cushions of down,
The finest lady in all the town,
And wear a velvet and satin gown"—
Thus dreams Jamie the gentleman.

"Trust ever in God," and "Be brave and true"—
Jamie has chosen these precepts two;
Glorious mottoes for me, and for you;
May God bless Jamie the gentleman!

If we take these two precepts of little Jamie, and follow them out, they will make us models of honor, just as they did with him.

Samuel was a model of early piety. And there were four good things about his piety. It made him— *a model of usefulness—a model of happiness—a model of perseverance—*and *a model of honor*. Let us follow his example in trying to serve God while we are young, and it will have the same effect upon us.

"Like Samuel let us say
Whene'er we read his word,
Speak, Lord! we would obey
The voice that Samuel heard;
And when we in thy house appear
Speak, for thy servants wait to hear."

DAVID, THE MODEL OF PRAISE.

"*Seven times a day will I praise Thee.*"—PSALM cxix: 164.

E might find a good many models in David's life and character. We might speak of him as the model shepherd. What care he took of his sheep! And when the lion, and the bear came, and ran away with one of his lambs, how bravely he went after them, and fought them, and brought his stolen lambs home again! We might speak of him as the model warrior. How nobly he offered himself to go and fight the great Philistine giant, when all the soldiers in Saul's army were afraid of him, and fled from him, as often as he came, and offered to fight them! We might speak of him as the model musician. He learned to play on the harp, when he was a boy taking care of his father's sheep. And he became so good a player, that he was known as one of the best musicians in the country. And when King Saul was troubled with an evil spirit, that made him sad and sorrowful, David was sent for, to come and play before the King. And he played so sweetly, that his

music used to cure the King. It took away his melancholy, and made him feel bright and cheerful again.

And then we might speak of him as the model King or ruler. He fought the battles of his people so bravely, and always got the victory over their enemies. He was like a father to his people. He was so kind to them, and took such care of them, and ruled them so faithfully, that he was a real blessing to all the people of Israel.

But we are going to pass all these things by, and to speak of David as *the model of praise*. He was remarkable for many things, but for nothing was he so remarkable as for the way in which he praised God. There are one hundred and fifty Psalms, in the book of Psalms in the Bible. David wrote nearly all of those Psalms; and he has more to say about praising God, in these Psalms, than about anything else. The word praise is found nearly a hundred times in these Psalms.

We do not any of us praise God as much as we ought to do. And anything, that may help us to learn to praise Him better, will be very useful to us. And so we shall speak of David as *the model of praise*. And there are *four* things about this model for us to speak of.

In the first place, David was a model of praise for— TEMPORAL—*blessings*.

We do not praise God, as much as we ought, for our temporal blessings. His mercies to us are new every morning. "He gives us life, and breath, and all things." He is pouring His benefits upon us all the time; and we should be constantly praising Him for these blessings. The light of day,—the air of heaven,—the use of our hands and feet, our eyes, and ears,—the food we eat,—the clothing we wear,—the health, and strength we have,—these are temporal blessings that God is giving us all the time. He gives them to us for nothing; and the least that we can do in return, is to thank Him, and praise Him continually for them.

Here are some illustrations of the way in which we should do this. The first is a story called—*The Contented Shepherd Boy*.

This boy was minding his sheep in a beautiful valley. He felt so happy that he was all the time singing out, to express the joy and thankfulness of his heart. Wherever he was, the glad echoes of his cheerful voice could be heard. One day the king of that country was out hunting. He was not known as the king, except by the friends who were with him. He heard this poor boy's merry songs, and thought he would like to have a little talk with him. So he made his way up to the boy, as he sat singing under a tree, while he was watching his sheep.

"Well, my boy," said the king, "tell me what it is that makes you so happy."

"Why shouldn't I be happy?" said the boy; "the king of the country is not richer than I am."

"Indeed!" replied the king. "Please tell me what you've got to make you so rich."

"Well, you see, sir, the sun in yonder clear blue sky, shines as brightly for me, as it does for the king. The trees on the mountains, and the grass and flowers in the valley do as much to please my sight, and make me glad, as they can do for him. Look at these two hands! why I wouldn't be without them for all the gold and silver that the king owns; and then I have the use of my eyes and my ears; I have all the food I want to eat, and all the clothes I want to wear, and what can the king have more than this?"

"You are right," said the king, with a smile. "But your greatest treasure is, that you have a contented, grateful heart. Keep it so, my young friend, and you will always be happy."

That boy had learned the lesson of thanking God for his *temporal* blessings, as David did.

Here is a story called—"*Every Day Blessings,*" that comes in very well here.

A gentleman was once stopped in the streets of London, by a stranger, who said to him: "Sir, did you ever thank God for the use of your reason?"

"I don't know that I ever did," replied the gentleman. "Then do it quickly," said the stranger, "for I have lost mine, and you may lose yours, if you are not thankful for it." We are very apt to forget to thank God for his daily blessings. And we do not know how much they are worth, till they are taken from us. We see this in the story of a little boy. He lived in Scotland. His name was James. When about eight years old, he had the smallpox. When he was getting better of it, his eyes were closed, so that he could not see. He was a sweet, gentle boy, and all the family loved him. He had a little sister named Annie, somewhat older than himself. She was very fond of him, and tried in every way to make him happy.

One day they took a long walk together, and sat down to rest, at the foot of a great tree. "Annie," said James, "what a pleasant day this is! The air feels so soft and warm to my face. And it is so nice to hear the water running over the smooth stones, and the sheep and the lambs bleating in the fields! Oh, how I wish I could *see* them again! And hark! there is a bird singing over our heads. How beautiful it used to be to sit down here, and look to the hills, and the clear blue sky; and to see the mill yonder, and the pretty ducks swimming in the pond! Oh, Annie, how hard it is to think that I shall never see these things again!" And then he burst into tears.

"Don't cry, Jamie dear," said his sister. "You may yet be able to see again. There was Daniel Scott, you know, who had the smallpox. He was blind for weeks; but then he got well, and now he sees as well as ever he did. And you know, as mother says, that God will do what is right about it. He can open your eyes if that is best. But if he leaves you to be blind, He can make you happy in some other way. And we will do all that we can for you. I'll walk with you, and read to you, and then it will not be so bad."

But poor James could not help thinking of his sad state. He sat there with his head upon his hands, and his elbows on his knees, and he kept on crying. The flood of tears pressed their way between his eye-lids, which had stuck together since his sickness; and when he lifted up his head, he called out, "Oh! Annie, I can see! I can see! There's the brook; and

DAVID, THE MODEL OF PRAISE.

there's the mill; and there are the sheep. Thank God, my eyes are open again and I can see."

After that Jamie never forgot to praise God for his eye-sight. And this is one of God's temporal blessings for which we should always praise Him.

Here is a story about a little girl who was not thankful for her daily blessings, and of the way in which her mother taught her the lesson of thankfulness. This girl's name was Kate; her mother's name was Mrs. Smith. At the close of the afternoon one day, Mrs. Smith called Kate to supper. As she sat down to the table Kate said: "I don't want any supper. There's nothing but bread and milk, and cake and berries. The same every night. I'm tired of them."

Mrs. Smith said nothing, but after supper was over, she put some things in a basket, and asked Kate to take a walk with her. She was going to visit a poor sick girl, who lived not far from their house. When they reached the place, they climbed up the tottering steps to the garret.

There, on a straw bed, near the only window in the room, lay the young girl asleep. She was so pale, and thin, and still, that she looked as if she was dead. But hearing footsteps woke her, and she opened her eyes. Mrs. Smith uncovered her basket, and gave the poor girl a drink of milk. Then she placed some bread, and cake, and berries on the table, and sat down beside the sick girl's bed, to watch the pleasure her visit had caused.

Kate's eyes filled with tears when she saw how eagerly the sick girl ate the supper, which she despised a little while before. That poor girl had not tasted a mouthful of anything since the morning.

Her mother had been away all the day working, and now came home wishing that she had something nice to bring to her poor sick child. But when she found how well she was cared for, her heart was overflowing with thankfulness. That supper seemed a feast to them. "If we can only keep a roof over our heads," said she, "and have a crust to eat, we ought to be thankful."

Kate never forgot what she saw and heard that night. It taught her the lesson of thankfulness. Let us all learn the same lesson. If we have a home to shelter us, and food to eat, let us never forget to praise God for His temporal blessings to us.

I will finish this part of our subject with some sweet lines on "*The Causes for Thankfulness.*"

"For all that God in mercy sends;
For health and children, home and friends,
For comfort in the time of need,
For every kindly word and deed,
For happy thoughts and holy talk,
For guidance in our daily walk,
   For everything give thanks!

"For beauty in this world of ours,
For verdant grass and lovely flowers,
For song of birds, for hum of bees,
For the refreshing summer breeze,
For hill and plain, for streams and wood,
For the great ocean's mighty flood,
   For everything give thanks!

"For the sweet sleep which comes with night,
For the returning morning's light,

> For the bright sun that shines on high,
> For the stars glittering in the sky,
> For these and everything we see,
> O Lord! our hearts we lift to Thee;
> > For everything give thanks!"

When David said, "Seven times a day will I praise Thee," we may well speak of him as a model of praise for temporal blessings.

But in the second place, David was a—MODEL OF PRAISE FOR SPIRITUAL BLESSINGS.

David was very thankful to God, for the temporal blessings bestowed upon him, as we have seen; but he was still more thankful for his spiritual blessings. He was always ready to praise God for these. There are many passages in the beautiful Psalms he wrote, which show this very plainly. This is what he means in one place, when he says that God's statutes—"are more to be desired than gold; yea, than much fine gold; sweeter also than honey, and the honey-comb." Ps. xix: 10. This is what he means again, when he says: "Because thy loving kindness is better than life, my lips shall praise thee. My soul shall be satisfied, as with marrow and fatness; and my mouth shall praise thee with joyful lips." Ps. lxiii: 3, 5. In another place he says: "Oh, how I love thy law; it is my study all the day." Ps. cxix: 97. "The law of thy mouth is better to me than thousands of gold and silver." Ps. cxix: 72. "I rejoice at thy word as one that findeth great spoil." Ps. cxix: 162. "My lips shall praise thee when thou hast taught me thy statutes." Ps. cxix: 171. "I will praise thy name for thy loving kindness, and for thy truth; for thou hast magnified thy word above all thy name." Ps. xxxviii : 2. We might quote many other passages for the same purpose; but these are enough to show us how truly David was a model of praise for spiritual blessings.

And it is easy to find illustrations of those who have followed David's example in this respect. Let us look at some of these. Here is one that we may call—

An Example of Thankfulness. We will suppose that you are going with me to visit a poor suffering Christian woman. We enter her room, where she lives by herself. The room is clean and airy. A bright little fire is burning in the grate. And in a corner of the room, you may see a woman, about sixty-four years of age, sitting up in her bed. Her hands are folded and stiff; and her whole body is crippled by the rheumatism, which she has had for thirty-eight years. For sixteen of those years she has not been able to be moved from her bed, nor to look out of the window, nor even to lift her hand to her face. But listen! with a cheerful voice she is thanking God for enabling her to use *one thumb*. She has a two-pronged fork fastened to a stick, with which she can take off, and put on her old-fashioned spectacles. By the same means, she can feed herself, and sip her tea through a tube, helping herself with that one thumb. And there is another thing she can do with her fork; she can turn over the leaves of a large Bible, which lies near her. A Christian lady, who visited her, lately asked her if she did not feel very lonely. In a pleasant, cheerful voice, she said: "I am alone, and yet not alone." "How can that be?" asked the lady. "Why, you see, ma'am, I feel that the Lord is always with me; and that I have much for which to praise and bless His holy name." "What is it that makes you feel so happy?" Now, mark what that poor sufferer said, in answer to this question: "Oh, it is the thought that my sins are forgiven me; and the thought of the wondrous love of Jesus, my blessed Saviour. I am content to lie here, as long as it is His blessed will that I should do so; and then, I know that He will take me to Himself forever."

What glorious praise that poor sufferer offered for her spiritual blessings!

Here is another illustration which we may call—

Poor Mary. She was left alone in the world, and had a hard time to get along. But she was a Christian, and had a heart always thankful to God for the spiritual blessings He had given her. One day, as she was returning to her lonely and desolate home, Mary overtook a rich lady who lived in the same neighborhood. She was a professing Christian too, but she had not learned the lesson of thanking God for her spiritual blessings. She had just lost one of her children, and was expecting to lose another. She was very sad and sorrowful. When poor Mary overtook her, the lady told her about her affliction, and talked on in such a way, that you might have thought she had not one single blessing left. Mary waited till she got through with what she had to say. Then she spoke very kindly, and lovingly to her, and tried to comfort her. She reminded her of the goodness and faithfulness of God, who had promised never to forsake His people. She exhorted her to be thankful for the many mercies she still enjoyed, and begged her to trust to the love of God, to give her all she needed.

By this time they had reached Mary's humble home. She asked the lady to step in; and taking her to an empty closet, she opened the door, and said, "Pray, ma'am, do you see anything there?" The lady answered—"No." She took her to another closet and repeated the question—"Pray, ma'am, do you see anything here?" The reply again was—"No." She took her to a third closet, and once more asked the question—"Pray, ma'am, do you see anything here?" The lady was a little displeased, and answered rather sharply—"No; why do you ask me these questions?" "Why, ma'am, those empty closets contain all that I have in the world. But why should I be unhappy? I have Christ in my heart, and heaven in my eye. I have God's own word of promise that 'bread shall be given me, and water shall be sure,' as long as I live in this world; and when I die, there is a bright crown of glory laid up for me in heaven. Should I not praise God for these great blessings?"

And, in this way, poor Mary tried to teach her rich neighbor the lesson of thankfulness to God for His spiritual blessings.

Here is a beautiful illustration of the lesson now before us, given by a little girl. She had been severely scalded, and was carried to a neighboring hospital, to linger there a while in great suffering, and then to die. Now most young persons would have been very sad and sorrowful under these circumstances. But this little girl was a Christian, and the knowledge she had of God's spiritual mercies to her, made her thankful and happy in the midst of her great sufferings. Night had come, and most of the patients, and the nurses too, were asleep in that hospital. But, as the clock struck—one—suddenly a low, sweet song was heard, coming from the cot, on which that suffering child was lying; and these were the words she sang:—

> "Jesus, the name to sinners dear,
> The name to sinners given;
> It scatters all my guilty fear,
> And turns my hell to heaven."

Then the voice was still for a while. But presently it was heard again, and seemed to sound more like heaven than earth, as it sang out these words:—

> "Happy, if with my latest breath
> I may but gasp His name,
> Preach Him to all, and cry in death,
> Behold, behold the Lamb!"

The nurse hastened to the bedside of her little charge; but before she reached it, the lips which had been singing were still in death. The child's spirit had winged its way to heaven. She died in the very act of praising God for the spiritual blessings He had given her.

I will close this part of our sermon, with some sweet and simple lines about:—

The Love of Jesus.

They contain the substance of all that I have been

trying to teach under this point of our subject; and I think the youngest scholar will be able to understand them:

> "My mother loves me dearly,
>   My father loves me well;
> But Jesus loves me better
>   Than ever I can tell.
>
> "My parents give me food, and clothes,
>   And many a loving kiss;
> But Jesus Christ, my Saviour,
>   Loves me much more than this.
>
> "With brothers dear, and sister,
>   And many a friend I'm blest;
> And they love me always fondly,
>   But, Jesus loves me best.
>
> "He came on earth to save me,
>   He takes me for his lamb;
> And He is always watching
>   Around me where I am.
>
> "His love gives all I have on earth,
>   His love gives all I see;
> But, most of all, in His sweet love,
>   He gave Himself for me.
>
> "So when, both night and morning,
>   I pray to God in heaven,
> And thank Him for the blessings
>   That He to me has given,
>
> "I'll say—'*For these, I bless Thee,*
>   Lord Jesus, God above;
> But, most of all, I thank Thee,
>   Lord Jesus, for thy love.'"

DAVID THE MODEL OF PRAISE.

DAVID, THE MODEL OF PRAISE.

In the second place, David was a model of praise for spiritual blessings.

In the third place, David was a model of—GROWING—*praise.*

When he had learned to praise God for His mercies, he went on praising Him more and more. When he first began to praise God, he only speaks of doing it once a day. He says: "My voice shalt thou hear in the *morning*." "I will sing of thy mercy in the *morning*." Ps. lix : 16. Then it seemed as if he thought that once a day, was not often enough to praise God; and so he speaks of his "prayer as being set forth as incense, and of the lifting up of his hands as an *evening* sacrifice." Ps. cxli : 2. Then he speaks of "praying and praising God in the evening, in the morning, and at noonday." Ps. lvii : 17. That was three times a day. And then, here in the words we have chosen for our text, he says: "*Seven* times a day will I praise Thee." This shows how the spirit of praise was growing in David. First he said he would praise God *once* a day; then *twice;* then *three* times; and now he says—"*Seven times* a day will I praise Thee."

Now we might think that seven times a day was often enough for praising God. But David did not think so.

The spirit of praise grew so strong in him, and his sense of God's mercies got to be so great, that we find him saying, in one place, "I will bless the Lord *at all times;*" and in another, "My praise shall be *continually* of thee." Ps. lxxi : 6.

And again he says, "I will hope continually, and

will praise Thee *more and more."* Ps. lxxi: 14. And so we may well speak of David, as a model of *growing* praise.

And if we look carefully at the book of Psalms, which David wrote, we can see plainly how the spirit of praise was growing in him all his days. When he first began to write the Psalms he had very little to say about praising God. In the first seven Psalms, the word praise only occurs once. But as he gets further on, he talks a great deal about praising God. And the further he goes, the more he has to say about it. And at last, it seems as if he could hardly speak of anything else but the thanks, and the praise that he owed to God. The last Psalm in the book is a very short one. It has only six verses in it; and yet the word praise is found in that short Psalm—*thirteen* times! He says: "Praise God in his sanctuary; praise him in the firmament of his power. Praise him in his mighty acts; praise him according to his excellent greatness. Let everything that hath breath, praise the Lord." How well we may say that David was a model of *growing* praise!

And we find it the same still. When people truly learn the lesson of praising God, they find that the spirit of praise grows in them, and like David they want to praise Him more and more.

Here are some nice stories which show us how true this is.

Our first story is one we may call—

"*Learning the Lesson of Praise.*" A clergyman, in England, had a poor woman connected with his church, who had never learned to thank God for

His mercies to her. She supported herself and family, as well as she could by washing. Her husband was a sober, industrious man, but his health was poor, and he was not able to do much work. Whenever the minister called to see this woman, whose name was Jones, he found her gloomy and sad, and complaining of her many trials. She seemed to think that she had nothing for which to praise God. So one day when he was visiting her, the minister thought he would try and teach her to begin to praise God for the mercies she had. When he first spoke about it, she shook her head, and said, "She didn't know what she had to thank God for."

"Why, yes, Mrs. Jones," said the minister, "there are at least two great mercies that you have. There, for instance, is your good health. Think what a great blessing that is! You never have to send for the doctor, and you are never interrupted in your work by sickness. Surely this is something to be thankful for! And then you have a good husband. He never gets drunk, and is always kind to you. He cannot work indeed, as much as he would like to do. But when he is able to work, instead of spending his wages at the tavern, he brings them home to you, and does all he can to help you. This is a great mercy. Now, I want you, when you say your prayers to-night, to thank God for these two great blessings. And then I want you to keep on doing this every day." She promised to do so, and then the minister left her.

It was several weeks before he had time to call on her again. But the next time he came to visit her, before knocking at the door, he was surprised to hear a merry voice singing cheerfully in the house. He had never heard anything of this kind there before; and he wondered what it could mean. Then he knocked, and Mrs. Jones opened the door. Her face lighted up with a pleasant, cheerful smile, as soon as she saw him.

"I am glad to hear you singing, Mrs. Jones," said the minister.

"Oh, yes, sir," she replied, "I feel very happy now. I'm very much obliged to you for teaching me to thank God for those two mercies. But you see, sir, when I began with thanking God for my good health, and my good husband, I found I couldn't stop there. I had to thank Him for my good children; and then for my good home. Then I had to thank Him for teaching me to know Him, and love Him, and for giving me the hope of heaven when I die. And now, when I begin to thank Him, I find so many mercies for which to praise Him, that I hardly know where to stop." And here we see what a growing thing the spirit of praise is, when once we begin to exercise it in the right way.

How Many Mercies in a Year. A little boy, who was very clever at figures, had heard so much about the goodness of God, that he thought he would try and reckon up how many mercies he received in a year. So he took his slate and pencil, and began to set them down.

"Let me see, there are 365 days in a year, and so I must put down 365 mercies. But then, I get more than one mercy a day. Why, every hour brings some mercy. So I must multiply 365 days by 24, the number of hours in a day, and this makes 8,760 mercies for the year. But then, God's mercies come oftener than once an hour. Why, every minute brings a mercy. And if I multiply God's hourly mercies by 60, the number of minutes in an hour, it makes my mercies for the year to be more than half a million. How great a number this is!"

"But let me count my greater mercies," said the little fellow. "There are my dear father and mother, who have been spared to me all these years. Two big marks for this. Then one for health preserved; another for food; another for clothing; and then for teachers, books, pleasant companions, and merry play, more still. And then there's the Bible, a big, broad mark for that. And then the Sabbaths, fifty-two every year. But oh, dear me! my slate is full, and yet I don't seem to be half through with counting my mercies. So I must give it up."

And this was just what King David himself was obliged to do. I don't know whether he tried to reckon up his mercies as this little boy did, by writing them on a slate. But I do know that when he was thinking about God's mercies to him, he found himself at a loss, and was obliged to say: "If I should count them they are more in number than the sand." Ps. cxxxix: 18.

And if we try to count God's mercies to us as David did, we too shall find them "more in number than the sand."

I will finish this part of our sermon with one more story. We may call it—

Prayer Turned to Praise. A dear little girl, was

kneeling one evening, at her mother's knee, to offer her evening prayer, and to thank God for the mercies of the day. Soon she reached the point where she was accustomed to say, "God bless my dear mother, and——" but there she stopped; her little hands were unclasped, and a look of agony, and wonder met her mother's eyes, as the words of hopeless sorrow burst from the lips of the poor child, and she said, with much feeling, "I can't *pray for papa any more.*" Ever since her little lips had learned to speak that dear name, she had been accustomed to pray for a blessing on it. It had always followed after the name of her mother. But now, that dear father was dead. This was the first time she had said her prayers since her father's death. Her mother waited for some moments. Then she asked the child to go on. "She looked at me for a moment," said the mother, and then, with a voice almost choked with her deep feeling, she said: "Oh, mother, I cannot leave him *all out*. Let me thank God that I *had such a dear father once;* so I can still go on, and keep him in my prayers."

This was very sweet. It shows us how we may turn our prayers into praise, and learn to thank God for the blessings we *have had*, as well as for those that we now have. And so we may well speak of David as a model of *growing* praise.

And then, in the fourth place, we have in David a model of—UNIVERSAL PRAISE.

Universal praise means praise for everything. When God makes us well, after we have been sick; or when He makes us successful in our business; or when He gives us kind friends who are able and willing to help us, we all feel that it is right for us to praise Him, and give Him thanks for these blessings. But, when God sends sickness upon us, or trials and afflictions of other kinds, very few of us ever think of thanking God for *these* things. Yet *this* is what David did. He had learned to praise God for everything He did to him. He says in one place, "*All* the paths of the Lord are *mercy* and *truth*." Ps. xxv: 10. By "the *paths* of the Lord" David meant His acts, His doings, what we call His providences, or anything that He does. David meant to say that whatever God does to His people He does in mercy and in love, and therefore we ought to praise Him for it. And so we see that David had learned to thank God for everything; and in this way he became the model of *universal* praise.

We see the same thing when he says: "It was good for me that I have been afflicted, that I might learn thy statutes." Ps. cxix: 71. And again when he says—"Thy judgments are good." Ps. cxix: 39. "At midnight I will rise, to give thanks unto thee, because of thy righteous judgments." Ps. cxix: 62. "Many are the afflictions of the righteous, but the Lord delivereth him out of them all." Ps. xxxiv: 19. In all these passages we see clearly how David was a model of universal praise. He had learned to thank, and praise God for everything that He did for him. And we should try to follow the model that David has set us in this respect. We find many examples of those who have learned to do this; and it is always pleasant to hear about them.

Here are some illustrations of this kind of praise.

The first story is about—"*The Man with One Leg.*" "Well, Uncle Philip," said a little boy one day, "what are you looking at so earnestly? I can't see anything but a lot of people going by. Is there anything to be learned from them, Uncle Philip?"

"Oh, yes, there is a very good lesson to be learned here. If we keep our eyes open, and our hearts ready, we may learn a lesson from everything we see."

"Well, I can't see what can be learned from looking at that crowd of people. Do tell me, Uncle Philip, what lesson you learn from looking at it."

"That I will gladly do," said his uncle. "Do you see yonder poor fellow, with the wooden leg?"

"Yes, I see him, but I can't tell what lesson is to be learned from that."

"There is a very good lesson we may learn from it. I don't know whether the poor fellow lost his leg from his own fault, or from his misfortune; but, if he has only made a right use of his loss, he will be able to get along faster on the way to heaven with one leg, than he used to do with two. And now, mind what I say, and you may learn a good lesson to-day. *Never pass by a man with only one leg, without thanking God that you have two.*" This will help us in following David's model of universal praise.

Our next story, which teaches us the same lesson, may be called—

Light Out of Darkness. A minister was visiting among the poor, in one of the crowded streets of the city of Glasgow, in Scotland. He entered one house where, in a small, but very clean and neat room, he found a blind man, who was busily at work making a mat. In looking at him he was very much struck, with the bright, and cheerful expression of the blind man's face. He thought he would like to have some talk with him, and try and find out what it was that made him look so happy. It turned out just as he expected, that the man was a Christian, and that it was his faith in Jesus which was filling his heart with joy, and lighting up his face with gladness.

But the history of that blind man was very striking. For thirty years he had lived in the world, without any thought of God, or any desire to serve and please Him. Though seeing with his bodily eyes, the eyes of his soul were blinded. But, at one time, by what men call an accident, he lost the use of both his eyes. The minister thought that the man must feel his blindness to be a great calamity, and he began to say such things to him as would be likely to comfort him under that affliction. But very soon the blind man interrupted him by saying: "Please, sir, don't go on talking in that way. You don't understand how I feel. The loss of my eyes was the greatest blessing I ever received. It stopped me in my course of wickedness. It led me to see what a sinner I was. It brought me to repentance. It taught me to love and serve Jesus. It gave me the hope of heaven, which fills my heart with joy and gladness. *Why, sir, I never saw till I was made blind.* And now, I thank God every day, for the loss of my eye-sight."

This is a good illustration of the point now before us. This man had learned the lesson of universal praise.

The Blessing of Affliction. A minister of the gospel had been very ill for six weeks. When he was getting better, one of his friends called to see him. He said to him: "I am very glad, sir, that God is raising you up again. But it will be a good while before you will be able to preach. And I hope you will not be too much troubled on account of your great affliction."

"Why, my friend," said the minister, "you don't understand my case at all. I feel better able to preach now, than I did before I was sick. I can say with David, 'It was good for me that I have been afflicted.' *This six weeks' sickness has taught me more about the Bible than ever I knew before.* As long as I live, I shall thank God for this sickness." That good man was learning the lesson of universal praise.

A good Christian lady, in England, once wrote some beautiful lines, that will come in very well here, at the close of our sermon. They are about—*What we should praise God for.* Listen to them:

> "For what shall I praise thee, my God, and my King?
> For what blessings the tribute of gratitude bring?
> Shall I praise thee for pleasure, for health, and for ease?
> For the spring of delight, and the sunshine of peace?

> "Shall I praise thee for flowers that bloom'd on my breast?
> For joys in perspective, and pleasures possess'd?
> For the spirits that heighten'd my days of delight,
> And the slumbers that sat on my pillow by night?

> "For this I *should* praise thee! but if only for this,
> I should leave half untold the donation of bliss;
> I thank thee for sickness, for sorrow, for care,
> For the thorns I have gather'd, the anguish I bear.

> "For nights of anxiety, watchings, and tears,
> A present of pain, a perspective of fears;
> I praise Thee, I bless Thee, my King, and my God,
> For the good, and the evil, thy hand hath bestow'd."

That is universal praise indeed! It is *thanking God for everything*.

And thus we have David set before us as the model of praise. And there are four good points about this model, for us to try and imitate. In the *first* place, he was the model of praise *for temporal* blessings; in the *second* place, he was the model of praise for *spiritual* blessings; in the *third* place, he was the model of *growing* praise; and in the *fourth* place, he was the model of *universal* praise.

Let us try to follow this model, and it will do us good all our days.

"Seven times a day will I praise Thee."

DAVID, THE MODEL USER OF GOD'S WORD.

"O how I love thy law! it is my meditation all the day."—PSALM CXIX : 97.

Y the *"law"* of God, of which David here speaks, we understand him to refer to what we call—"the word of God," or so much of the Bible as was then written. Of all the servants of God, mentioned in the Scriptures, we read of none who seemed to love, and delight in God's word, and who had so much to say about it as he did.

This 119th Psalm, from which our text is taken, is the longest chapter in the Bible. It contains 176 verses; and in almost every one of these verses, David has something to say expressive of the feeling with which he regarded the word of God. He never makes use of either of the two words that we most commonly apply to God's word, viz.—the Bible, or the Scriptures. But he uses a variety of terms, when speaking of what we mean by the Bible. In one place he calls it—the *word* of God; in another—his *law*—his *commandments*—his *precepts*—his *testimo-*

nies—his *statutes*—his *judgments*, and so on. But these all mean in substance, the same thing. They all refer to the word of God, or, as we call it, the Bible. And if David had so much to say, in praise of the small portion of God's word, which had been written in his day, what would he have said if he had known the whole Bible, as we have it now—including the Proverbs—and the Prophets—and the Gospels—and the Epistles—and the Revelation of St. John? And the great reason why David thought so much of the small portion of the Bible which he had, was that he believed, with the apostle Paul, that—"all Scripture is given by inspiration of God"—(2 Tim. iii : 16)—and with the apostle Peter, that the men who wrote the Scriptures—"spake as they were moved by the Holy Ghost." (2 Peter i : 21.) And the meaning of what these two apostles have here said, is—that both the *thoughts* made known to us, by "the holy men of old," who wrote the Scriptures, and the *words*, in which they expressed these thoughts, are God's. They not only thought what the Holy Ghost led them to think; but they expressed those thoughts, in the words which the Holy Ghost taught them to use. "They *spake as they were moved by the Holy Ghost.*" The Bible contains God's thoughts to us, expressed in God's words.

And it is this, which makes the Bible so different, from any other book that ever was written. This was what David believed about the Bible. This was what the apostles Paul, and Peter, both believed about it. And if this was the way in which David looked, upon the small portion of the Bible which was written in his day, we do not wonder to hear him say of it in the words of our text: "O how I love thy law! it is my meditation all the day."

David would have been quite ready to unite, in all that one has said, about the word of God in these sweet lines:—

> "Thy thoughts are here, my God,
>   Expressed in words divine,
>   The utterance of heavenly lips
>   In every sacred line.
>
> "Each word of Thine a gem,
>   From the celestial mines,
>   A sunbeam from that holy heaven,
>   Where holy sunlight shines."

Or as another writer thus speaks:—

> "This holy book I'd rather own
>   Than all the gold and gems,
>   That e'er in monarch's coffers shone,
>   Than all their diadems.
>
> "Nay, were the seas one chrysolite,
>   The earth one golden ball,
>   And diadems all the stars of night,
>   This book outweighs them all."

In the 119th Psalm, where our text is found, David speaks of about forty different ways, in which he made use of the word of God. And in view of all these, we may well speak of him as—*the model user of God's word*. It would make a long sermon if we should undertake to speak of all the points. We shall not attempt to do this. But out of them we may select —*seven*—of which to speak. In the model which David sets us, he points out seven different ways in

DAVID, THE MODEL USER OF GOD'S WORD. 203

which he made use of the word of God. And we should try to follow this model, if we wish to secure to ourselves all the benefits, which God intends that we should derive from His word.

The first use, that David made of God's word was, for—MEDITATION—or to give him something to think about. In our text he says: "O, how I love thy law! it is my *meditation* all the day." This means that he was in the habit of reading some of it every morning, and then of remembering it, and keeping it in his mind all through the day.

And this is a very proper use to make of God's word. This is what we should all try to do. We have many striking examples of the way in which this has been done by God's children, in different parts of the world.

The Rev. William Romaine, a useful clergyman of the Church of England, for the last thirty years of his life, read and studied, no other book than the Bible. Surely, like David, he was making it his meditation all the day!

Joshua Barnes, a good English merchant, always carried a New Testament in his pocket. He read that Testament through one hundred and twenty times.

A pious English physician used to read fifteen chapters of the Bible every day. He read five chapters in the morning; five at noon; and five at night.

A pious French nobleman, named De Renty, always read three chapters of the Bible in the morning, kneeling on his knees, and with his head uncovered.

Alphonso, King of Spain, read over the whole Bible, together with a large commentary—fourteen times.

And a well-known Christian prince, of Austria, read over the whole Bible twenty-seven times.

These men were following David's example, in meditating on God's word all the day.

Here is a good story about a Scotchman. We may call it—

Feasting on God's Word. "Where have you been reading this morning, Uncle?" asked little Sandy.

"Weel, Sandy," said the old man, "I hae been getting a wonderful feast yesterday and to-day, out of the last two verses of the eighth chapter of Romans."

"And haven't you read any more than those two verses in two days?" asked Sandy in surprise.

"Oh, you see, Sandy," said the old man, "there's a mine of golden treasure in these verses, and I've been trying to dig down to the bottom of it. I've been doing wi' these verses as I do wi' the sugar-plums your Aunt Mary makes me, when I've a sore throat. Now and then she puts one of them in her mouth. But she jist gies it a chew or twa, and then it's done with. But I lay mine in my cheek, and let it lie, and slowly melt away, and do me good for half a day.

"And there's jist the same difference in the way folks use God's blessed word. Some gallop through a chapter, and then turn away and forget it. But that's nae my way. I like to tak' a sweet, wee bit of a verse, and do wi' it jist as I do wi' the sugar-plums. I let it lie in my soul, as the plums do in my mouth, and melt slowly away; and so it fills my soul wi' sweetness, for a day, or a week, or a month at a time. This is what I call—feasting on the word of God."

That old Scotchman was making the very same use

of God's word, that David did, when he said: "O, how I love thy law! it is my meditation all the day."

Here are some sweet lines, written by the late Miss Frances Havergal, on the precious promise—

"*Certainly I will be with thee.*"

They show us how she meditated on God's word, just as David and the old Scotchman did.

"Certainly I will be with thee!" Father I have found it true;
To Thy faithfulness and mercy I would set my seal anew,
All my life Thy grace hath kept me, Thou my help indeed hast been;
Marvellous the loving kindness every day and hour hath seen.

"Certainly I will be with thee!" Blessed Spirit, come to me;
Rest upon me, dwell within me, let my heart Thy temple be!
Through all the days before me, Holy One with me abide!
Teach me, comfort me, and calm me; be my ever present Guide.

"Certainly I will be with thee!" Starry promise in the night!
All uncertainties like shadows, flee away before the light.
"Certainly I will be with thee!" He hath spoken, I have heard!
True of old, and true this moment, I will trust Jehovah's word.

The first use that David made of God's word was for—*meditation.*

The second use that David made of God's word was for—LIGHT.

He says in the 130th verse of this 119th Psalm: "The entrance of thy word giveth *light.*" David was all in the dark about his soul, till he became acquainted with the word of God. And we are all in the same condition. We are born into this world with our souls in the dark. We are in the dark about ourselves; about God; about heaven, and the way to get there.

And we never can get any light on these great matters till we come to the word of God for it. But as soon as we come here, for instruction, the light begins to shine around us. In the 105th verse of this Psalm, David says: "Thy word is a lamp unto my feet, and a light unto my path." It shows us the way in which God would have us walk; and tells us how we can get strength to walk in that way. Here are some illustrations of the way in which God's word throws light on the path of those who are walking in darkness. The first of these may be called—

Light on the Traveler's Path. An American gentleman, who was a Christian, was traveling by himself in the Holy Land. At Jerusalem he was taken sick with malarial fever. There was no friend near him. The wide ocean was rolling between his family and himself. And when he thought that perhaps he might die there, a stranger among strangers, it made him feel very sad and low-spirited. One day, when he was just in this state of feeling, a stranger called at the house and asked to see him. Without giving his name, after a short conversation with him, he proposed to read a portion of Scripture. The request was granted, and the stranger read the 121st Psalm; and then, without saying a word, he went away. This Psalm is very short. There are only eight verses in it; but they are all very beautiful. The last two verses in the Psalm read thus: "The Lord shall preserve thee from all evil: He shall preserve thy soul. The Lord shall preserve thy going out and thy coming in, from this time forth forevermore." Now this short portion of God's word had a singular effect on that sick man. If the angel Gabriel had come down from heaven, with a message from God unto him, it could not have given him more light, and comfort, than he found from this portion of God's word. His gloom and sadness all disappeared. He became bright and cheerful. He soon got quite well, and went on his way rejoicing.

Our next story may be called—

The Great Problem. A young man, who was a student in one of the colleges at Oxford, England, was very fond of mathematics. He was the first of his class in this branch of study, and felt very proud of his success. He was constantly asking his classmates to give him some hard problem to solve. He had one classmate who had lately become a Christian, and who was very anxious that his mathematical friend should be a Christian too.

So he came to his room one day, and said to him: "John, here's a very important problem, which has occupied my mind a great deal of late. I wish you would help me to solve it." Then he handed him a piece of paper, carefully doubled up, and went away.

As soon as his friend was gone, John eagerly unfolded the paper; but, instead of a question in mathematics, he found written there this question from the Bible:

"What shall it profit a man, if he gain the whole world and lose his own soul; or what shall a man give in exchange for his soul?"

This made him very angry. He tore the paper up, and threw it in the fire. Then he turned to his studies again. But he could not get that great question out of his mind. It led him to see how sinfully he was acting in neglecting his soul. He never rested till he had turned in penitence and faith to Jesus; and so saved his soul. He afterwards became an earnest and successful minister. And all the good, resulting from his life and labors, was brought about by the light which shone from that single passage of God's word.

I have one other illustration under this part of our subject. We may call it—

The Wonderful Lamp. A little ragged errand-boy was busy one day, in the city of London, with a piece of chalk in his hand, trying to write on a wooden gate this verse from the Bible: "*Thy word is a lamp to my feet.*" He was so busy with his work, that he did not notice a kind-looking old gentleman, who, after walking slowly past him twice, returned, and stood behind watching him.

"M-y," said the little fellow, repeating the letters aloud, as he wrote them with the chalk; "f-double e-t, feet."

"Well done, my little man, well done," said the old gentleman. "Where did you learn that?"

"At the ragged school, sir," said the boy, who was half frightened, thinking perhaps that the old gentleman would hand him over to the police, for writing on the gate.

"Don't be afraid, my boy. I'm not going to hurt you. So you learned that text in the ragged school? Do you know what it means?"

"No, sir," said the boy.

"What is a lamp?"

"A lamp? Why, a lamp! It's a thing that gives light."

"And what is the word here spoken of?"

"It's the Bible, sir."

"That's right. Now how can the Bible be a lamp and give light?"

"I dun'no," said the boy, "'cept you set it on fire."

"There's a better way than that, my lad. Suppose you were going down some lonely lane, on a dark night, with an unlighted lamp in your hand, and a box of matches in your pocket, what would you do?"

"Why, light the lamp, sir," said the boy, surprised that any one should ask such a simple question.

"What would you light it for?"

"To show me the road, sir."

"Very well. Now suppose you were walking behind me one day, and saw me drop a shilling, what would you do?"

"Pick it up and give it to you, sir."

"But wouldn't you want to keep it yourself?"

"I should want to; but I wouldn't do it."

"Why not?"

"Because that would be stealing, and the Bible says we mustn't steal. And is the Bible called a lamp, because it shows us the right way to walk in?" asked the boy.

"That's just it, my lad. And now do you think it worth while to take this good old lamp, and let it light you right through life?"

"Yes, sir."

"Why?"

"Because if I'm honest, I sha'n't stand no chance of going to prison."

"And what else?"

The boy thought a moment, and then said:

"If I mind the Bible, I shall go to heaven when I die."

"Yes, that's the best reason for using this lamp. It will show you the right way to heaven. Good-by, my lad. Here's a shilling for you. Mind you use this lamp."

"Sir," said the little fellow, clasping the shilling, and taking off his ragged cap—"I'll mind."

The second thing for which David used the Bible was for—light.

The third thing for which David used God's word was for—CLEANSING.

In the 9th verse of this 119th Psalm, David asks the question how a young man can cleanse his ways. And the answer which he gives is, that it can only be done by the right use of God's word. And it was just this use of that word, which led David when he was repenting of his sin, to offer this prayer:—"Wash me thoroughly from my wickedness, and cleanse me from my sin." Ps. li : 2. And the apostle Paul teaches us the same lesson, when he tells us that Christ purifies and cleanses His church,—"by the washing of water, by the word." Ephesians v : 26. What he means by this is, that the word, or truth of God has a purifying power like water; and that just as things when washed in water are made clean by it; so those who make a right use of God's word, find that it has a power to purify their hearts, and make them clean.

And Jesus Himself taught us the same lesson, when, in praying to the Father for His people, He said: "Sanctify them through thy truth; thy word is truth."

John xvii: 17. To sanctify, means to purify, or to make clean. And God has appointed His word, or truth, to be the means of cleansing the hearts and souls of His people, and of making them pure and holy. Let us look at some examples of the power there is in the word of God to cleanse from sin. Our first illustration may be called:

The Power of God's Word. A colporteur in Turkey visited a hospital. Among the patients he saw a poor Turk lying on his bed very ill. He went up to the man, intending to speak a few kind words to him; but he frowned at him so fearfully, and uttered such terrible curses, that he had to turn away.

He spoke to the nurse about him. She said: "He is the most dreadful man we ever had in the hospital. I give him his medicines, and dress his wounds. But he is all the time cursing me, so that I am afraid to go near him."

Then the colporteur thought he would offer him a copy of the New Testament in Arabic. He opened it, and held it up before him. When the Turk saw that it was a book printed in his own language, the frown on his face passed away, and a pleasant smile took the place of it. He held out his hand to receive the book, and it was given to him.

Immediately after this the colporteur had to leave that place for some time. On his return he went to the hospital to inquire about the sick soldier. "Sir," replied the nurse, "I never saw such a change in any man, as the reading of that book made in him. His rough manner all passed away. His scowling face became bright and pleasant. He took his medicine without a word of cursing, and was kind and gentle. As for the New Testament you gave him, he never would let it go out of his hand. He was reading it all the time, till he died two days ago. And just before he died he said he was so happy, because *that book had taught him how to get his sins pardoned.*" He used God's word as David did, to get his soul cleansed from sin.

Here is an interesting story that illustrates this point very nicely. We may call it—

"*What did the Angels Blot it out With?*" A merchant in New Orleans had been successful in business, and was very well off. He was born in New England, and had a pious mother who had taught him faithfully the truths of God's holy word. But, when he grew up, and moved away from home, he became acquainted with a number of gentlemen who said they did not believe the Bible. They were what we call infidels. He adopted their views, and became an infidel too. He had given up going to church, and did not have a Bible in his house. But he had a bright little boy about seven years of age. This was the only child he had. His name was Theodore, and his father was very fond of him.

"One evening," says this gentleman, "when I came home, Theodore was lying on the bed partly undressed. My wife and I were sitting by an open fire in an adjoining room. She had been telling me that Theodore had been naughty that day, and that she had punished him for it.

"All was quiet, when suddenly he broke out into a loud crying and sobbing. I went in and asked him what was the matter. 'I don't want it there, father! I don't want it there!'

"'What, my child—what is it?'

"'Why, father, I don't want the angels to write down in God's book, all the naughty things I have done to-day. I don't want them there; I wish they could be blotted out;' and then, in great distress, he broke out crying again.

"What could I do? To turn away from the dear child, in his heart-breaking sorrow, was impossible. There was nothing in the teachings of infidelity that would meet the case, and give the distressed child any comfort. And so, in spite of myself, I was obliged to fall back on what my dear mother had taught me about the Bible.

"'Well, you need not cry, my dear child; you can have it all blotted out, if you want.'

"'How, father? how?' he asked.

"'Why, get down on your knees, and ask God for Christ's sake, to blot it all out, and He will do it.'

"I did not have to speak twice. He jumped out of bed, and was on his knees in a moment. He was silent for a while, and then looking up to me, he said: 'I don't know what to say. Father, won't you come and help me?'

"What was I to do? I had not offered a word of prayer to God for years. But the dear boy's distress was so great, and he pleaded so earnestly, that, big man as I was, I got down on my knees, alongside my sorrowing child, and asked God to blot out his sins. Then we got up, and he laid himself down on the bed again. In a few moments he said—'Father, are you sure it's all blotted out?' And then, in spite of my infidelity I was compelled to say: 'Why, yes, my dear boy, the Bible says so; if you are really sorry for what you have done wrong, and if, from your heart, you have asked God for Christ's sake, to blot it out, you may be sure that He will do it.'

"A smile of pleasure passed over his face, as he quietly asked: 'But father—*what did the angels blot it out with?*'

"Again putting my infidelity aside, I answered—'With the precious blood of Christ.'

"Then he lay down and went quietly to sleep.

"When I went into the next room, and told my wife what had taken place, both our hearts were melted. We wept like children. Then we kneeled down side by side, and asked God for Christ's sake, to blot out *our* sins, and make us His dear children."

Here we see what cleansing power there is in the word of God. And this was the third use that David made of this word.

The fourth use that David made of the word of God, was for—STRENGTH.

In the 28th verse of this Psalm, David's prayer to God is: "Strengthen Thou me according to Thy word." There are many places in the Bible, in which God promises to give His people strength. One of the sweetest of these is found in the 10th verse of the 41st chapter of Isaiah. Here God says: "I will strengthen thee; yea, I will help thee."

If we have the Lord Almighty for our Helper, what is there that we cannot do? The apostle Paul said: "I can do all things through Christ strengthening me." And if we make a right use of God's word, to get the strength from it, which it is designed to give, then, like David and St. Paul, we shall find it easy to do all that God tells us to do.

Let us look at some examples of the strength and power, that God's people have found in the word of God. And the first example furnished us here, we find in the case of our blessed Saviour. There He is in the wilderness, for forty days to be tempted of Satan. And notice now the way in which He met those temptations. As He was God, He might have said to Satan, at the beginning of those temptations, what He did say to him, at the close of them—"Get thee hence, Satan;" and he would have been obliged to go. But He allowed Satan to go on tempting Him, on purpose that He might show us how we must meet temptations, so as to get the victory over them. Jesus did not get the victory over Satan by using the power that was in Him, as He was God. If He had done this, He would have been no example to us. But He met all those temptations, and got the victory over them, simply by the strength which He found in the word of God. Every time that Satan came, and tempted Him to do something that was wrong, Jesus quoted some passage of Scripture against him. "It is written"—"It is written"—"It is written"—was His answer all the time. This gave Him the victory. And if we hope to get the victory over temptation, as Jesus did, we must do it in the same way. The strength to be found in the word of God, is the only thing that can make us successful here. Here is a story which shows how a little boy found strength from the Bible to resist temptation.

This boy's name was Billy Jones. He was a feeble-minded boy, with very little education. His mother was a good Christian woman, though very poor. She had taught him a great deal about the Bible. He had committed the Ten Commandments to memory, and used to repeat them to his mother every Sunday.

One day, Billy was sent on a message to the house of Mr. Graham, who was the richest man in that neighborhood. As he passed under the kitchen window, he saw something bright and shiny, lying in the grass. He picked it up, and found it was a beautiful silver spoon. He had never had any silver in his hand before. He thought, for a moment, what nice things he might buy with it. But when he remembered the eighth commandment—"Thou shalt not steal"—he hid it away in the sleeve of his coat. Then he went into the kitchen of Mr. Graham's house and delivered his message. After this he asked to see Mrs. Graham.

He was taken into the parlor, where Mrs. Graham was with some company. When she saw him, she was astonished, and said: "Well, my boy, and what do you want to-day?"

Billy went up to her, and taking the spoon out of his sleeve, put it in her hands, saying very slowly as he did so: "Thou shalt not steal."

Mrs. Graham and her friends were greatly surprised.

"And pray where did you find the spoon, my little man?" asked Mrs. G.

After a pause, he said: "Under the kitchen window—Billy found it. 'Thou shalt not steal.'"

Then the lady thanked him, and gave him half a dollar as a reward for his honesty. When Mr. Graham heard of it, he was so much interested in little Billy, that he had him placed in an institution for the feeble-minded, where he was well taken care of, and educated.

Here we see how this boy found strength from the word of God to help him do what was right.

Here is another story, showing—

How a Student Resisted Temptation. The members of the Junior class, in one of our colleges, had met in a student's room, to spend the night in drinking and rioting. Among them was one who had been very successful in his recitations. He was at the head of his class. But the day before, for the first time since entering college, he had failed in his lesson. This made him feel gloomy and sad. All the other students were merry and joyful. One of his classmates said to him: "Come, Bob; drink some of this wine. It'll make you feel better."

Just then the tempter whispered in his ear: "Drink once, and forget the past." A great struggle was going on in his mind. "Shall I drink—or shall I not?" he said to himself. He was stretching out his hand, to take hold of the glass, when this passage of Scripture came into his mind: "Resist the devil, and he will flee from you." He paused. He withdrew his hand. He shook his head, and left the room. He was saved from learning to drink. That young man continued a successful student. He graduated at the head of his class, and is now the president of a college. And all this resulted from the strength he received from the word of God, to enable him to resist temptation, and to do what was right.

The fourth use that David made of God's word was for strength.

The fifth use that David made of the word of God was for—JOY.

In the 14th verse of this Psalm he says: "I have rejoiced in the way of Thy testimonies as in all riches." In the 24th verse he says: "Thy testimonies are my delight." In the 54th verse he says: "Thy statutes have been my songs in the house of my pilgrimage." And in the 162d verse he says: "I rejoice at Thy word as one that findeth great spoil." No stronger language could possibly be used, to show what joy David found in the use of God's word, than that which he here uses.

And when the apostle Paul declared that he "counted all things but loss for the excellence of the knowledge of Christ Jesus," he was only telling what joy he found in the word of God. And all, who learn truly to understand the Bible, find it to be indeed the source of their highest joy.

Here are some good illustrations of the point now before us. The first story may be called—

The Hidden Treasure. A good man visited a house in Germany, and found it very wretched. There was no fire—no furniture—no food. Everything bore the appearance of the greatest poverty. But, looking round, he saw, in a neglected corner, a dust-covered copy of the Bible. And, as he was going away, he said to the members of the family: "There is a treasure in this house that will make you all rich, if you find it." As soon as he was gone they began to search the house, expecting to find a jewel, or a bag of gold. But they found none. Again and again the search was renewed; but in vain.

One day, when tired of searching, the mother of the family, lifted up the old Bible and set it on the table. She opened the lid of that neglected book; and there, written on the first blank leaf, were these words from the Psalms of David: "*Thy testimonies are better to me than thousands of gold and silver.*" "Ah!" she said, "I wonder, if *this* can be the treasure that the stranger spoke of?" She told the rest of the family what she thought about it, and suggested that they should begin, and read the Bible every day. They did so, and God blessed the reading of His word to the salvation of their souls. And a good while after, when the stranger visited them again, what a wonderful change he saw in that home! There was plenty, in the place of poverty. Peace and contentment were seen, where there used to be only misery and murmuring. With grateful joy they said to him: "We have found the treasure of which you spoke, and it has proved to us all that you said it would be."

Our next story may be called—

The Secret of Happiness. An old negro, in Virginia, was remarkable for his good sense, and his clear knowledge of the Bible. He was always bright and cheerful. He seemed to have a fountain of joy in his heart that never failed. One day a gentleman was on a visit to the owner of this plantation. While there he heard a good deal about that cheerful, happy negro. He thought he would like to have a talk with him, and try to find out what it was that made him always seem so merry-hearted. So the next time he met him, he said: "Sambo, you always appear to be so bright, and joyful, that I cannot understand it. Won't you please tell me the secret of your happiness?"

"Why, Massa," he replied, "when any trouble comes on Sambo, he jes' fall right flat on de blessed Lord's precious promises, and looks up to Him for help; and it always comes." This was an excellent answer. Here is a secret worth knowing. Yes, and worth *following* too. Like David, that old negro was using the word of God, for his joy and happiness. And seeing that this is the effect which follows from the right use of the word of God, we may well take up here the sweet lines some one has written about it, which read thus:—

> "Thank God for the Bible! whose clear shining ray
> Has lighted our path, and turned night into day;
> Its wonderful treasures have never been told,
> More precious than rubies, set round with pure gold.
>
> "Thank God for the Bible! in sickness or health,
> It brings richer comforts than honor or wealth;
> Its blessings are boundless, an infinite store;
> We may drink at its fountain, and thirst nevermore.
>
> "Thank God for the Bible! sent down from above,
> Revealing to mortals God's infinite love;
> A fathomless sea with its bright shining shore,
> Where the glorified dwell and are safe evermore.
>
> "Thank God for the Bible! rich treasures untold,
> Are laid up in store in its city of gold,
> That beautiful home of the saved and the blest,
> Where no sorrow can come, where the weary find rest.

> "Thank God for the Bible! how dark is the night
> Where no ray from its pages sheds forth its pure light:
> No Jesus—no Bible—no Heaven of rest—
> Oh, how could we live, were our lives so unblest?
>
> "There are millions who wander in darkness to-day,
> No Jesus—no Bible—no knowledge to pray;
> God help us to feel, and to act, in His sight,
> To render our thanks now, by giving them light."

The fifth use, that David made of the word of God, was for—joy.

The sixth use, that David made of the word of God, was for—TRUST.

In the 42d verse of this Psalm, David says: "I trust in thy word." He had tried it, and found he could rely upon it, with entire confidence. It had never failed or disappointed him. If any body had come to him, and tried to shake his trust or confidence in God's word, he would have said at once: "It's not worth while to talk to me in that way. I know that God's word *is* true, and I trust it with my whole heart, because I have tried it, in troubles and difficulties of all kinds, and it has always proved true."

Suppose we should meet a sailor, who has just returned from a long voyage. He is on his way from the ship to his home, and under his arm, in a little square box, he is carrying the compass, by which he has found his way across the sea. He tells us how he prizes that compass, and how great his confidence in it is. And suppose we begin to talk with him, and try to shake his faith in that compass. We point to it laughingly, and say: "How foolish it is to think so much of such a little thing as that! Just look at that needle, and see how it trembles and shakes! Of what use can that little needle be? Why not throw that compass away, and find something else to trust to, when you go to sea?"

He would say to us in reply: "Well, you can laugh at me as much as you please. But I *know* what I am about. Experience has taught me the worth of this compass. I have sailed round the world, trusting to it for guidance, and it has never disappointed me. In storm and in calm,—by day and by night,—in summer and in winter, it has led me in the right way, and brought me safe home. And so nothing that any one may say, can, for a moment, shake my trust in this compass." And this is just what every true Christian is ready to say about the word of God:

> "Yes, yes, this blessed book is worth
>   All else to mortals given;
> For what are all the joys of earth
>   Compared to those of heaven?
> This is the guide our Father gave
>   To lead to realms of day—
> A star whose lustre gilds the grave—
>   'The light, the life, the way.'"

The Bible is not only our compass, but our anchor too. Here is an illustration of what I mean. We may call it—

An Anchor to the Soul. In a gale off the coast of England, a vessel was being driven ashore. Her anchors were gone, and she no longer obeyed the helm. A few moments more, and she would be dashed against the rocks. In the midst of the terror and confusion that prevailed, there was one man who remained perfectly calm. He saw that the wreck was inevitable. He believed that death was near, and was quietly waiting for its approach.

A friend came up to him and asked: "How can you possibly be so calm, in the midst of this great danger? Don't you know that the anchor is gone, and that we are drifting on the rocks?"

"Yes, I know it," was his calm reply "but then you see, I *have an anchor to my soul;* and whatever happens to the ship, my best interests are all safe." That is the way in which we ought to trust God's word.

Some people find their trust in God's word and the comfort which that trust would give, very much disturbed by the things in the Bible which they cannot understand. Here is an illustration of this part of our subject. We may call it—

A Lesson from a Cow. The deacon of a church in New England, called on his pastor one day, to have a talk with him about the Bible.

In the course of their conversation the deacon said: "You see, Parson, as I am reading my Bible, I find many things in it that I can't understand. I stop and think about them. But the more I think about them, the harder they seem. And then, instead of finding strength and comfort from the Bible, I go away in weakness and trouble. Now, what am I to do?"

"Come with me to the barn, deacon," said the minister, "and I'll show you what to do."

When they reached the barn, the minister pointed to a cow, that was quietly standing in the stall and eating hay. "There," said he, "is my cow Dulcy. Just watch her a moment, and she will teach you a lesson in theology. There, see, she has just found a piece of wood in the hay. And what does she do? Does she stop, and try to chew the wood? No; but she just lays it aside, and goes quietly on eating the hay. Now she finds a thistle, and now an ugly weed. But she does not trouble herself about them. She merely thrusts them aside, and goes on eating the nice, fresh, juicy hay. Now, deacon," said the minister, "just follow the example of this cow. When, in reading your Bible, you meet with things which you can't understand, don't stop and bother yourself about them. Treat them as the cow does the weeds that she finds in the hay. Put them aside, and go on carefully reading the pure, simple truth 'as it is in Jesus,' or as St. James calls it—'the engrafted word which is able to save your soul.'" The sixth use that David made of God's word was to—*trust* it; and we must do the same.

*The seventh use that David made of the word of God, and the last of which we shall now speak, was for—*PEACE.

In the 165th verse of this Psalm, David says: "Great peace have they that love thy law." And when he said this, he was speaking from his own experience. He says in our text: "O how I love thy law!" And he found peace in loving that law. And if we love God's law, as David did, we also shall find peace in it. When we know and love God's law, it will lead us to Jesus. He is the Prince of peace. He made peace through the blood of his cross, and He gives peace to all His people. And when this peace is given, it always comes through the knowledge of

His word. Here is an illustration of this in a little story which we may call—

The Watchword. In one of the great rock galleries of the fortress of Gibraltar, two British soldiers, were acting as midnight guards, or sentinels, at each end of a long tunnel in the fortress. One of them was a happy Christian, rejoicing in the peace which he had found in Jesus. The other was distressed with the burden of his sins. He had long felt the need of a Saviour; but he had never come to Jesus, and was a stranger to peace.

In the silence of the night, these soldiers were going their rounds. One of them was meditating on the atoning blood of Christ, which had brought peace to his soul. The other was groaning under the burden of sins, and longing to get rid of that burden. Suddenly an officer came in sight. In passing the former of these sentinels, he paused, and asked for the watchword. The startled soldier, forgetting for the moment what the watchword was, and thinking only of the peace that filled his soul, and of the source from which it sprung, exclaimed: "The precious blood of Christ!" But, correcting himself at once, he gave the true watchword, and the officer passed on, greatly wondering, no doubt, at the soldier's first utterance. But the words he spoke, had rung out distinctly through the gallery. They entered the ears of the other soldier, like a message from above. It seemed as if an angel from heaven had spoken to him. "The precious blood of Christ!" He felt that this was what he needed. In penitence and faith he turned to Jesus, while treading his lonely round. His burden rolled off at the foot of the cross, and his soul found rest. Peace in believing, was his happy experience from that hour.

I have only one other story to tell about this peace. Here we see how the peace which Jesus gives, can comfort his people under the most trying circumstances. We may call it—

The Dying Soldier. During one of the battles of the Crimean war, an English officer saw a soldier lying on the ground, and weltering in his blood. Going up to him, he said in a kind way: "Can I do anything for you, my friend?"

"There is one thing for which I would be much obliged," said the dying man. "In my knapsack you will find a New Testament. Please open it at the 14th chapter of St. John. Near the end of the chapter you will find a verse beginning with the word 'peace.' Be kind enough to read it to me."

The officer found the place, and read these sweet words: "Peace I leave with you, my peace I give unto you: not as the world giveth, give I unto you. Let not your heart be troubled, neither let it be afraid." John xiv : 27.

"Thank you, sir," said the dying man. "I have that peace—I am going to that Saviour—God is with me—I want no more," and with these words upon his lips, he died.

We have spoken now, of *seven* ways in which David made use of the word of God, viz. : for *meditation;* for *light;* for *cleansing;* for *strength;* for *joy;* for *trust*, and for *peace*. Let us all try to follow David's example here, and then we shall be making the best use of the Bible. And we shall feel the truth of one who asks:

What is the Bible Like? And who answers the question in this way:

"It is like a large, beautiful tree, which bears sweet fruit for those that hunger, and affords shelter and shade for pilgrims on their way to the kingdom of heaven.

"It is like a casket of jewels and precious stones, which are not only to be looked at, and admired, but used and worn.

"It is like a telescope, which brings very near the far-off things of the unseen world, so that we can see something of their beauty and importance.

"It is like a treasure-house, full of all sorts of useful and valuable things, which can be had without money and without price.

"It is like a deep, broad, calm-flowing river, the banks of which are green and flowery, where birds sing, and lambs play, and dear little children are loving and happy."

I would conclude what I have to say on this subject, by quoting some sweet lines which contain the substance of all I have been trying to say about

THE BIBLE.

"My Book! my Book. my grand old Book! by inspiration given!
Thy ev'ry page from age to age, reveals the path to heav'n;
My Lamp of Light! in nature's night thy unbeclouded ray
Has turned the gloom of death's cold tomb to everlasting day.

"My Chart! my Chart! my changeless Chart! by thee I guide my bark,
A simple child on ocean wild, o'er mountain billows dark;

By thee I steer my safe career, with canvas all unfurl'd,
And onward sail before the gale, to yonder blissful world.

"My Staff! my Staff! my trusty Staff! I'll grasp thee in my hand,
As faint and weak on Pisgah's peak, I view the promised land;
Not sadly told, as one of old, to see—but to explore,
My hold I'll keep through Jordan's deep till safe on Canaan's shore.

"My Sword! my Sword! my two-edged Sword! by thy unerring might,
I deal my foe the deadly blow, in faith's unequal fight;
Thy tempered blade, that lent me aid in every conflict past,
Shall make me more than conqueror, through Him who loved, at last.

"My Book! my Chart! my Staff! my Sword! heav'n speed thee on thy way,
From pole to pole, as ages roll, the harbinger of day,
Till Christ 'the Light,' shall banish night from—'this terrestrial ball,'
And earth shall see her Jubilee, and God be all in all."

NOTE.

Some persons may be ready to say: "Well, and what good did David's use of the Bible do to him? Notwithstanding all he says about it, he yet fell under the power of the great sin that marred his life."

I admit the truth of this statement, and desire to meet it honestly and fairly.

And the best way of doing this, that I know of, is to affirm, what none can deny, that God often allows evil to take place, and then brings good out of it.

DAVID, THE MODEL USER OF GOD'S WORD.

We have an illustration of this, in God's dealing with our world. He allowed sin to enter it. Without His permission, it never could have entered. But the entrance of sin led to the plan of salvation through Jesus Christ. This, in the end will bring more glory to God, and more happiness to the world, and to the universe, than ever could have been secured, in any other way.

And we see that it is often so with His people in this world, when He allows them to fall into sin. He overrules it for good. He did this in David's case. It is easy to see *three* good results, that have been brought out from David's sin.

One of these is the proof thus afforded, *that human nature is the same in all ages.* If the good men, whose histories are given in the Bible, such as Noah, and Abraham, and Moses, and David and Peter, had not fallen into great sins, we should have been tempted to say, that their nature must have differed from ours; and this thought would have been a great discouragement to us, in our struggles against sin. But, when we read of their great failures, we feel sure, that, in themselves, they were no better than we are. Each of them, was a stone, taken from the same quarry of corruption, in which we ourselves were found originally. And then, the thought, that, at least they gained the victory over this fallen nature, encourages us to hope for the same blessed result in the end.

Another good thing that resulted from David's sin, is seen in—*the illustration it affords of the power of the grace of God.*

By the sin which David committed, he fell to the

lowest depths, in the great pit of human transgression. Yet the grace of God was a chain, long enough to reach him there; and strong enough to lift him out from that horrible pit. He was led to repentance, and restored to God's favor. He was cleansed from his sin, and saved. There could not be a more striking illustration, of the power of the grace of God, than David's case affords. And what that grace did for him, it is able to do for any of God's children. It has been an unspeakable blessing to the church, in all ages, to have had such an illustration of the power of God's grace.

And then another good thing resulting from David's sin, is—*the help it has afforded to penitents.* If David had not fallen into his great sin, he never could have written the 51st Psalm. That is the Psalm in which he confesses his sin, and pleads for pardon. And persons repenting of their sins, in every age, have made use of this Psalm, and have found the greatest help and comfort in using it. No language can tell what a blessing this Psalm has been, to untold multitudes of people, through all the centuries that have passed away, from the days of David to the present time. And when we put all these things together, we cannot but wonder at the marvellous way in which God brings good out of evil.

It does not lessen the evil of our sins when God makes them work for good in His own wise and wonderful way. And if any should say that, in speaking thus, we are encouraging men to go on in sin, it is only necessary to look at David's life, after he committed his great sin, to see the error of such a state-

NATHAN TELLS DAVID HE SHALL BE PUNISHED FOR HIS SIN.

ment. When the prophet Nathan came to David, to reprove him for his sin, he said: "Because by this deed thou hast given great occasion for the enemies of the Lord to blaspheme, the sword shall never depart from thine house." And so it came to pass. He had nothing but sorrow and trouble, in his family, and in his kingdom, from that time, till the day of his death. And it was all the sad result of his sin. And as these things were taking place, one after another, how often David must have been compelled to shed bitter tears, over that sin, from which they all sprung! They must have made him feel—deep down to the very depths of his soul, how true it is: "That, *the way of the transgressor—is hard.*"

JONATHAN, THE MODEL FRIEND.

"Jonathan—thy love to me was wonderful."—2 SAMUEL i : 26.

THESE words David used, in the lamentation which he wrote, when he heard of the death of his friend, Jonathan. We seldom hear anything said about Jonathan. And this is surprising, when we remember what a remarkable man he was. He was a remarkable soldier. His courage was very great. We have a striking illustration of this in the 14th chapter of the first book of Samuel. At that time the Philistines had gained great victories over the Israelites. They had put garrisons of soldiers all through the land of Israel. They had taken away from the Israelites their swords and spears, and would not let any blacksmiths remain among them, for fear they would make swords for them to fight with. When things were in this sad state, Jonathan made up his mind one day, that he would try his hand with their enemies, and see if he could not get a victory over them. He told his armor-bearer what he was going to do, and asked him to go with him, and help him. He agreed to do so, and they two went out by themselves, and made an attack on one of the garrisons of the Philistines. Their enemies were afraid of them, and ran away. Jonathan and his companion went after them, and killed a number of the Philistines. Then the Israelites heard of it, and great numbers of them came, and joined Jonathan and his companion. They attacked the other Philistine garrisons. The Lord sent an earthquake at that time. This frightened the Philistines. They all ran away; and the end of it was, they were defeated and driven back into their own country, and a glorious victory was gained by the Israelites. And all this was owing to the courage of Jonathan, when he made his bold attack on the Philistines that day, with none but his armor-bearer to help him.

And then, in addition to being so brave a soldier, he was an uncommonly good son. We might speak of him as the model son, and there is a great deal in his history that could be brought out to illustrate this view of his character. But the most interesting thing, in the life of Jonathan, is the friendship that existed between him and David. And so, I wish to speak of Jonathan as—*The Model Friend.* And there are *three* points about this model, that well deserve our attention.

*In the first place, Jonathan was the model of a—*LOVING—*friend.*

A friend is good for nothing unless he really loves us. And the better he loves us, the more his friendship is worth.

But Jonathan's friendship for David had this quality in it, to a remarkable degree. The first time that he ever saw him, was on that memorable day when David went forth alone to fight the great giant Goliath. Day after day, that giant had stalked forth from the army of the Philistines, and had challenged any soldier from Saul's army to come out and fight him. But no one dared to go. They were all afraid of him. Even Jonathan, brave soldier as he was, was not willing to engage in a single-handed fight with that huge monster. But at last David came, a mere shepherd boy, without sword, or shield, or armor, and with nothing in his hand but his sling, he went out alone to fight that mighty giant, all covered as he was with his shining armor of steel and brass. We can easily imagine the scene that presented itself between those two armies. See, yonder comes forth the enormous giant. The ground shakes beneath his heavy tread. All the soldiers, in both armies, are watching that sight. And no one is looking at it with greater interest than Jonathan. And as he saw that stripling boy go forth to such a fight, he must have wondered to himself, how it could be possible for him to get the victory over that prodigious enemy! And when he saw David put the stone in his sling, and run to meet the giant, how he must have trembled for him! But the next moment, that stone is hurled against the giant. It smites him in the forehead. He stumbles, and falls thundering to the ground. David runs up, and stands upon his huge body. He draws the giant's sword, and cuts off his head with it. And now we can imagine what a loud "hurrah"—rang forth from the

JONATHAN PROMISES TO BE DAVID'S FRIEND.

JONATHAN, THE MODEL FRIEND. 235

soldiers of Saul's army, before they started to chase the flying Philistines. And then Jonathan fell in love with David. It was love at first sight. But it was real, true, heart-felt love. We read that Jonathan loved David "as his own soul." He sought him out, after the battle was over, and told him that he wanted to be his friend, from that day. And then they made a covenant, or agreement with each other, to be true, and loving friends, forever. And as proof of his friendship and love, Jonathan gave to David the robe that he was wearing, and his sword, and his bow, and his girdle. And then, through all the years of David's trouble, while Saul was persecuting him, and trying to kill him, Jonathan showed himself his loving friend. And when at last Jonathan was killed in battle, David mourned for him, and wrote a most beautiful and touching lamentation over him. In this, the words of our text are found, in which he says: "I am distressed for thee, my brother Jonathan; very pleasant hast thou been to me; thy love to me was wonderful, passing the love of women."

And thus we see how truly Jonathan was the model of a loving friend. We should follow the example that Jonathan has set us, and try to show the same sort of love to our friends.

Let us look at some illustrations of what loving friends will be, and do.

A Loving Friend. Colonel Byrd of Virginia, fell into the hands of the Cherokee Indians, when our Government was at war with them. He was condemned to death, and was led out to execution. One of the chiefs in that tribe, had been the Colonel's friend. As the executioners approached to put the Colonel to death, this chief came out, and standing before him, said: "This man is my friend. Before you can get at him, you must kill me." This saved his life.

A Little Hero. A boy in a town in Germany, was playing one day with his sister, when the cry was heard—"A mad dog! a mad dog!" The boy saw the dog coming directly towards him; but instead of running away, he took off his coat, and wrapping it round his arm, boldly faced the dog, holding out his arm covered with the coat. The dog flew at his arm, worrying over it, and trying to bite through it, till men came up, and killed him.

"Why didn't you run away from the dog, my little man?" asked one of the men.

"I could easily have done that," said the brave boy, "but if I had, the dog would have bitten my sister."

He was truly a loving friend and brother.

Damon and Pythias. There is a well-known story of two men, who lived about four hundred years before the birth of Christ, that comes in very nicely here. Their names were Damon and Pythias. They were educated men, and what were called—philosophers—in those days, and were very warm friends. Some one accused Damon to Dionysius, the king of the country, of doing something that made him very angry. Kings, in those days, had the power of life and death in their own hands. So Dionysius ordered Damon to be put to death. Before this sentence was executed, Damon begged to be allowed to go home, and arrange the affairs of his family. The king said he might go, if he could get some one to take his place in prison, and to die for him, if he did not come back by the time fixed for the execution.

As soon as his friend Pythias heard of this, he came and offered to take his place. He was put in prison, and Damon went to visit his family. The day fixed for the execution arrived, and Damon had not returned. He had to cross the sea, to get back, and the wind had been ahead for several days. A platform had been erected, on which the execution was to take place, and the king sat by, on a sort of throne. Pythias was brought out for execution. He asked permission to say a few words to the crowd of spectators. Permission was granted.

"My countrymen," said he, "this is a happy day to me. I am not only willing, but glad to die in the place of my friend Damon. I am thankful that the wind has kept him back. He will be here to-morrow. And it will be found that he has done nothing wrong. He is an honest, upright, honorable man, and I am glad of the opportunity to shed my blood in order to save his life. Executioner, do your duty."

Just as he had finished speaking, a voice was heard in the distance crying—"Stop the execution!" The crowd around the scaffold, took up the cry, and exclaimed, in a voice of thunder—"Stop the execution!" The execution was stopped. Presently, panting, and out of breath, Damon appeared. He mounted the scaffold. He embraced his friend Pythias; and said how happy he was that a change of wind had allowed him to get there just in time to save his life. "And now," said he, "I am ready to die."

"If I may not die *for* you," said Pythias, "I ask the king to let me die *with* you; for I have no wish to live any longer in this world, when my friend Damon, whom I have loved so truly, is taken out of it."

This touched the king so much that he pardoned Damon, and became the warm friend of those two noble men.

The Little Substitute. I have one other story to illustrate this part of our subject. A teacher in a day-school had to punish one of his scholars, for breaking the rule of the school. The punishment was that the offending boy should stand, for a quarter of an hour, in a corner of the school-room.

As the guilty boy was going to the appointed place, a little fellow, much younger than he, went up to the teacher, and requested that he might be allowed to take the place of the other boy. The teacher consented. The little boy went, and bore the punishment due to the other boy.

When the quarter of an hour was passed, the teacher called the little boy to him, and asked if his companion had begged him to take his place. "No, sir," he replied.

"Well, don't you think that he deserved to be punished?"

"Yes, sir; he had broken the rule of the school, and he deserved to be punished."

"Why, then, did you want to bear the punishment in his place?"

"Sir, it was because he is my friend and I love him."

The teacher thought this was a good opportunity for teaching his scholars an important lesson.

"Boys," said he, "would it be right for me now, to punish that boy who has broken the rule of the school?"

"No, sir," answered the boys.

"Why not?"

"Because you have allowed his friend Joseph to be punished in his place."

"Does this remind you of anything?" asked the teacher.

"Yes, sir," said several voices; "it reminds us, that the Lord Jesus bore the punishment of our sins."

"What name would you give to Joseph for what he has now done?"

"That of a substitute."

"What is a substitute?"

"One who takes the place of another."

"What place has Jesus taken?"

"That of sinners."

"Joseph has told us that he wished to take his friend's place, and be punished instead of him, because he loved him. Can you tell me why Jesus wished to die in the place of sinners?"

"It was because he loves us."

"Repeat a passage from the Bible which proves this."

"'The Son of God, who loved me, and gave himself for me.'" Gal. ii : 20.

Jonathan was the model of a loving friend. But Jesus is the most loving of all friends. We may well look up to Him, and say, in the language of the hymn:

"One there is, above all others,
  Well deserves the name of Friend;
His is love beyond a brother's,
  Lasting, true, and knows no end."

In the second place, Jonathan was the model of—a GENEROUS—*friend.*

Jonathan was the oldest son of Saul, the king of Israel. He was what men call, "the heir apparent," of the throne of Israel. This means that he was the one to be made king, when his father should die. Jonathan knew this. He fully expected to be king, on the death of his father. And all the people of Israel expected it too. But God had determined to take the kingdom away from Saul, and his family, because of his disobedience. The prophet Samuel had been sent by God, to anoint David to be king of Israel, instead of Saul. When Saul heard of this, he was very angry, and tried in every way to kill David.

But it was very different with Jonathan. When he found out that it was the will of God, that his friend David should take his crown, and throne, and be king instead of him, he was not at all angry. He made no objection to it. He never thought of quarreling with David about it. He knew that it was right for God to do just what He pleased; and he submitted, at once, to the will of God, although it took the crown of Israel away from him. He said to David, when they were talking about this matter: "Thou shalt be king over Israel; and I will be next to thee." 1 Sam. xxiii : 17. Noble Jonathan! Generous Jonathan! It does our hearts good, and helps to make us better, just to *think* of such friendship! Another example of generous friendship like this, is not to be found, anywhere, in the history of the world. How well we may speak of Jonathan, as the model of generous friendship!

And now let us look at some other illustrations of this same kind of friendship. Our first story may be called—

Willie Winkie's Sacrifice. Willie was a bright little fellow, about ten years old. His father had a Scotchman named Sandy, who worked about the place, and attended on Willie, when he had nothing else to do.

"Oh, Sandy!" said Willie to him, one day, "I'm so happy, I don't know what to do. Papa has promised me a new hobby-horse. It's to be just the biggest I can find in all the town, with the longest mane and tail, and a beautiful saddle and bridle. Mamma is going to take me down town this afternoon to pick it out."

Then Willie stopped, and looked at Sandy, and noticed that his face seemed sad. Then he said:

"What makes you look so sad, Sandy? Aren't you pleased about my pony?"

"Oh, yes, Master Willie, I'm always pleased with anything that pleases you. But I can't help feeling sad when I think of my own little Jamie. He can't walk a step, because his legs are so badly crippled."

"Please tell me all about it, Sandy; I'm so sorry."

"It's going on two years since the big wagon ran over him, as he was crossing the street; and he has never put a foot on the ground since. Yesterday he was worse, and the doctor said he never would live through the hot weather, unless we could give him a good bit of fresh air every day. I made bold to ask him how we could do this, when he couldn't walk, and was too big to be carried. He said if we could only get one of those wheeled wagons, which they make for such as he, with nice soft cushions in them, he could work it with his hands, for they are all right, though his legs are so bad. But bless you, those wagons cost a heap o' money; and I'll never be able to buy one. So you see, I'm like to lose my laddie, and he's the only one I've got." And then Sandy had a good cry. This set Willie to crying too, for poor Sandy's suffering boy. He went straight to his mother, and told the sad story. Then he said:

"Mamma, dear, can't we help poor Jamie?"

"I don't see how we can, Willie. The doctor says Jamie can't live through the warm weather, unless he can be taken out in the open air every day, for a good long while."

"Couldn't papa buy one of those little wagons for him?"

"No, dear, he couldn't indeed. He can hardly afford the expense of your new pony. But he said you had been such a good boy, and had waited patiently so long for it, that he would try and get it for you."

Willie was silent. Then he went up to his room for awhile. When he came back his mother saw that he had been crying; but with a determined look, he said, quietly:

"Mamma, I'm not going to have any new hobby-horse."

"Why not, my boy?"

"If I don't get one, perhaps papa will take the money and buy a wagon for poor Jamie, that will help to save his life. Do you think he will?"

"My precious, darling boy! I know your father will be delighted to do it."

When his father came home they talked the matter over. Willie and his mother went and bought the wagon, and took it round to Sandy's house.

With the tears streaming down his cheeks, Sandy said: "I'll never forget it of ye, Master Willie—never, never!"

So Willie went without his hobby-horse. But the wagon which was bought with the money saved poor Jamie's life; and that made Willie happier than a dozen hobby-horses could have done.

The Confederate Soldier. In one of the battles in Virginia, during the late war, a Union officer fell, severely wounded, in front of the Confederate breastworks. He lay there crying piteously for water. A noble-hearted Confederate soldier heard his cry, and resolved to relieve him. He filled his canteen with water, and though the bullets were flying across the field, and he could only go at the risk of his life, yet he went. He gave the suffering officer the drink he so greatly needed. This touched his heart so much, that he instantly took out his gold watch, and offered it to his generous foe. But the noble fellow refused to take it.

"Then give me your name and residence," said the officer.

"My name," said the soldier, "is James Moore, of Burke County, North Carolina."

Then they parted. That soldier was subsequently wounded, and lost a limb. In due time the war was over, and that wounded officer went back to his business, as a merchant in New York. And not long after, that Confederate soldier received a letter from the officer, to whom he had given the "cup of cold water," telling him that he had settled on him $10,000, to be paid in four annual instalments of $2500 each. $10,000 for a drink of water! That was noble on the part of the Union officer. But to give that drink of water at the risk of his own life, was still more noble on the part of that brave soldier. I never think of it, without feeling inclined to take off my cap and give a rousing—"Hurrah!"—for that noble Confederate soldier.

The Noble Engineer. Two freight trains, on the Philadelphia and Erie Railroad, came into collision. Christian Dean was the engineer of one of those trains. Both he and his fireman were fastened down beneath the wreck of the locomotive. Dean was held by one of his legs, close by the fire of the engine. His fireman was nearly buried under the pieces of the wreck. When they were discovered, Dean had managed to reach his tool-box, and was making every effort to get the fireman out. When he saw the men who had come to help them, Dean said to them: "Help poor Jim! Never mind me." The fireman was taken out, as soon as possible; but he was unconscious. Then Dean was taken out. And it was found that during all the time he had been working to relieve his friend, the fireman, the fire was burning his own leg to a crisp. It was literally roasted, from his knee down, and had afterwards to be cut off. And yet the noble fellow, unmindful of his own sufferings, was only thinking about his companion, and trying to relieve him. This was a generous friend indeed!

I have only one other story on this point of our subject. We may call it—

The Spirit of Christ. Thomas Samson was a miner, and he worked very hard every day for a living. The overseer of the mine said to him, one day: "Thomas, I've got an easier berth for you, where there is not so much work to do, and where you can get better wages. Will you accept it?" Most men would have jumped at such an offer, and would have taken it in a moment. But what did this noble fellow do? He said to the overseer: "Captain, there's our poor brother Tregony: he has a sickly body, and is not able to work as hard as I can. I am afraid his work will shorten his life, and then what will his poor family do? Won't you let him have this easier berth? I can go on working as I have done." The overseer was wonderfully pleased with Samson's generous spirit. He sent for Tregony, and gave the easy berth to him. How noble that was! It was indeed the very spirit of Christ. Now, all the four stories we have here, show the same generous spirit that Jonathan had in his friendship with David. He was the model of a generous friend.

There is one other point for us to notice, in Jonathan, and that is that he was *the model of a*—FAITHFUL —*friend.*

Jonathan and David lived in very trying times. It was a time of war; and they were surrounded by many and great difficulties and dangers. But, in the midst of all those trials, Jonathan's friendship for David never failed, and never faltered. He went to meet him whenever he could, in the woods, or on the mountains. He did, and said everything in his power, to help and comfort him. And, until the day of his death, he remained unchanged,—the faithful friend of David. And we should try to imitate the example of Jonathan in this respect. Let us aim to be faithful friends to those we love.

We have many beautiful illustrations of faithful friendship, which it is very pleasant to think of.

We find examples of faithful friendship among animals, that are well worthy our imitation. I have one story about a horse, and one about a dog, that come in very well under this head of our subject.

The Arab and his Horse. The Arabs, you know, have some of the finest horses in the world. They treat them very kindly. They are very fond of their horses; and the horses get very much attached to their masters. An Arab chief, whose name was Abon-el-Marah, had a remarkably fine horse. He was greatly attached to this animal, and treated it almost like one of his family. Once, while engaged in battle, this chief was wounded and taken prisoner, together with his horse.

On the evening of the first day after the battle, the chief had his limbs bound by a leather strap, and was left to sleep on the grass, outside of the tents in which the Turks were sleeping, who had taken him prisoner. The pain of his wound kept him awake during the night. A large number of horses had been fastened by ropes, not far from where he lay. He heard them neighing and snorting. And, among the rest, he heard, and recognized, the neighing of his own horse. Then he wanted very much, to go and speak once more to the horse that had been so long a faithful friend to him.

His limbs were so bound, that it was impossible for him to walk. But by dragging himself painfully along, on his hands and knees, he managed at last, to reach the horse. He spoke to him kindly, as he would have done to a friend. "I am to be a slave," said he, "but you shall be free; and I hope you will soon get home to the tents you know so well." Then he gnawed, with his teeth, the cord of goat-hair that held him fast. Soon the beautiful animal was free. "Now go," said his master. But seeing his beloved owner, wounded, and bound, as he lay on the ground, he bowed his head and smelt of his master. Then he grasped, with his teeth, the leather girdle which bound him. Holding it firmly in his mouth, he started for home, carrying his master with him. He galloped away, and never paused, or stopped to rest, but went on, and on, mile after mile, till he brought the Arab chief back to his own tents. When he had arrived there, he gently laid his master on the sand, in the presence of his wife and children, and then the noble horse fell down, and died from the great exertion he had made. That was a beautiful illustration of faithful friendship.

And now for the story of—

The Faithful Dog. This story is connected with the history of the celebrated city of Pompeii, which was overwhelmed by the eruption of Mount Vesuvius, in the first century of the Christian era. A rich citizen of Pompeii had a noble dog, whose name was Delta. He had saved his master's life three times. The first time was when he was nearly drowned in the sea. The dog plunged in after him, caught hold of him, and brought him safe to land. The second time was when he was attacked by robbers. He sprang upon the robbers, and drove them off from his master. The third time, was when a fierce she-wolf attacked his master, in a grove near the city of Herculaneum. He had nothing with which to defend himself. But the brave dog nobly fought the wolf off, and saved his master from being torn to pieces. After this, the master of this noble animal died. Then the dog attached himself to his son, who was but a boy. When the fatal day of that eruption came, and the fiery storm began to come down on Pompeii, this faithful dog stretched himself over the body of his young master, to try and protect him from the burning ashes which were falling fast around. The dog died; and his young master died. But seventeen hundred years after, when the ruins of Pompeii were uncovered, the skeleton of that faithful dog was found, stretched over the skeleton of his master. There was a collar round the neck of the dog, on which was found inscribed his name—Delta, and the three incidents above described. What a noble illustration of a faithful friend, we have in the history of that dog!

The Faithful Comrade. Some time ago, a very fine church was built in a market-town of Belgium. It took a long time to build it. But at last it was nearly finished. Only one thing remained to be done, and this was to have the weather-vane fastened to the top of the steeple. There was only one way in which the thing could be done, and this was for one of the workmen to take his stand on the top of the staging, and then let another man climb up on his shoulders, and stand there while he fastened the weather-vane in its place. This was a very dangerous thing to do, and yet, it seemed to be the only way in which it could be done!

When the time came for undertaking this dangerous work, a vast crowd of people assembled in the great square around the church, and all the windows of the houses in the neighborhood, were filled with people eager to see how the work was done.

The two workmen, chosen to manage this dangerous matter, were old friends, very much attached to each other. They went deliberately up the staging till they reached the top. One of them,—a stout, broad-shouldered man, placed himself firmly on his feet, and took hold of a pole of the staging with one hand. Then he stooped down, while the other man climbed cautiously up on his shoulders. This man had his tools in a bag, that was slung over his shoulders. As soon as he was ready, his friend, who was supporting him, handed him up the iron weather-vane. This was fixed in the place it was to occupy. Then there was handed to him the pan of hot coals, with the melted lead, by which the vane was to be fastened in its place. And so, in that perilous position he began to do his work. And while this was going on aloft, the crowd below were gazing in silent and breathless anxiety. They were afraid that the brave fellow might lose his balance, and be dashed to the earth. Many a heart was lifted up in secret prayer that God would protect him.

It took the brave man a long time to do his work. The moments seemed like hours, to the anxious gazing crowd. The broad-shouldered man stood in his place, as motionless as a rock. And many in that crowd, as they watched him, were saying to themselves: "Hold on! don't move! or your friend is lost!" But he did not move. And the man standing there on his shoulders, went quietly and steadily on with his work. At last it is done, and he carefully descends from the shoulders of his friend. When the crowd saw this, many of them exclaimed—"Thank God! Thank God!" And then they all united in a rousing "Hurrah!" which rang through the town.

The man who had done the work walked briskly down the staging; but his broad-shouldered friend who had supported him, came down very slowly. Every little while he stopped, and leaned against the staging, as though he could not walk any further. Still he kept on. But, as soon as he reached the foot of the scaffold, he fell, fainting to the ground. He was carried into a neighboring house, and a doctor was sent for. When they came to examine him, they found that his shoulders, and arms, and breast, were covered with terrible burns. While his comrade, whom he had borne on his shoulders, was at work, the melted lead, with which the work was done, was falling down, drop by drop, on this brave man. But, although he was suffering fearful agony, he never moved a limb. He knew that the least motion on his part, would cause his friend to totter and fall. And so, in the midst of all his terrible suffering, he stood perfectly still.

He was a faithful friend indeed, and fully worthy to take rank with Jonathan, the noble prince of Israel!

One other, very short story will finish this subject.

A gentleman gave his two little children in charge of a negro servant, to be taken to a distant port. The vessel in which they sailed was wrecked, and had to be abandoned. The boats were so crowded that there was not room for the negro and the children. He had to take his choice, either to leave the children to go down with the sinking ship, or to go down himself. In a moment he decided that the children should be saved. He kissed them; gave them in charge of one of the sailors; told him to tell his master that he had been faithful to his trust, and then, bravely waited to go down with the foundering vessel. This was a beautiful illustration of true faithfulness. And, negro though he was, he was worthy to be the companion of the princely Jonathan.

We may always think of Jonathan as—the model friend. He was the model of a *loving* friend—of a *generous* friend—and of a *faithful* friend. Let us try to imitate his example,—and then we shall be real treasures—to our friends.

ELIJAH, THE MODEL REFORMER.

"Elijah the Tishbite."—1 Kings xvii : 1.

ELIJAH was one of the most remarkable men, of whom we read in the Bible. The name of Tishbite, here given to him, is supposed to refer to the town of Tishbe, in which he was born. And this is the first time that his name is mentioned. Not a word is said about his education, or early history. We are not told when he was appointed to be the prophet of the Lord; nor how long he had been engaged in the duties of his office. He is a full-grown man, and actively at work in the service of God, when he is thus introduced to us as—"Elijah the Tishbite."

He was raised up in the providence of God, to do a very remarkable work. The Israelites had fallen into idolatry. The public worship of the God of their fathers had been given up, and the worship of the idol Baal, had taken its place. And God had raised up Elijah to change this state of things, and bring the people back to the worship of the true God. He was to bring about a reformation in Israel. And this is the point of view from which we propose to look at the life, and work of Elijah. We shall speak of Elijah as "*the model reformer.*" And we all have work to do in the way of reformation. Our work may not be the reformation of the church, or of the nation, to which Elijah was called. But if we become Christians, and engage in the service of God, we shall have a work of reformation to carry on, in our own hearts and lives, and we shall need just the same qualities, in carrying out this work, which Elijah exercised, in doing the great work, entrusted to him.

And when we look at Elijah, as the model reformer, we can see four points about this model, which we must try to imitate, if we hope to be as successful in our work, as he was, in carrying on the work he had to do.

Elijah was, in the first place, a model of—PROMPTNESS.

Whatever God told him to do, he went to work at once, and did it. When he was told to go and tell Ahab, the king, that there would be no rain for three years, although he knew that it would make him very angry, he went right away and did it. And, three years after this, when he was sent to deliver God's message to Ahab, although he knew that the king had been searching for him everywhere, that he might kill him, yet, he went, without a moment's delay, and did just what God had told him to do. He was prompt. And the lesson of promptness is a very important lesson for us to learn, and practise, both in the service of God, and in all our daily duties. Let us look at some illustrations of promptness and of the good that results from it.

Our first story may be called—

Promptness Leads to Success. A few years ago, the owner of a large drug-store, advertised for a boy. The next day the store was thronged with boys applying for the place. Among them was a queer-looking little fellow, accompanied by his aunt. "Can't take him," said the gentleman; "he's too small."

"I know he's small," said the aunt, "but he is prompt, and faithful." After some consultation, the boy was set to work. Not long after, a call was made on the boys, for some one to stay in the store all night. The other boys seemed reluctant to offer their services. But this boy promptly said—"I'll stay, sir."

In the middle of the night, the merchant went into the store to see that all was right, and found the boy busy at work cutting labels. "What are you doing, my boy?" said he. "I didn't tell you to work all night." "I know you didn't, sir. But I thought I might as well be doing something."

The next day the cashier was told to "double that boy's wages, for he is prompt and industrious."

Not many weeks after this, a show of wild beasts was passing through the streets, and naturally enough, all the hands in the store rushed out to see them. A thief saw his opportunity, and entered by the back door to steal something. But this prompt boy had stayed behind. He seized the thief, and after a short struggle captured him. Not only was a robbery prevented, but valuable articles stolen from other stores were recovered.

"Why did you stay behind," asked the merchant of

this boy, "when all the others went out to see the show?" "Because, sir, you told me never to leave the store when the others were absent; so, I thought I'd stay." Orders were given once more: "Double that boy's wages, for he is not only prompt, and industrious, but faithful." That boy is now getting a salary of twenty-five hundred dollars a year, and before long he will become a member of the firm. He was following Elijah's model of promptness, and it helped to make his fortune.

Here is a good story of a boy whom we may call—

The Minute Boy. A shipping-merchant, in New York, had purchased a cargo of wheat at the West. He was expecting it on, and wished to ship it at once for Charleston, S. C. His agent there had sent him word, that the price of wheat was likely to fall, and that the sooner he could get it to the South, the better. This made him very anxious to get it off immediately on its arrival.

At last it arrived; but, the day on which it came, happened to be a holiday. The men who usually worked for him, had gone off to spend the day in pleasure, and could not be had to handle the wheat.

The merchant was very much worried about it. But just then he heard a knock at his office door. "Come in," said he. A young man entered. His clothes were poor, but clean, and neatly patched.

"I understand, sir," said the boy, "that you wish to have a cargo of wheat loaded?"

"I do," replied the merchant.

"Well, sir, I shall be pleased to do it for you."

The merchant looked at him with surprise, and said:

"You! you! and pray, sir, how long before you will be ready to begin?"

"Just *one minute*, sir."

"My lad," said the merchant, "if you load that wheat to-day, I will give you two hundred dollars."

Instantly the boy stepped out. The next minute ten strong men came up, and went to work under the boy's direction. The work was done in good time, and the boy received his two hundred dollars. That boy had learned the lesson of promptness. This was the beginning of his course; but he rose to be one of our very first merchants.

I have one other story on this part of our subject. It may be called—

Ten Minutes' Delay. This story refers to the late young Prince Napoleon. When his father lost the empire of France, he went with his wife, the Empress Eugenie, and his son, the young prince, to live in England. The English were very kind to them. After his father's death, when war broke out between England and the Zulus in southern Africa, the prince, to show his gratitude to the English, offered to go to Africa, and help them fight the Zulus. He went, and just here the story comes in.

It seems that this young prince had never learned the lesson of promptness. When he was told to do anything, he always used to ask for ten minutes' delay. When told to go to bed at night, he would ask to sit up ten minutes longer. When called to get up in the morning, he would beg for ten minutes' more sleep. He did this so constantly, that his mother used to call him—"Mister ten minutes."

One day, when he was in Africa, a squad of six soldiers, under the command of Captain Carey, was ordered off some miles, to examine a particular part of the country. The Prince went with them. They reached the spot, and got through with their examination. Then Captain Carey ordered the men to remount their horses and return. But the Prince, as usual, begged for ten minutes' delay. Before these ten minutes were over, a party of Zulus came upon them. They fired a volley; and Prince Napoleon fell dead, with nineteen bullets in his body! He lost his life through that miserable habit of delay. If he had only learned the lesson of promptness, which we are considering, humanly speaking, he might have been alive to-day. I will finish this part of our sermon, with quoting some simple lines which put this important lesson in its proper light. They are headed—

WITH ALL YOUR MIGHT.

If you have any task to do,
Let me whisper, friend, to you,
    Do it.

If you have anything to say,
True and needed, yea or nay,
    Say it.

If you have anything to give,
That another's joy may live,
    Give it.

If you know what torch to light,
Guiding others through the night,
    Light it.

If you have any debt to pay,
Rest not either night or day—
    Pay it.

If you have any grief to meet,
At the loving Father's feet,
　　Meet it.

If you are given light to see
What a child of God should be,
　　See it.

Whether life be bright or drear,
There is a message sweet and clear,
Whispered down to every ear—
　　Hear it.

Elijah was a model of promptness. Let us try to imitate his example, in this respect, and we shall find it very useful.

But, in the second place, Elijah was a model of— PATIENCE—*as well as of promptness.*

When God wanted Elijah to work, he was, as we have seen, *prompt* to do, whatever he was bidden to do. And when he was told to wait, for the further manifestation of God's will, he waited patiently. When the long three years' drought came on the land, God told him to go and hide himself "by the brook Cherith" near Jordan. He went, and remained there in patience, till he was ordered to leave.

I have often seen pictures of Elijah at the brook Cherith. These pictures represented the prophet as sitting under the shadow of a tree, with a pleasant brook flowing by, and a beautiful landscape all around. And I used to think that it was in some such lovely place, that Elijah spent his long days of patient waiting. But the men who drew those pictures, had never seen the brook Cherith, and knew not what it was like.

ELIJAH AT THE BROOK CHERITH.

When I was in the Holy Land, I learned better. In going down from Jerusalem to Jericho and the Jordan, we passed by the brook Cherith. On reaching the spot, I guided my horse gently along to the edge of a fearful precipice, and looked down. There was a dark valley, or chasm, hundreds of feet deep. The side of the valley, near where I stood, went down almost perpendicularly. From the other side of the valley, a steep, rocky mountain rose up like a wall of stone. At the bottom of this valley, I could see a little brook, winding its way through. *That*, was the brook Cherith. How gloomy, and dark it looked! And all around was lonely, and wild, and desolate! It gave me a chill to look at it then; and it gives me a chill now to think about it. And that lonely and dreary-looking valley, was the place where God told Elijah to go, and hide himself from Ahab. There he went, and there he stayed, for eighteen months, or two years. And during all those long and lonely days and months, he saw no one, and had no one to speak to. The ravens brought him bread and flesh in the morning, and bread and flesh in the evening, and he drank of the brook. God told him to go there, and he went. God told him to stay there, and he stayed. He never worried, nor murmured; but waited patiently till God's time should come for him to change his place. How well Elijah had learned the lesson of patience! And, in the work of reformation which we have to do, in our own hearts and lives, one of the most important things for us is, to learn well this lesson of patience. Let us look at some illustrations of this part of our subject.

We may begin with a little story called—

One Day at a Time. A certain lady met with a very serious accident. A surgical operation was necessary, which would confine her to her bed for many months. When the surgeon had finished his work, and was about taking leave of her, she said to him: "Doctor, how long will I have to lie here helpless?"

"Oh!" said the doctor, in a cheerful way—"only one day at a time."

This thought gave her comfort; and during the weary weeks, and months that she lay suffering there, she learned the lesson of patience, by often saying to herself—"Only one day at a time."

I think it was Sidney Smith who said that taking "short views" of things was the best way to learn patience. And one, wiser far than he, taught us the same lesson, when he said: "Take, therefore, no thought for the morrow, for the morrow shall take thought for the things of itself. Sufficient unto the day is the evil thereof."

This is just the same as saying—"Only one day at a time."

A Patient Sufferer. There is a poor suffering Christian woman, living near Hartford, Conn., who is one of the best examples of patience that I have ever heard of. She has been confined to her bed for years, in great suffering. She is entirely helpless, and has nothing to live on, but what is given by her friends. Yet she is always cheerful, and patient. Her name is Chloe Lankton. Listen to this letter, which she wrote last summer to a friend, who had sent her some money.

NEW HARTFORD, CONN., July 21, 1881.
"MY DEAR FRIEND:
"Your note is received, with its check for $15. Many thanks to you for your kind gift. My heart overflows with gratitude for all the kindness received from you in years past. You have added greatly to my comfort, God bless you! I still live, and suffer as usual, sometimes much worse than others. God still sustains me under all my heavy trials. It is forty-eight years this month, since I have been entirely confined to this bed of pain and suffering. Jesus only knows what I have suffered. But I feel resigned to the will of God. I will trust him to the end.
"Your grateful friend,
"CHLOE LANKTON."

What an illustration of patience we have here! Nearly fifty years she has lain, poor and helpless, on that bed of suffering! When we feel tempted to murmur, under our lighter trials, let us think of Chloe Lankton, and try to learn the lesson of patience.

The Pansy. Here is a little fable which illustrates the point now before us very sweetly. It is about the trouble that arose one time in the garden of a certain king. The trees in that garden all began to murmur and complain The oak tree complained because it did not bear flowers. The rosebush found fault because it bore no fruit. The vine was full of complaints because it could not grow up by itself, like the oak, but had to lean against the wall.

One day, when the king came into the garden, he found the trees, and plants all discontented and impatient.

"I never bore a flower in my life," said the oak, "and I am of no use in the world."

"I might just as well die," said the rosebush, "for I never bear any fruit."

"What good can I do in the world?" said the vine. "I never can stand by myself, but always have to go leaning on something else."

Then the king saw a little flower, called a pansy, which was looking very bright and cheerful.

"My darling little flower," said the king, "what makes you look so fresh, and happy, while all the rest are murmuring and complaining?"

"I thought," said the little flower, "that you planted me here, because you wanted me to be a nice, good pansy, and so I made up my mind that I would try to be the best little pansy in all the garden." How beautiful that was in the pansy! It had learned the lesson of patience, and was practising that lesson.

Let us remember this. God has put us all where we are. He knows what is best for us; and He wants us to be patient, and try to serve Him just there. As the Catechism says, we must—"do our duty in that state of life, unto which it has pleased God to call us." And if we learn to do this, we shall be practising the lesson of patience.

But, in carrying on his work of reformation, Elijah was, in the *third place, a model of*—CONFIDENCE; and we should try to follow his example, in this respect.

At one time, in the life of Elijah, there had been no rain in the land of Israel for more than three years. The people were suffering greatly, for the whole country was parched, and dried up. The time had come when God had promised to send rain. And Elijah had great confidence in God's promise. He felt sure, that whatever else might happen, His promise would never fail. But then, he knew that it is not enough merely to have faith in God's word. We must not rest in our confidence alone. There is always something for us to do, at the same time that we are trusting to God. Elijah saw that the proper thing for him to do, was to pray for the rain, which God had promised to send. So he resolved to pray till the rain came.

He was at the foot of Mount Carmel, which overlooks the Mediterranean Sea. And while he was engaged in prayer, he told his servant to go up to the top of Carmel, and look out over the sea, for some sign of the promised rain. While his servant was on his way, Elijah was engaged in prayer. After awhile the servant came back, and said there was no sign of rain. Then he told him to go again, and he kept on praying. He came back the second time, and said: "I see nothing." "Go again," said the prophet, and still he prayed. He came back the third time, with the same report. "Go again," said his master, and went on with his prayers. He came back the fourth time, and said: "I see nothing." "Go again," said the prophet, and continued his prayers. He came back the fifth time, and said: "There is nothing." "Go again," said the man of God, and he prayed on. He came back the *sixth* time, and said— "Still there is no sign of rain." Now, most men would have got tired by this time, and would have given up, saying: "It's not worth while to try any longer." But Elijah was a man of confidence in God. And just *here*, we see how beautifully his confidence shines forth. He never, for a moment, thought of giving up. He felt perfectly sure that God's promise could not fail, and that the rain would come. So he said to his servant—"Go again the seventh time," and he went on praying. His servant came back the seventh time, saying: "I see a little cloud, rising out of the sea, like a man's hand." Then Elijah knew that his confidence was rewarded, and the rain was coming. And presently that little cloud spread itself out till—"the heavens were black with clouds, and there was a great rain."

Here, we see how truly Elijah was—a model of confidence. And we must learn to imitate this point of his model character, and have the same kind of confidence in God, if we hope to serve Him acceptably as Elijah did.

Let us look at some other illustrations of what this confidence is, and of the way in which it leads people to act.

When Martin Luther, the great reformer, was on his way to the city of Worms, where the Emperor, Charles V., had summoned a great Council to try him, some of his friends tried to persuade him not to go there. They were afraid if he ventured to go, he would be thrown into prison, and put to death. But Luther's confidence in God was so great, that he never had a moment's fear. He said to those who were trying to keep him back: "If there were as many devils in Worms, as there are tiles on the roofs of its houses, I would still go there." What noble confidence that was!

A Child's Life Saved by Trust in God.—A maid-servant in India, who was a heathen, was received into a Christian family, to have the charge of the children.

She attended prayers in this family, and so learned to know something about the God whom Christians worshipped. She used to take the children out, and was well acquainted with all the places in that neighborhood. She was gentle and kind to the children, and the family liked her very much.

One day, when she was out with the children, they went farther in their walk than usual, and being tired they all sat down on the grass to rest. One of the little ones strayed away, and not returning at once, the nurse said she would go and look after her, and told the other children to stay where they were, till she returned.

She ran off, calling the child by name as she went. Presently she heard the child's voice, answering her call. Very soon they met, but judge of her surprise when she saw a great fierce-looking tiger, coming up towards the child. She ran at once and bravely took her stand between the child and the tiger. In a moment the thought came into her mind, I must trust my master's God. Then she threw herself on her knees, and in an agony of feeling offered up this short prayer: "Oh! my master's God, save my master's child, for Jesus' sake! Amen."

She rose from her knees, and looking towards the tiger, saw that it had turned round, and was walking away into the thicket. Here we see what a blessing confidence in God is.

I have one other story under this part of our subject. It shows us how much comfort a poor colored woman found from exercising simple confidence in God. Her name was Nancy. She supported herself by washing, and was very poor. But still she was always cheerful and happy. One day a Christian man, who had never learned to have proper trust in God, and was always worrying about the future, stopped to speak to her.

"Ah! Nancy, how can you sing away, and always be so happy? I should think that when you looked forward to the future, it would take away all your happiness. Suppose, for instance, that you should be sick, and not able to work; what would become of you? Or, suppose your present employers should move away, and no one else would give you any work to do; or suppose—"

"Please stop!" cried Nancy. "Massa, I neber supposes. De Lord is my Shepherd, and I *knows* I shall not want. And honey," she added to her gloomy friend, "it's dem *supposes*, as is makin' you so mis'ble. You orter give dem all up, and jus' trus' in de Lord."

This is true. That poor woman was imitating the point of Elijah's model now before us. She had learned, and was beautifully practising the lesson of confidence in God.

And then, in the fourth place, Elijah was—a model of—COURAGE.

There came a time in Elijah's life, when he had to engage in a very trying work—a work in which great courage was needed. He told the king to call all the people of Israel together, and all the prophets of Baal—four hundred and fifty in number—that they might settle the question whether the Lord was God, or Baal. There was the whole nation of Israel, and all the prophets of Baal on one side, in this matter, and

Elijah alone, on the other—and yet, without a moment's fear, he went bravely on to do what God had told him to do.

Was the Lord Jehovah, or was the idol Baal the true God?—*that* was the question they had to settle. And *this* was the plan which Elijah proposed for settling the question. He said, let us build two altars—one for the priests of Baal, and one for me. We will put the wood on the altar, and the sacrifice, but no fire. Then we will each call on our God, to send down fire from heaven, to consume the sacrifice, and the God who answers by fire, we will agree beforehand to acknowledge as the true God. *This* was the understanding. Then Elijah told the prophets of Baal to begin first, as they were many. So they built an altar, and put the wood upon it, and laid the sacrifice upon the wood; and then they began to pray to their god Baal, to send down fire upon the altar. They kept on praying till noon; but there was no answer. Then Elijah made sport of them. He said: "Cry louder, for he is a god. Maybe he is away from home; or perhaps he is asleep, and must be wakened up. Then they cried louder, and cut themselves with knives, till the blood gushed out. They kept doing this, till three o'clock in the afternoon. But there was no answer to their prayers; and no fire came down from heaven.

And now Elijah's time was come. He called the people near to him. He built an altar, and put the wood and the sacrifice upon it. And then, to show that there was no cheating about it, he had twelve barrels of water poured over his altar. Then he kneeled down, and prayed to the God of Israel. He asked Him to hear his prayer, and to turn the hearts of the people away from their idols, and to prove that He was the true God, by sending down fire from heaven. His prayer was answered; and, while he was yet speaking, the fire came down from heaven, and consumed the sacrifice, and licked up the water that was about the altar.

When the people saw this, they cried out: "The Lord, He is the God! The Lord, He is the God!"

Then Elijah said: "Take all the prophets of Baal. Let not one of them escape. And bring them down to the brook." And they were brought down to the brook Kishon, and Elijah slew them there. Thus Elijah's work of reformation was finished. He engaged alone in that struggle—one man against four hundred and fifty; and yet he was not afraid. Truly he was a model of courage! And we must have just the same kind of courage, if we hope to be successful, in the work of reformation we have to carry on in our own hearts, and lives. Let us look at some examples of courage, and of the good it will enable us to do.

Courage in Telling the Truth. Charley Mann was playing one day after school. A ball that he threw smashed a large pane of plate-glass, in the window of a drug-store. He did this without intending it. He was very much frightened, and at first he ran away. But presently he said to himself—"What am I running away for? I didn't mean to do it. It was an accident. I'll just go back, and tell the truth." He did so. Charley was a brave boy. He told the whole truth. "The ball that I was playing with," said he, "slipped out of my hand before I knew it. I'm awful sorry for it. If I had money I would gladly pay for it. But I have no money. If I can pay for it by working, I'll do anything you want me to do." So it was arranged that Charley should run on errands, and sweep the store out every day, and keep the pavement clean. He was to be allowed a dollar and a half a week for this work, and he kept steadily on with it, till he had earned enough to pay for the broken pane. But by this time, the keeper of the store had got so fond of Charley, for his honesty, and industry, and truthfulness, that he was unwilling to give him up. He took him into the store, and made Charley his clerk, and gave him a good salary. In talking about it to his mother, one day, Charley said:

"What a lucky day it was for me, when I broke that window!"

"No, my dear boy," said his mother, "the lucky thing about it was, not that you broke the pane, but that you had the courage to go back and tell the truth about it, and offer to do the right thing." That was true.

I have only one other story to tell. Please pay special attention to this story. I am sure you will feel that it is worthy of it, when you find out who the boy was to whom it refers. We may call it—

The Brave Boy. Some years ago, on the frontiers of Ohio, there lived an industrious boy. He was the son of a poor widow. But he had the courage always to do what he knew was right and to refuse to do what he believed was wrong.

One day, a companion of his, proposed that they

should spend the coming Sabbath, in going to a neighboring village, and visiting a mutual friend.

"Not on Sunday," said the boy.

"Why not?"

"Because it isn't right."

"If you and I never do anything worse than that, Jim, we'll be pretty good fellows."

"We shouldn't be any better certainly for doing that."

"Nor any worse either in my opinion," said his friend.

"My mother wouldn't consent to it," said James.

"I don't know whether mine would or not, and I don't care—I shouldn't ask her," said his friend.

"I never go anywhere, or do anything, against my mother's advice," said James. "I know what she thinks about the Sabbath, and I respect her feelings. I shan't go on Sunday."

"And you can't go any other day, because you have so much to do," said his companion.

"Rather than go on Sunday, I'll not go at all," said James. "If I had no scruples of my own about it, I should have no comfort in going against my mother's wishes."

This ended the matter. Boys, follow the example of this brave boy. Always respect the Sabbath, and like this heroic boy, have the courage to refuse to do anything that you know will be displeasing to your Christian parents. The noble, and courageous boy, whose example I now hold up for your imitation was—*James A. Garfield*—our late loved, and honored, and martyred—President. He had learned the lesson of courage. And it was *that*, with God's blessing, which helped to make him the great, and good man that he rose to be.

And thus we have considered the character of Elijah the model reformer. There are four good points in this model. He was a *model of promptness*—a *model of patience*—a *model of confidence*—and a *model of courage*. Let us pray for grace to follow his example in these respects, and it will make us successful in the reformation of our own hearts and lives.

ELISHA, THE MODEL HELPER.

"*My father, my father! the chariot of Israel, and the horsemen thereof.*"—2 KINGS xiii : 14.

DURING the last sickness of the prophet Elisha, these words were spoken by the king of Israel, who was visiting him. The time had come when Elisha was to die. He was a very old man, and had made himself useful to the people of Israel all his days. He had prayed for them when they were in trouble. He had given them wise counsel, when they knew not what to do. He had performed many miracles for them, and had been a help to them, in a great variety of ways. He did not have a work of reformation to do, like that which Elijah had performed. But, like our blessed Saviour, "he went about doing good." He healed the sick; he raised the dead; he fed the hungry; he gave good water for the thirsty to drink; he comforted the sorrowing; and brought relief and deliverance to those who were oppressed with trouble. The mission on which he was sent, was a mission to help people. And he fulfilled this mission most faithfully. So we may well speak of Elisha as—*the Model Helper*. And, in this respect, it will be well for us all to try and imitate the model he has left us. There is work here for us all to do. No matter whether we are old, or young; rich, or poor; sick, or well; there will always be some about us, who need our help; and we can make ourselves both happy, and useful, by trying to be helpers as Elisha was.

And when we look carefully at the model which Elisha has set before us, we find *four* good points in it; or four things about his way of helping, in which it will be well for us to follow his example.

In the first place, Elisha was the model of—a READY —*helper.*

Some people will help their friends when they are obliged to do so, but they are not ready, or willing helpers. Our Saviour tells us of one of these men. He spoke a parable about him. He said, suppose you have a friend. You go to him at midnight, and say, please lend me some loaves, for a friend of mine has come to visit me, and I have nothing to set before him. And the friend to whom you apply for help, says, "Oh, don't bother me now. My children are with me in bed, and I cannot get up to help you." But, if you keep on asking for help, and teasing him about it, after awhile he will be tired of hearing you; and then he will get up, and give you the help you need. This man would be a helper, indeed, but not a *ready* helper. He was not willing to help, till he was obliged to do it. But it was different with Elisha. He was always *ready* to help. He never had to be asked twice for help.

One day, the Shunamite woman came, in great distress, to tell him of the death of her son. He sent his servant Gehazi, to go to her house at once. And then he followed himself, with the poor sorrowing mother. He raised her son to life again, and so gave her the help she needed. Thus he proved himself a *ready* helper. And we should try always to be ready in giving the help that is asked of us.

And now, for our encouragement, let us look at some examples of ready helpers.

Here is a story which we may call—

A Ray in the Dark. It illustrates this part of our subject very nicely.

"During my last voyage to India," says an English missionary, "I was sitting in my state-room alone one evening. The wind was rising. The sea was rough, and not being much of a sailor, I was getting to feel very uncomfortable from sea-sickness. Suddenly the cry of—"A man overboard!" made me jump to my feet. I heard a great tramping overhead, caused by the men running about. I made up my mind not to go on deck, lest I should be in the way of the crew, who were trying to save the poor man. I said to myself: "What can *I* do?" In a moment I unhooked my lamp, that hung at the side of my cabin, and held it close up to the bull's-eye window, that its light might shine upon the sea. As I did this, I said to myself: "Perhaps the feeble light of this lamp, may help to save the poor fellow from drowning."

In a short time I heard the joyful cry, "All right: he's safe." And when I went up on deck, the next morning, judge of my surprise and joy, to find that

ELISHA BRINGS THE WOMAN'S SON TO LIFE.

my little lamp had been the means of saving the poor man's life; for it was by the light which shone from it, that he was enabled to see, and grasp the knotted rope, which had been thrown over for him to take hold of. Now this minister was a ready helper. And this is what we should strive to be. Let us always be ready to lift up our light, and "let it so shine," that men may see the way of salvation, the rope thrown out for them to take hold of. And then, in the bright resurrection morning, we shall find that our little light has helped to save some soul from death, when we least expected it.

Helping a Fellow up. A little boy was lying on the ground, crying as if his heart would break. Another little boy, named Tommy, was trying to comfort him.

"What are you doing, Tommy?" asked a lady who knew him.

"Oh, I'm only trying to help a fellow up," said Tommy. That is just the right thing to do. We may all take it as our life motto, to help a fellow up. Wherever we go, we shall always find some poor fellow, who needs to be helped up.

What would have become of Martin Luther, when he was a young man, singing in the streets for his bread, if some one had not put out a hand and helped a fellow up? There are hundreds of useful men and women, to-day, doing great good, who never would have been where they are, and what they are, if there had not been some one, in their time of need, ready to help them up. Let us make it our business in life to be—ready helpers.

I have just one other illustration of this part of our

sermon. The title of it may be expressed in two little words—

Do It. Not long ago, a good Christian lady died in New York, whose name was Mrs. Doremus. She had been a dear loving servant of the blessed Saviour, for more than fifty years. She was a ready helper, in every good work. She had been so useful that she was known in all parts of the world. She taught the children in a mission school. She helped the poor; she comforted the sick; she visited the orphan children in the asylums, and made them glad; she went into the homes of old and worn-out people, and cheered the sorrowing hearts she found there; and helped in all good works. Wise and good missionaries, and ministers called her—mother—because she helped them in their work, and was so true, and wise, and kind, and unselfish. Her long life was a life of blessing to others; for she was so full of love to Christ, and joy in serving Him, that her example was like sunshine to warm and brighten everywhere.

Somebody asked her, one day, how she could do so much work? She gave her answer in the use of the two little words, we have put at the head of this article, saying: "When I have anything to do—I—*do it.*" "*Do it,*" that was the secret of her great usefulness. She was a ready helper. She began when she was young, to love and serve Jesus. And He showed her how to help people; and taught her, when she had anything to do, to—*do it.* Let us try to follow the example of this good woman; and then we shall be imitating the model which Elisha has left us, when we think of him as—*a ready helper.*

But, in the second place, Elisha was the model of—a KIND—*helper.*

One day, a poor widow woman came to him in great distress. She was in debt for a sum of money, which she could not pay. The man to whom she owed it, had threatened if it was not paid, to take her two sons, and sell them as slaves. This would break the poor mother's heart. So she came to the prophet Elisha, telling him her sad story, and asking him to help her. He had no money to give her; and he might have said:

"I am very sorry for you, my friend. If I had any money, with which to pay your debt, I would gladly give it to you. But, I have no money, and I can do nothing to help you out of this trouble." But Elisha was too kind-hearted to treat her so. Then he asked her what she had in her home. She said she had nothing but a jar of oil. Elisha told her to go home, and borrow from her neighbors, as many empty oil jars as she could get, and then to begin and pour out the oil from that one jar, and he would ask God to increase the oil, till all those jars were filled ; and that then she could go and sell the oil, and pay her debt, with the money this would bring her, and thus she could save her sons from being sold into slavery. She did so ; and the oil never gave out till all those empty jars were filled. In this way she not only had money enough to pay her debt, but there was a good deal left for herself, and sons to live upon. This shows what a kind helper Elisha was.

One day, when he was in the city of Jericho, the men of that city came to him and asked his help. They were dependent for their supply of water, on a large fountain, outside the walls of their city. But, the water from that fountain was not very pleasant, or wholesome to drink, and it had the strange effect of making the land barren, as it flowed through it. They asked Elisha to heal that fountain, and relieve them of this great trouble. He took a vessel full of salt, and threw it into the fountain, asking God to heal the water. He did so, and as the Bible history tells us, "there was no more death, or barren land," from that fountain. Its water continues fresh and good, unto this day. I can bear witness to the truth of this statement. For when in the Holy Land, while visiting the ruins of Jericho, we went to Elisha's fountain, and drank of its water, and found it very pure and pleasant. What a kind helper Elisha was, when he did this good deed for the men of Jericho! And so, he went about all his days, proving himself to be a kind helper wherever he went. And we should try to follow his example, by kindly helping those around us, who are in trouble.

Here are some illustrations of the way in which we may do this.

I Like to Help People. One day, an old lady was trying to get over the crossing, of a crowded street, in the city of New York. She had a basket, and several parcels to carry, and was afraid to venture off the pavement. As she stood on the curbstone, wondering how she could ever get over, a bright little fellow, about twelve years old, came along. He saw her trouble, and going up to her, kindly said: "Please ma'am, let me help you over." He picked up her parcels, and walked by her side, across the street. When they got over, he laid down the parcels, and taking a piece of strong string out of his pocket, he tied the parcels together, so that they could be easily carried, and then handed them to the old lady, saying: "Now, ma'am, you can get along better with them."

"My dear young friend," she said, "how can I ever thank you enough, for your great kindness to me?" "Oh, never mind, ma'am about the thanks," said the little fellow, "*I like to help people.*" That dear boy was proving himself a real kind helper.

Kind Words. One summer afternoon, a little match-girl, with a basket on her arm, stood at the entrance of one of the large railway stations in London. "Buy a box, please, sir," she kept saying as she stood there. But the busy crowd took no notice of her. At last, one gentleman stopped a moment to look at her. "Buy a box, please, sir," said the little girl. "No, I don't want any," he said, and was about to hurry on, when the hungry look of the poor child touched his heart. He remembered a bag of biscuits, which his little daughter had put in his pocket, for his luncheon, before he left home that morning, and which he had been too busy to eat. So he took the bag out of his pocket, and handed it to her, saying, as he did so, "Here, my darling, are some biscuits for you." She took them, without a word of thanks, which rather surprised him. After going a few steps, he turned to look at her again. There she stood, with the bag in her hand, and her eyes filled with tears, and he heard her saying to herself: "He called me *darling*, he did."

Oh, what a help, and comfort those few kind words were to that poor child! That gentleman was a kind helper.

I have just one other story, under this part of our sermon. It is about the great Duke of Wellington, and shows what a kind helper he was.

The Boy with his Toad. One day, the Duke was taking his usual walk in the country, when he heard a cry of distress. He walked to the spot from which the cry came, and there he found a chubby, rosy-faced little boy, lying on the ground, bending his head over a tame toad, and crying most pitifully.

"What's the matter, my little lad," asked the Duke.

"Oh, please, sir, here's my poor toad. I bring it something to eat every morning. But they are going to send me off to school, ever so far away. Nobody will bring it anything to eat when I am gone, and I'm afraid it will die."

"Never mind, don't cry my lad—I'll see that the toad is well fed, and you shall hear about it, when you are at school."

The boy thanked the gentleman heartily, dried up his tears and went home, without knowing who the kind gentleman was. But, after he had been a week or two at school, he received one day, a letter written as follows:—

STRATHFIELDSAYE, July 27, 1837.

"Field-Marshal, the Duke of Wellington, is happy to inform William Harris, that his toad is alive and well."

Five times, during that school-term, Willie received similar letters from the great Duke. And when vacation time came, and he returned home, he found his toad alive and well. The Duke of Wellington was a kind helper, as Elisha was.

Let us all try to imitate the model helper in this point of his character, by being *kind* helpers.

But, in the *third* place—*Elisha was the model of—a* USEFUL—*helper*.

During the lifetime of this good prophet, there was a sort of theological seminary, in the city of Jericho. They used to call it "the school of the prophets." A large number of young men attended this school. At one time they found that their building was too small, and that it was necessary to enlarge it. So a number of them went into the woods, in order to get the timber necessary to make the alteration. They invited Elisha to go with them, and he went. While they were engaged in this work, one of the young men was busy cutting down a tree, by the bank of a river. As he went on chopping, his axe flew off its handle, fell into the water and sank to the bottom. As the axe was not his own, but one that he had borrowed for that occasion, he was greatly distressed at the thought of losing it. He turned to Elisha, and exclaimed: "Alas! my master, for it was borrowed!" The prophet plucked off a twig, and threw it into the water. In a moment, the heavy iron axe came floating up to the top of the water, like a chip. The man got his axe, and went on with his work. Here we see what a useful helper Elisha was.

He went out with the sons of the prophets again, on another occasion. They were going to have a sort of picnic in the woods, and they had a cook along with them to get their dinner. He undertook to prepare them some soup. But, in making it, he put in some vegetables that he was not acquainted with. These proved to be poisonous. And at dinner-time, as soon as they began to eat the soup, they were taken sick. Then one of them turned to Elisha, and said: "Oh, thou, man of God, there is death in the pot." "Bring me some meal," said the prophet. The meal was brought. He took a handful, and sprinkled it in the pot. Immediately the poison was removed, and they all enjoyed their dinner very much.

And so this man of God spent all his days in showing himself to be a useful helper.

Now let us look at some illustrations of the great good that we may do, if we try to follow his example.

What are You Doing? A gentleman met a little boy, hauling a baby in a small wagon.

"My little fellow," said the gentleman, "what are you doing to help anybody?" The boy stopped a moment, and then, looking up at the gentleman, he said:

"Why, I'm trying to help mother, who is sick, by making the baby happy, so that he won't trouble her."

That little fellow was making himself a useful helper.

A Scene in a Railway Station. This story is told by a lady who was present. It was a bleak, snowy day. The train was late. About a dozen females, old and young, were in the ladies' waiting-room. Just then, a poor old woman, shaking with palsy, came in. She had a basket on her arm, full of papers of pins, and tapes, and cakes of soap, and such things, which she was offering to sell; but no one bought anything. The poor old body stood for a minute, looking through the window, as if unwilling to venture out into the storm again. Then turning round, she went about the room, as if trying to find something. A lady in black, sitting on one of the sofas, saw the old woman, and going up to her, said, in a kind way: "Have you lost anything, ma'am?"

"No, dear. I'm lookin' for the heatin' place, to have a warm 'fore I goes out again. But my eyes is poor, an' I don't seem to find the furnace nowheres."

"Here it is," said the lady, as she led her to the opening, where the furnace heat came out. Then she placed a chair for her to sit on, and showed her how to warm her feet.

"Well, now, ain't this nice?" said the old woman, spreading out her ragged mittens to dry. "Thanky, dear! this is proper comfortable, ain't it? I'm most frozen to-day, being lame, an' wimbly; an' not sellin' much, makes me feel a kind of down-hearted."

The lady smiled, and then went to the counter, and bought a cup of tea, with some rolls, and carrying them herself to the old woman, she said, in the kindest possible way: "Won't you have a cup of tea, my friend; it's very comforting such a day as this."

"Sakes alive! an' do they give tea in this depot?" asked the old woman, in a tone of innocent surprise, which brought a smile to the faces of all in the room. "Well, now, this is jest lovely," she added, as she went on sipping her tea with a relish. "This smoothes all the wrinkles out of my poor old heart."

And while she was warming and refreshing herself, the lady in black looked over her basket, and picked out some soap, and pins, and shoe-strings and tape, and cheered the old soul by paying her well for them.

The kind act, and gentle words, of that lady in black, not only cheered and comforted the poor old woman, but they had a good effect on all the people in that room, and taught them a lesson that they would never forget. She was proving herself a useful helper, and showing others how they might do the same.

I have one other illustration under this part of our subject. We may call it—

The Good One Man Can Do. The pastor of a village church, in speaking to a friend one day, said: "There is a man in our church, a carpenter, who does more good, I really believe in our village, than any other person who ever lived in it. He cannot speak very well in our meetings, and he doesn't often try. He is not a rich man, and never has much money to give to any object. But, a new family never comes into the village, that he does not find them out. He calls on them, gives them a hearty welcome, and kindly offers to do for them anything in his power. He is always on the look out, to give strangers a seat, in his pew at church. If any one is sick in the neighborhood, he calls at the house, and offers to sit up at nights, and to attend to any business for him; and I've sometimes thought that he and his wife keep house-plants, through the winter, just on purpose to have bouquets of flowers to send to sick people. He finds time to speak a pleasant word to every child he meets in the street. All the children of the village know him, and love him. And when he is driving his one-horse wagon, with no other load, you will often see the children climb up into it till it is full. He has brought more scholars into our Sabbath-school, than any other half dozen people in the village. He really seems to take delight in helping people, in all sorts of ways. And I never meet him in the street, but it does me good to look at him.

Now, certainly this good village carpenter had learned to follow the example Elisha left us. He was proving himself to be a useful helper. Let us all try to tread in his steps, and be useful helpers to all about us.

In the fourth place, Elisha was the model of—a POWERFUL—*helper.*

When he went about trying to help people, he did not do it in his own strength. He felt that he had the arm of God to lean upon. And, when leaning on that arm, he was not afraid of anything. And this was just the way the apostle felt, when he said: "I can do all things through Christ strengthening me." And what was true of St. Paul, is just as true of you and me. If we wish to be true helpers we must get the same strength that the great apostle had; or the same power that Elisha had.

We may speak of two illustrations found in the life of Elisha, of the power which he had as a helper.

One day, a splendid chariot drove up to the door of Elisha's house. Sitting in that chariot was a famous soldier. He was the captain—or as we should say, the general—of the army of the king of Syria. He had fought many battles, and gained many victories. He was one of the greatest men of his day. But, poor fellow! what good did all this greatness, and glory do for him, when he had that dreadful disease—the leprosy. His name was—Naaman. His wife had a little girl, who waited on her. This girl had been carried away, as a captive from the land of Israel. One day, when hearing how much her master Naaman suffered, from his terrible disease, she said to her mistress: "Oh, how I wish my master would go and see the prophet Elisha, who is in the land of Israel! for he could cure him of his leprosy." These words, of his wife's waiting-girl, were told to Naaman. It seemed to him too good to be true. But still he thought it was worth trying. He made up his mind to go and visit the prophet. He took the long journey from the city of Damascus, to the city of Samaria, where Elisha lived. On arriving at Samaria, he inquired for Elisha's home. Then he drove up to the house, and stopped his chariot in front of the door. When the servant came to see what was wanted, he told him to go and tell his master, that Naaman, the great captain of the king of Syria, was there; and that he wanted him to cure him of his leprosy.

Naaman thought, that as soon as the prophet heard what a great man was waiting at his door, he would come out in a moment, and call upon his God, and wave his hand over the place where the leprosy was, and heal him at once. But Elisha didn't care at all for the man's greatness. He saw what a proud man he was; and resolved to try and humble him. And so, instead of coming out to see him, he merely sent his servant, and said: "Tell him to go down to the river Jordan, and wash himself seven times in the water of that river, and his leprosy will be healed."

This made Naaman very angry. He was turning away, to go back home, in a great rage. But his servants came and talked with him. They said: "Master, if the prophet had told you to do some great thing, would you not have done it? And if by simply washing in Jordan, your leprosy can be cured, had you not better do it?" He listened to them. He went. He washed, and in a moment he was made well. Then his heart was full of gratitude, and he drove back as fast as he could go, to thank the prophet, for the great good he had done him.

Why, all the doctors in the world could not have cured Naaman's leprosy. And when Elisha did it so simply, and so quickly, he proved himself—a powerful helper.

On another occasion, during the life of Elisha, three kings—the king of Israel, of Judah and of Edom, raised a great army, and went to fight the king of Moab. They had to march through a desert country. Their supply of water failed them. They were in danger of perishing from thirst. Elisha had gone with them. The kings called on him for help. He prayed to God. Then he told the kings to dig great trenches, all round about where their army was encamped, and that on the next morning, God would fill these trenches with water. The soldiers were all set to work. Great trenches were dug all about their camp. And, by sun-rise the next morning, the water came. The trenches were filled. The army was saved, and a great victory was gained over their enemies. Here we see what a powerful helper Elisha was.

We cannot expect to work miracles, as Elisha did;

but, if we have God's almighty arm, to lean on, this will be sure to make us—powerful helpers. Let us look at some illustrations of the different ways in which this may be done.

Willie's Prayer. A little boy, about five years old, whose name was Willie, used to be very fond of having his mother sit down by his bedside, and talk to him before he went to sleep at night.

One night, just after he was in bed, she said to him: "Willie, dear, mamma is too sick to talk to you, to-night."

"Ma," said the little fellow, "God can make you well, can't He? Shall I ask him?"

"Yes, darling," said his mother.

Then the little fellow started up in the cold room, and kneeling down on the bed-clothes, folded his tiny hands together, and prayed thus:

"Oh, good heavenly Father, please to make dear mother well by morning, for Jesus' sake, Amen."

Then he crept back into his bed, and in a few moments he was fast asleep.

Next morning he woke, with the earliest light, and turning to his mother asked:

"Are you quite well this morning, mamma?"

"Yes, darling, I feel very well indeed this morning."

"Oh! I knew you would," said Willie, clapping his hands for joy. "I knew you would, for I prayed to God to make you well, and Jesus always hears little children when they pray." Willie was a little fellow, but he took hold of God's arm by prayer, and *that* made him a powerful helper.

A Little Girl, and her Bible. Some time ago, a

crowded train of cars was going from Boston to Springfield. In one of the cars was a lady with her little girl, about eight or nine years old. She was a good child, and was trying to love and serve the blessed Saviour. She had in her hand a Bible, which had been given her as a Christmas present, and which she was very fond of.

Not far from them, was a company of young men, who had just been recruited for the United States army. They were talking very loudly, and swearing dreadfully. One of them, in particular, who seemed to be their leader, swore worse than all the rest. The mother of the little girl was greatly distressed by those horrible oaths. She looked around to see if she could get a seat in another part of the car; but every seat was occupied. She knew not what to do. Presently, her little daughter whispered to her mother, "Let me go and give them my Bible."

The dear child, stepped timidly out from her seat, and going up to the young man, who had been the loudest swearer, she presented him with her Bible. She was a little, delicate-looking creature, and as she laid the book in his hands, she did not say a word, but she looked right into his face, in an earnest way, which seemed to say: "Oh, sir, please don't swear any more!" And then she went back to her seat.

Now, if an angel from heaven had come, and spoken to those young men, it could hardly have had a greater effect upon them. They quieted down at once. Their loud talking ceased. They stopped their swearing. Not another oath was heard through that journey.

The young man, who had received the book, seemed

particularly touched. The first time the train stopped, he got out and bought a paper of candy. He came and gave it to the little girl. Then he stooped down and kissed her, and said: "I thank you, my dear child, for your Bible. I'll keep it, and read it every day; and when I do so, I'll always think of you."

Now, what a powerful helper that little girl was! How much good she did by that one simple act!

I will close now, with a very nice story. We may call it—

The Cabin Boy Hero. Charley Wagner—the hero of this story—lived in the town of Plymouth, England. His mother was a widow, and Charley was her only child. He had a great desire to go to sea, but his mother was not willing to have him go. They often talked about it; but she told him one day, not to say anything more on the subject, till he had finished his schooling. Charley agreed. And though he often thought about it, he never mentioned it again, but went diligently on with his school duties. His mother tried to comfort herself with the hope that he had given up the idea of going to sea. But it was not so.

At length the time came when he got through with going to school. Then he said: "Now, mother, can't I go to sea?" "My dear boy," she said, "how can you think of going away, and leaving me all alone? What shall I do without you? It will break my heart, Charley, to have you go." And then she burst into tears.

"Well, don't cry, mother, and I'll think about it."

Then he kissed his mother, and went to take a walk, and make up his mind what to do. He got out into the country, and sat down under a tree, to think it all over.

"I never shall be happy," said he to himself, "unless I do go to sea; but mother will never be happy if I go. Oh, dear me, what shall I do?" He lifted up his heart in prayer, and asked God to guide him in the right way. It was a great struggle for Charley. But at last, he said to himself: "Well, I can't expect God to bless me, unless I honor and obey my mother. Then I'll give it up." That was a noble triumph for Charley. He gained a great victory over himself that day. And *that*, is the noblest of all victories. He went home, and said: "Mother, I have given up the thought of going to sea, and I'll go into uncle John's store to-morrow, as you wish me to do."

His mother was greatly delighted. She kissed him, and said: "Thank you, my dear boy, and I am sure that God will bless you for this."

So Charley went into his uncle's store, and became a clerk there. He was diligent, and industrious, and worked hard every day. But he never could get over his longing for the sea. Plymouth is a seaport town, and the docks there are always full of vessels loading, and unloading. Charley often used to get up in the morning, a good while before breakfast, and walk down to the docks for exercise, and to see the ships.

One morning he was there very early. The men were not at work yet. There was a vessel, lying a little distance from the wharf, with a plank leading up to it. He saw a little boy coming down the plank, to play on the wharf. Charley was walking on, when suddenly he heard a splash. The little fellow had fallen overboard. In a moment Charley threw off his coat and shoes, and plunged in after him. He was a good swimmer. He caught the child, and came up to the surface of the water with him. The sailors threw him a rope, and they were both drawn out of the water.

Now, it happened that this little boy, was the son of the captain of that ship—his only child—and he was very fond of him. He thanked Charley very heartily, for saving his child's life. Then he said: "Come into the cabin, my brave boy, and I'll give you some other clothes to put on, while yours get dried." The captain's name was Marshall. He had a long talk with Charley, while his clothes were getting dried. In the course of his talk, he found out all about Charley's desire to go to sea. As soon as he could spare time, he went to see Charley's mother, and had a long talk with her about him. He begged her to let Charley go to sea with him. "I'd like to have him, as my cabin-boy, and I'll take the greatest care of him. And, as my own little boy's mother is dead, I will leave him in Charley's place, Mrs. Wagner, and will pay you well for taking care of him." His mother, finally consented, and to Charley's great delight, he was shipped, as a cabin-boy on board of Captain Marshall's vessel.

This happened at a time when there was war between England and France. The French had men-of-war all over the sea, on purpose to seize the English merchant vessels, as prizes. Of course it was not safe then, for single merchant vessels to go to sea. So they used to go out in companies of four or five, and the Government would send a man-of-war along with them to protect them. Four other vessels went to sea with Captain Marshall's ship, and an English man-of-war went along for their protection.

They had only been about two days out at sea, when they saw a fleet of French men-of-war, come sailing towards them. The captain of the English man-of-war saw in a moment, that it would be impossible for him to protect the vessels under his charge, from this French fleet. So he ordered the captains of the vessels to separate, and each to go off in a different direction, and try to get away from the Frenchmen. They did so. Captain Marshall's ship was a very fast sailer. He put on all sail, and hoped he might be able to get out of reach of the French man-of-war. But after awhile, he saw that one of the French ships was coming after him. She was a fast sailer too. She gained on him in spite of all his efforts. Pretty soon she came near enough to fire a shot across his bows. This was to tell him to stop. He had to do it. The Frenchman came up alongside of him. They threw out their grappling-irons, to bind the two ships together, so that they could go from one vessel to the other, without having to use their boats. There was very little discipline on board the French men-of-war, at that time. The sailors did pretty much as they pleased. So, as soon as the two vessels were fastened together, nearly all the French sailors hastened on board the English ship, and went below to help themselves to whatever they could find.

Just then, a bright idea came into Charley Wagner's mind. He called the crew of Captain Marshall's ship around him, and told them what he wanted to do. The men were delighted. They said: "Charley's our captain. Give us a signal when you are ready, by throwing up your cap, and we'll do whatever you tell us." Presently up went Charley's cap—and he went on board the French man-of-war, with all the crew of Captain Marshall's ship. They made prisoners of the few Frenchmen on board. Then they took off the grappling-irons, and got away from the English ship. In the meantime the French officers and men began to come up on deck; and what was their surprise to find that the English sailors had got possession of their man-of-war, and they were left prisoners on board of an English merchantman. Oh, how angry they were! How they swore, and gnashed their teeth with rage! But there was no help for it. Then Charley got a speaking-trumpet, and standing on the quarter-deck, he called out to the French officers and crew: "Throw overboard all your swords, and pistols, and guns, or we'll blow you out of the water." There was nothing else for them to do; so overboard went all the arms the Frenchmen had. Then he sent two boats to bring Captain Marshall, to take command of the French man-of-war, and twenty sailors, to help manage the vessel. They came. Charley felt proud when he handed the command of the French man-of-war, over to his good friend Captain Marshall. And Captain Marshall felt glad that he had taken Charley to sea with him. Then the captain gave orders to put the vessels about, and return to England. They soon arrived there, and entered the harbor of Plymouth— a great French man-of-war, the prize of an English merchantman! And this, too, brought about by a brave cabin-boy—and that, on his first voyage to sea! Such a thing had never been known before in English history. All England rang with the praises of the cabin-boy. Don't you think Charley's mother was glad that she let him go to sea? I rather think she was. After this Charley was made a midshipman in the English navy. He did well there; and rose higher, and higher, till at last he became an admiral. The king knighted him, and he was well known in the English navy as—Admiral, Sir Charles Wagner. That was glorious. Charley proved himself a powerful helper. And this all came, through God's blessing upon him, for gaining the victory over himself first, and for honoring and obeying his mother.

Now, we have Elisha as the model helper; and we have spoken of four points in this model. He was first—a *ready* helper; second—a *kind* helper; third—a *useful* helper; and *fourth*—a *powerful* helper. Let us all ask God to give us grace to follow his example; and then our lives will be spent for the good of those around us, and for the glory of God.

EBED-MELECH, THE MODEL OF KINDNESS.

"*Ebed-melech.*"—JEREMIAH xxxviii : 8.

ZEDEKIAH, the king of Israel, had a servant, who was an Ethiopian, or a colored man. The time here referred to was one of great trouble in Israel. The king of Babylon had invaded their country, and was now besieging the city of Jerusalem. God had sent the prophet Jeremiah with a message to the king and princes of Israel. He told them that God wished them to give up their city to the king of Babylon. But they would not listen to what the prophet said. The princes were very angry with Jeremiah, for the message which he brought them from God. They took him prisoner, and put him down in a deep, dark dungeon, where there was no one to attend to him, or give him anything to eat, and where he sank in the deep mire. No one took any notice of poor Jeremiah, but this good servant of the king—Ebed-melech. He felt very sorry for him; and kindly made up his mind that he would try and get him out of the dungeon.

He went and spoke to the king about it. He told him that the prophet would surely die, if he were left in the mire of that dark, and dreadful dungeon. This dungeon was under ground. There was no door to it. The only way of getting in and out of it, was through an opening in the top, like those we see in our coal vaults.

The king told Ebed-melech to take some men with him, and a strong rope, and go, and lift Jeremiah out of the dungeon. He did as the king told him; and so the life of Jeremiah—the prophet of the Lord—was saved through the kindness of this humble servant of the king—Ebed-melech. He was the only one, among all the inhabitants of Jerusalem, who showed any kindness to Jeremiah in his time of trouble. And so I wish now to speak of Ebed-melech, as the *model of kindness*.

This is a good model for us all to study, because we can all show kindness to those about us, if we only try. And I wish to speak of *three* reasons, why we should try to imitate this model of kindness.

We should do so, *in the first place, because it is*— EASY—*to show kindness*.

Some things are very hard to do. We know, for how many years, the Government of England, of our own country, and of other nations, have been trying to find the way to the North pole. How much money has been spent, and how many valuable lives have been lost, in these attempts! And yet they have never succeeded. Getting to the North pole is a very hard thing to do. Some things can only be done by those who have plenty of money. When a railroad has to be built, across a great country like ours, millions of money are needed for it: and nothing can be done without it. But, it is very different with the work of showing kindness. There is nothing hard about this. We do not need much money to do it. The poor can show kindness, as well as the rich. Ebed-melech had not much money. He was a poor colored man—the servant, or slave of king Zedekiah; and yet he managed to show real kindness to the prophet Jeremiah. He was the means of saving his life.

And if we learn, while we are young, to show kindness to those who are in trouble, we shall find that it is an easy thing to do.

Let us look at some examples of the easy way in which we may show kindness.

Helping and Thanking. It happened one day, that an old Scotchman was taking his grist to the mill. It was in sacks, which were thrown across the back of the horse. In going along the horse stumbled, and the sacks of grain fell to the ground. The old man had not strength enough to lift the sacks up, and put them on the horse's back again. He looked around to see if there was one near to help him. Presently he saw a person on horseback, coming along the road; and he thought he would ask him for help. But the horseman proved to be a nobleman, who lived in the great castle near by, and the old man thought it never would do to ask such a favor of him. But that nobleman was a gentleman. He had learned to practice this point of the model we are considering. He knew how easy it was to show kindness. And so, without waiting to be asked, when he saw the old man's trouble, he instantly got off his horse, and came and helped the farmer, whose name was John, to lift his sacks of grain, on to the horse's back again. When this was done, John—for he was a gentleman too—took off his cap, and making a respectful bow, said: "My lord, how shall I ever thank you, for your very great kindness?"

"Verily easily, John," replied the nobleman. "Whenever you see any one in trouble, as you were just now, help him out of it, and that will be the best way of thanking me."

We ought to practice this point of the model before us, because it is easy to show kindness.

A Woman's Love. A murderer sat in his cell in the jail, repeating over and over again to himself the sentence pronounced by the judge:

"You are to be hanged by the neck till you are dead, *dead*, DEAD—and may God have mercy on your soul!"

But there were no tears in the prisoner's eyes, and no penitence in his heart. His dark face grew blacker, and his wicked heart became harder still, as he went on repeating those dreadful words, and cursing both God and man.

Ministers had come to him, with gospel messages of divine mercy; but he spurned their words, and told them to come no more into his presence. "Why, man," said one of them, "you are condemned to die; and in a few weeks, you will be launched into eternity, and how can you stand before God, with all your sins unpardoned?"

"That's my business," was his answer; "I wish no

further conversation with any of you." And he waved his hand impatiently for them to depart.

A report of this interview was published in the papers the next day. Among those who read it was a timid, delicate Christian woman. As she read the report, the tears dropped on the paper, and the earnest desire came into her heart to tell the poor condemned man, that she was sorry for him. But she said to herself: "I can't do it. I never was in a jail in my life; and I wouldn't know what to say. And then I should be sure to cry. Oh, I wish I could go and speak a few kind words to him, without weeping!"

This desire grew stronger in her every day; and one morning she gathered a beautiful bouquet of flowers, from her garden, and went to the jail. The jailor admitted her to the prison. Then he threw open a window, through which, without entering, persons could converse with the prisoner; and calling him by name said: "Here is a lady who wishes to see you." But as soon as she found herself standing, face to face, with the hard-featured, gloomy-looking murderer, the good woman's courage and voice entirely failed her. She could not utter a single word; but handing the poor prisoner the bouquet, she burst into tears.

The sight of the flowers, and the weeping woman, had a strange effect on the prisoner. It brought fresh to his memory scenes long passed. It called up the picture of a dear home across the sea, and of a fond Christian mother, who wept over him at parting. His hard heart was touched and softened. And while the woman wept outside the cell, he cried, with a great, deep, bitter cry, as the tears flowed down his face: "God be merciful to me a sinner." God heard his cry, and visited the heart of the prisoner, with pardon and peace. That good woman's kindness and tears had melted his hard heart, and he was led like a little child to Christ. How easy she found it to show kindness to that poor man! And how much good it did to him!

I have one other illustration of this point of our subject. We may call it—

The Baby's Sermon. Three children in a certain family, had been up in their mother's room, after breakfast one morning, learning their text for the day. They had learned it perfectly, and were coming down stairs for a play in the garden, when Nannie and Frank, the two elder children, fell to quarreling. The cause of the quarrel was, which of them should carry the great rubber ball down stairs. Nannie wanted it, because she had first thought of it; and Frank wanted it, because he was the oldest.

"You're a mean, selfish boy," said Nannie.

"You're a naughty girl," said Frank.

"I'll just tell papa what a horrid boy you are," said Nannie.

"And I'll tell mamma I wish she would sell you to somebody. I don't want such a sister," answered Frank.

"I don't love you one single bit," said Nannie.

"And who wants you to?" asked Frank.

And so these naughty children went on, from bad to worse, saying all sorts of unkind, unpleasant things to each other.

While this was going on, their little brother, "Baby Ben," as he was called, was coming down stairs behind them. Slowly he came, one foot at a time, holding on to the banister, with his little fat hands. As he listened to the angry words, he looked greatly surprised, and his big blue eyes opened wider and wider. The children stopped to finish their quarrel, at the foot of the stairs. Frank was trying hard to get the ball away from Nannie, and she had hold of his hair, and was pulling it, as hard as she could, when Baby Ben stopped on the lowest step, and preached his little sermon to them.

"Ickle children," said he, "lub one anudder." That was all he said. It was the text they had just been learning in their mother's room. It had a strange effect on those naughty children. For a moment nobody said anything. Then Nannie dropped her hands. Her face flushed, and holding out the ball—

"Here, Frank," she said, "you can have it. I'm going to be good."

"So am I," said Frank. "You shall have the first toss, Nannie. I'm awful sorry I was so cross." And so they went off, hand in hand, to have a good time in the garden; while the baby curled himself up in papa's big chair, in the study; and there the nurse found him, fast asleep, with his thumb in his mouth.

Now, it was an easy thing for little "Baby Ben" to repeat that text, and you see what a good effect his kindness in repeating it, had upon his brother and sister. He was beginning early to learn the lesson of kindness.

Ebed-melech was the model of kindness; and the

first reason why we should try to imitate this model, and learn this lesson is, that kindness is *easy.*

The second reason why we should try to imitate this model, and learn this lesson is, that kindness is—USEFUL.

Ebed-melech's kindness was useful to Jeremiah, because it saved his life. He lived for years after this, and was the means of doing a great deal of good to the people of Israel, who were living then. If we knew more of the particulars of his history, it would be easy for us to point out the usefulness of his saved life. As the prophet of the Lord, his business was to make known God's will to the people of Israel. And all the good he did, in this way, through the remaining years of his saved life, was the result of Ebed-melech's kindness.

But then Jeremiah has been useful to the church of God, ever since that day, by the prophecies which he wrote. And a large portion of those prophecies was written after the day in which Ebed-melech saved his life. And this shows us how great the usefulness was of Ebed-melech's kindness.

And in learning to show kindness to others, there is no telling how much good we may do. And when we think how useful our kindness may be, we see a good reason why we should try to learn the lesson of which we are now speaking.

Let us look at some illustrations of the usefulness of showing kindness.

Betsey Brown—or, The Power of Kindness. A good minister of the gospel, whose name was Wortley, was settled in a New England village. He tried to do good to all the people with whom he became acquainted.

But, there was one person in his neighborhood, whom he desired very much to bring under the influence of the Gospel; yet he found it impossible to get near her. Her name was Betsey Brown. She was a wicked, swearing woman, who kept a drinking saloon, and a gambling table, and who would knock a man down in her bar-room, if he said anything she disliked. But all this only made Mr. Wortley feel more anxious to do her good. He thought about her constantly, he prayed earnestly that God would open some way for him to reach this poor woman. He not only prayed for her himself, but he asked many of the members of his church to unite with him in praying for her conversion.

One day Betsey fell down, and sprained her knee very badly. She suffered greatly from this sprain. It confined her to her chair; she could not walk a step, and for the first time in her life, she was unable to help herself. This was a terrible blow to that active woman. She fretted and fumed like a chained tiger. No friend or relative lived with her. Her temper was so cross, and disagreeable, that she could get no one to nurse her. A poor woman in the neighborhood, who was fond of Betsey's liquors, would occasionally come in and do little jobs for her.

And now the good minister, Mr. Wortley, thought that this would be the time for him to call. So one day, as Betsey sat alone, and uncared for, there was a knock at her door. She was so softened by hunger and pain, that, without asking, "Who's there?" she said—"Come in!"

To her great surprise, in walked the minister. He kindly expressed his sympathy with her, in her misfortune, and asked if there was anything he could do for her.

"I don't suppose you can do anything, except read the Bible and pray," said Betsey sharply; "but there hasn't been a soul near me to-day, and I'm starving."

The minister knew what to do. He began by starting a fire, and making her a cup of tea. Betsey was dumb with surprise, and then her hard heart began to soften. When Mr. Wortley brought to her the meal he had prepared, he found her crying like a child.

"To think that you should do this for such a wicked woman as I be!" she sobbed out.

God had graciously touched her heart. She was led to see her sins, and to repent of them. She listened as for her life, while the good minister talked to her of Jesus. This was the first of many long talks, which ended in her becoming a Christian. And what a change that made in Betsey Brown! She was indeed "a new creature in Christ." And it seemed as if she could not do enough, to make up for her former wickedness. There was no more liquor-selling, or gambling in her house. And, the same room, where dreadful oaths, and curses, and wicked songs, used to be heard, resounded now with the voice of prayer and praise. She became an active missionary in the village, and was the means of doing good to some whom no one else could reach. And all the good thus brought about, was the result of the kindness showed by Mr. Wortley, when he went to visit her in her trouble. Surely that kindness was very useful.

Here is a story which illustrates this point of our subject very well. We may call it—

The Deacon's Singing School. A deacon, connected with a church in a New England village, was getting ready to go out one very cold winter night. As he stood buttoning up his overcoat, and putting the mufflers over his ears, his wife said: "Where are you going, husband?"

"I have heard of a poor widow woman, two or three squares off, who is in great suffering. She has five little children, two of them are sick, and they have neither fire nor food. I thought I would step around and look into the case. Perhaps I can start a singing school there."

"Go, by all means," said his wife, "and lose no time. If they are in such need we can give them some relief. And let me know what I can do to help. But it's nonsense for you to talk about starting a singing school. You know nothing about music. You never raised a tune in your life."

While she was talking away her husband had gone out into the piercing cold of that wintry night. When he was gone, she sat down in front of the great blazing wood fire, and busied herself in mending a pile of the children's clothes. Very busily and quietly she worked away. But, all the time, she was puzzling herself, by thinking what her husband could have meant, by starting a singing school in the home of that poor widow! It was so queer! What *could* he mean by it?

At last she grew tired of the subject, and said: "Well, I won't bother myself about it any more. He'll tell me what he means, when he comes home. I only hope we may be able to help the poor widow, and make her sad 'heart sing for joy.'" And then she started, and said to herself: "There, can *that* be what he meant? the widow's heart made to sing for joy! Wouldn't that be a singing school? It must be so. It's just like John. He might well take up the language of the patriarch Job, and apply it to himself, when he said: 'The blessing of him that was ready to perish came upon me, and I caused the widow's heart to sing for joy.' How strange it is that I should have found out John's meaning, by just quoting those words of Job!"

And then she went on with her work, feeling very happy. Presently she heard her husband's footsteps. She sprang up and opened the door, exclaiming, as she did so:

"Well, John, and did you start the singing school?"

"I reckon I did," was his reply, as soon as he could take off his wrappings; "but I want you to hunt up some flannels and things to help keep it up."

"Oh, yes! I will; I know what you mean. I have thought it all out; making 'the widow's heart sing for joy' is your singing school. What a precious work it is, John. My own heart has been singing for joy, all the evening, because of your work; but I do not mean to let you do it all alone. I want to help you in drawing out some of this wonderful music."

How useful the kindness of that good deacon was, to that poor widow, and her suffering children! And this is a kind of work in which we may all engage. We may start singing schools of this sort, without knowing anything about music. And in this way, we may make ourselves very useful. I will finish this part of our subject, by quoting some simple lines. They are headed—

A CHILD MAY BE USEFUL.

"I may, if I have but a mind,
  Do good in many ways;
Plenty to do the young may find,
  In these our busy days;
Sad would it be, though young and small,
If I were of no use at all.

"One gentle word that I may speak,
  Or one kind, loving deed,
May, though a trifle poor and weak,
  Prove like a tiny seed;
And who can tell what good may spring
From such a very little thing!

"Then let me try each day and hour,
  To act upon this plan;
What little good is in my power,
  To do it while I can.
If to be useful thus I try,
I may do better by-and-by."

But there is a third reason why we should try to imitate the model Ebed-melech has set us, or learn to show kindness, and that is because kindness is—PROFITABLE.

We see this in the case of Ebed-melech himself. His kindness to the prophet Jeremiah, in taking him out of that terrible dungeon, where he had sunk in the deep mire, was the means of saving his own life. That was the reward of his own kindness.

God sent word to Ebed-melech, by the prophet Jeremiah, that when the city of Jerusalem should be taken by the Assyrians, He would put it into their hearts to show kindness to him by sparing his life. And so it came to pass. The princes, and nobles, and great men of the nation, were all put to death. The king had his sons killed before his face. Then his eyes were put out, and he was carried captive to Babylon. And to the day of his death, he never could forget the last sad sight, that he witnessed, before his eyes were put out. It was the mangled, and bleeding bodies of his dead sons. How sad, and sorrowful a recollection this must have been to him!

But Ebed-melech had his life given to him as a reward for the kindness which he showed to the prophet Jeremiah. Surely he found out that it was profitable to be kind. And it is very easy for us to find illustrations of the same sort. Let us look at some of these. Here is one that we may call—

The Beggar Boy and the Flowers. A little boy was standing near the gate, in his father's garden. On the outside of the gate was a ragged little fellow, looking through the railing at the beautiful flowers that were blooming there.

"Go away, you beggar boy!" said the boy in the garden. "You've no business to be looking at our flowers."

The poor boy's face reddened with anger, to be spoken to so rudely, and he was about to answer in the same style, when a bright young girl, sprang out from an arbor near, and looking at her brother, said: "How could you speak so roughly, Herbert? I'm sure his looking at the flowers won't hurt them." And then turning to the boy outside the gate, in the kindest possible way, she said:

"Little boy, I'll pick you some flowers, if you'll wait a moment." Then she gathered a beautiful bouquet, and handed it to him through the iron grating in the gate. He thanked her heartily, and turned away, with his face all lighted up with surprise and pleasure.

Twelve years pass away. That young girl has grown up to be a woman, and is married. One summer afternoon, she was walking with her husband in the garden, when she saw a young man, in a workman's dress, leaning over the fence, and looking earnestly at her and the flowers. She said to him: "Are you fond of flowers, sir? It will give me great pleasure to gather some for you."

The young man looked at her fair face, and then said: "Twelve years ago, I stood here, a ragged boy, and you showed me the same kindness that you are showing me now. Your sweet flowers, and your kind words, made a new boy of me; yes, and they made a new man of me, too. Your bright face has been a light and comfort to me, in many a dark hour; and now, thank God, though that boy is still only an humble, hard-working man, yet he is an honest, grateful, God-fearing man, and he owes it all, through God's blessing, to your kindness."

Tears stood in that lady's eyes, as she heard these words; and turning to her husband, she said: "God put it into my heart to do that little kindness, and see how great a reward it has brought!" Certainly this shows that kindness *is* profitable.

Here is another illustration. We may call it—

Kindness Rewarded. Some years ago, as the mail-train, on the Baltimore and Ohio Railroad, in charge of the late Captain George A. Rawlings, conductor, was approaching Doe Gully tunnel, the engine struck and killed a cow belonging to a poor woman, the widow of a watchman on that part of the road, who had lost his life in the service of the company.

The accident soon brought to the spot, a number of people, living in that neighborhood. Among these were the widow of the watchman, and her five little children. They were crying most piteously over their loss.

Rawlings, the conductor, had a heart full of tenderness, and he went to work, at once, to take up a collection. The passengers, and the men of the train, gave very gladly, and soon he had collected over seventy dollars, which he handed over to the widow, that she might buy a new cow.

With tears in her eyes, she said:

"Thank you! thank you, sir, a thousand times! I shall never forget your kindness to the poor widow and her children; and I feel sure it will come back to you some day or other."

Time rolled on, and the incident was almost forgotten, when one night, Rawlings left Cumberland on his east-bound trip, in a terrible rain-storm. After passing through Doe Gully tunnel, he saw a fire blazing on the track, some distance before him. He knew that this was a sign of danger, and gave the signal to put on the brakes and stop the train.

As soon as possible, the train was stopped, just a little distance from where an immense landslide covered the track. It lay like a young mountain, all over the road. Near the fire stood the widow, for whom conductor Rawlings had raised the subscription, so long before, when her cow was killed. She held a blazing pine knot in her hand, which she was waving about, as she shouted: "Where's the conductor? Where's the conductor?"

Presently Rawlings appeared. She went up to him and said: "I told you, Mr. Rawlings, I would never forget your kindness, to the poor lone widow, and her children. I heard the fall of the rocks and earth across the track. I knew you were coming; that in the darkness of night you could not see what had taken place, and that your train would be dashed in pieces, and many lives be lost. So I went out in the storm and started the fire, that you might see it in time to save the train. God bless the man who was kind to the poor widow, and her children, when they were in trouble."

Now, certainly, conductor Rawlings understood that day, how profitable to him was the kindness he had showed to the poor widow so long before!

I have just one other illustration to give, under this point of our subject. We may call it—

How God Works. This story is about a certain king, whose name was Rhoud. He lived in the north of Europe, some centuries ago. At the time to which our story refers, there was great trouble in his kingdom. There were many enemies of the king, who were plotting to take away his life.

One day, the king was taking a walk through the woods. A prince, whose name was Regan, was his companion. They were talking about the troubles in the kingdom. As they were going on, through the beautiful woods, they heard something scream pitifully in one of the trees.

"It is a bird up yonder tree," said the king; "it screams because it is in some trouble."

"Let it scream," said Prince Regan. "Just now we have more important things to think about, than a little bird up a tree."

"The nearest duty first," said the king. "There is nothing more important now, than to show kindness to that little creature in its distress. Regan, I must climb up that tree."

"But suppose you should fall and be killed, what a shame it would be, to have it said that our king lost his life for the sake of a little bird!"

"Many a life has been lost for less," replied the king, as he prepared to mount the tree. By the prince's help he managed to get hold of the lower branches. Then he went slowly up, higher and higher, till finally he came to where the bird was. It was a pretty little goldfinch, which had caught its leg in a crack of one of the branches of the tree, and could not get it loosened. The king took it carefully out, and came down safely, with the little goldfinch in his hand. He stroked its feathers tenderly, saying as he did so: "It shall be my adopted child, and the playmate of my little daughter Agnar."

He took the bird home, and had a beautiful cage made for it. "How childish the king is!" said one of his officers. "When war is at the door, and he is surrounded by great dangers, he finds time to save a little bird, and takes care of it himself."

In the meantime, his enemies were still plotting

against him. Two of the servants in the king's palace, had been bribed to help them, in carrying out their plans.

One day, when the king was out hunting with his men, his enemies made an arrangement by which they hoped to secure the death of the king, during the following night. Their plan was this: in the ceiling of the king's bed-chamber, and directly over the bed on which he slept, was a very heavy beam of timber. This was loosened, and yet held in its place in such a way, that whenever they desired, it could be made to fall across the king's bed, and so crush him to death. Then they thought, it would be supposed that the king had met his death by accident. People would say that the ceiling over the king's bed was weak, and had fallen during the night.

The king returned from his hunting late at night. He went to bed weary, and soon fell asleep, and probably would never have risen again, had not the little bird suddenly awakened him by its screaming. He sprang from his bed, to see what was the matter. He soon found that he had forgotten that morning, before going a hunting, to give the little creature any water to drink, or any food to eat; and at evening, on his return, he was so tired that he went to bed without thinking of the bird. He took the cage in his hand, and said: "You dear little creature! and did I save thy life only to let thee perish with hunger?"

Then he poured some water into the little glass, and put some seed in the little box in the cage.

And while he was doing this, the beam fell from the ceiling, with tremendous noise, and striking the bed, crushed it flat to the floor. The noise was heard all over the palace. The soldiers, sleeping in the palace-yard awoke, and drew their swords. The frightened servants rushed into the king's chamber, with torches flaming in their trembling hands. As soon as they saw the ruins of the bed, they exclaimed: "The king is killed! King Rhoud is crushed to pieces!"

But on looking round, they saw the king standing unhurt, with the bird-cage in his hand. He smiled on them and exclaimed: "Do not fear, my friends; God has kept his hand over me."

When Prince Regan heard of all this—how the beam had fallen, and how the little bird had saved the king's life—he was amazed beyond measure. Then fixing his tearful eyes on the king, he said: "How wonderfully God works! I never again shall doubt that there is a Providence in all things." The king answered with a smile, "Then you can see, Regan, that we should not despise little folks. If a king can save a bird, then the bird can save the king." Surely King Rhoud must have felt that his kindness to that little bird was profitable to him! It not only saved his life, but it led to the discovery and punishment of the wicked men who were plotting against him.

Now let us remember the subject we have been considering—*Ebed-melech the model of kindness*. And let us remember the three reasons why we should try to imitate this model, and to learn this lesson. The first reason is, because kindness *is easy;* the second, because *it is useful;* and the third, because *it is profitable*. May God give us all grace to learn, and practice this—easy—useful—and profitable lesson!

NEHEMIAH, THE MODEL MAN OF BUSINESS.

"I am doing a great work, so that I cannot come down."—NEHEMIAH vi : 3.

NEHEMIAH, a prince of Israel, spoke these words. He had been taken captive; and when first we read of him in the Bible, he was acting as cup-bearer to the king of Persia, in his royal palace at Shushan.

One day, some Jewish friends came to see him. They had lately returned from Jerusalem. Nehemiah asked them how they found things in that holy city. They told him that the walls of Jerusalem were all thrown down; that the city was in ruins, and that the people there, were in great poverty and distress. This troubled him greatly, and made him feel very sad and sorrowful.

Then he asked the king to let him go to Jerusalem, to get the walls built up, and the city recovered from its ruins. The king consented. He appointed Nehemiah the governor of Jerusalem, and gave him letters to some of his officers in that region, to secure for

NEHEMIAH ASKS THE KING TO LET HIM GO TO JERUSALEM.

him the help he would need, in carrying on the great work he had undertaken.

On arriving at Jerusalem, he found things there in a very sad state. But he called all the chief men of the Jewish people together, and engaged them to help him. Then they began at once, to rebuild the walls, and repair the ruins of the city.

The enemies of the Jews tried to hinder them, in many ways. But in the midst of all the dangers and difficulties, that surrounded him, Nehemiah went on patiently, perseveringly, and bravely, till the walls were rebuilt, and Jerusalem was again in a safe and prosperous condition. He acted so wisely, and was so successful in his work, that in putting Nehemiah among our "Bible Models," we may well speak of him as—

"*The Model Man of Business.*" And this is a good model for us to study. For as we grow up to be men and women, we shall all have business of some kind to attend to; and if we hope to be successful in that business, whatever it may be, we must set the best examples of business men before us, and try to imitate them. But I know of no better example in this matter, than we find in Nehemiah. He may well be called—"The model man of business."

And in studying this model, there are *four* good points for us to notice.

In the first place, as a business man, Nehemiah was a model of—EARNESTNESS.

We see this in him, when he used the words of our text, and said: "I am doing a great work, so that I cannot come down."

He was very busy then, in building up the walls of Jerusalem. The enemies of the Jews wanted very much to hinder that work. They threatened to attack Nehemiah and the Jews, while they were at work. But it was impossible to frighten them in this way.

Then they tried to get Nehemiah to come and meet them, pretending that they wanted to talk over matters with him. But he knew that if they could only get him in their power, they would be apt to kill him. So his answer to them was,—"I am doing a great work, and I cannot come down." So he went on with his work, bravely, and perseveringly, till it was done. He labored on for twelve years, for the good of Jerusalem, till he had finished the work which he went there to do. And here, we see, how earnest Nehemiah was as a business man. And *we* must be earnest too, if we wish to be good boys and girls, or men and women of business.

Let us look now, at some other examples of this point of Nehemiah's model.

How Charley Built the Church. A minister had an appointment to preach, in the country. On getting out of the cars at the station, according to the direction given him, he told the driver to take him to "Ebenezer Chapel." "Ebenezer?" said the driver; "oh, you mean little Charley's chapel, don't you?" "No," said the minister, "I mean Ebenezer." "Yes, but we about here, always call it—'Little Charley's Chapel.'" "And why do you call it so?" asked the minister. "Because little Charley laid the foundation-stone. You see, sir," continued the driver, "it happened in this way. A few years ago, we wanted a new chapel. A meeting was called, to talk the matter over. A good deal was said, at that meeting, about how the money could be raised. But the times were hard; and the people were poor; and labor and materials were very dear. So they resolved that the chapel could not be built; and then the meeting broke up.

"But a day or two after the meeting, a little boy about nine years old, came to the minister's door, and rang the bell. The minister himself opened the door, and found the little fellow there. His face was all flushed, and the perspiration thick on his forehead. In front of him was his little toy wheelbarrow; and in the barrow were six new bricks. He had wheeled his load up a long, steep hill, and was out of breath, so that he could hardly speak. 'Well, Charley,' asked the wondering minister, 'and what is the meaning of this?' 'Oh, please, sir,' said Charley, 'I heard you wanted a new chapel, and were about giving it up; so I begged these few bricks, from the men who are building a house down in the village, and thought they would do to begin with.'

"With tears in his eyes, the minister thanked Charley for what he had done. Then he called another meeting of the people, about the chapel. Charley's bricks were piled up on the table, in front of the minister. He told the story of what Charley had done. Then he made a little speech to them about it. He said—'If they were all as earnest in the business of building the chapel, as that little boy was, the work would soon be done.' This had a great effect on them. They resolved that the chapel should be built: but Charley laid the first stone. It is a big chapel. It will hold a thousand people, and cost more than ten thousand dollars, and now it is out of debt."

"And what has become of little Charley?" asked the minister. Here the old man's voice choked, as he said: "If you'll let me pull up at the church-yard, sir, I'll show you Charley's grave. There are many graves there, but you may always tell Charley's, by the bright flowers upon it. He was the pet of the Sunday-school, and the children never let a day go by, without putting fresh flowers on his grave. He used to live close by the school, and he died the very day on which the last dollar of the chapel debt was paid. It was a summer's day, and he made them set his window open, that he might hear them sing. He asked them to sing a bright, happy tune, which was a favorite of his; and he died, as he was trying to join them in singing it from his little bed.

"He sang the first verse of the hymn on earth; but, we all believe that he finished it in heaven."

Now certainly Charley was earnest in the business of building that chapel.

Earnestness in Conquering a Bad Habit. A working man, who was trying to be a Christian, had got into the habit of chewing tobacco. He put his hand in his pocket one day, took out his plug of tobacco, and threw it away, saying as he did so, "That's the end of it." But that was not the end of it. A bad habit, that has long been followed, is not so easily overcome. The longing for the tobacco came back to him, with great power. He would chew camomile, toothpicks, quills, and various things to keep his jaws in motion, as he used to do with tobacco. But this did not relieve him. He suffered dreadfully. At last he said to himself: "It's no use suffering so much for a bit of tobacco; I'll go and get some." So he went and bought another plug, and put it in his pocket. "Now," he said, "when I want it awfully, I know what I'll do." Well, very soon he did want it awfully. Then he took the plug in his hand, and lifted up his heart in prayer to God for strength to get the victory in this struggle. Then looking at the tobacco, he said: "I love you. But are *you* my master, or am I yours? You are a *weed*, and I am a *man*. You are a *thing*, and I am a *man*. *I'll master you, if I die for it!*" Every time the desire for the tobacco came over him, he would take it in his hand, and pray over it, and talk to it, in this way. This was kept up for six or eight weeks. Then, he threw the tobacco away, and felt that he no longer had any desire for it. By the help of God, and by his own earnestness he had gained the victory over his old enemy. And if we try to follow his example, we shall find that, in the business of overcoming bad habits, earnestness, and the help of God, will be sure to give us the victory.

The first point of Nehemiah's model, as a man of business, was his—*earnestness.*

In the second place, as a business man, Nehemiah was a model of—UNSELFISHNESS.

He gave up his office under the king of Persia, and the salary he was receiving there, that he might go to Jerusalem, to help his poor countrymen. Now, if he had been a selfish man, he would have said: "I am very sorry that Jerusalem is in ruins, and that my countrymen there are in so much trouble. I should like very much to help them. But if I go there, I shall have to give up my salary, and I can't afford to do that." But Nehemiah did not care about his salary. He was quite willing to let that go, if he could only help to build up the walls of Jerusalem, and be a comfort to the poor Jews there. And this shows us what an unselfish man he was!

And then, during the twelve years that he remained at Jerusalem as governor of the city, he was entitled to receive a salary, every year. But this could only have been made up to him by the people of that city. And they were so poor that it would have been very hard for them to do it. So he refused to take any salary. And he stayed there, through all those years, at his own expense, working hard all the time, to build up the city, and to do good to the people, who lived there. And here we see that he was indeed a model business man because of his—unselfishness.

And this is a good model for us to imitate. Let us look at some other examples of unselfishness. Our first story may be called—

The Unselfish Brother. A boy whose name was Jean Sedaine, lost his father, when he was thirteen years of age. They were living in France, about fifty miles from the city of Paris. He was left with a little brother, about five years old. His brother's name was Pierre. They had a mother living in Paris; and after his father's death, Jean's first desire was to get to Paris, with his little brother, and try to find their mother. This happened before the days of railroads. People used to travel then, in large stages. In France, these were called—diligences. Jean went to the office of the diligence, and asked what the fare was to Paris. They told him how much it cost. Then he found that he only had money enough to pay for one seat. So he took all the money he had to pay for his little brother; and he made up his mind that he would follow on foot, as fast as he could. It was winter time when this took place.

Jean overtook the diligence, the first time it stopped, at an inn, to change horses. As soon as he came up to it, he found his little brother crying from the cold. He had no shawl, nor anything to keep the poor fellow warm. So he nobly took off his own coat, and wrapped it round his brother, willing to walk in his shirt sleeves, if only the little fellow could be made comfortable. This touched the hearts of the other passengers, and brought tears to their eyes. They took up a collection among themselves, and soon had money enough to pay for Jean's passage. They gave him a seat by the side of his brother. This made them both feel very happy.

Here is another story that illustrates this part of our subject very well. It may be called—

The Unselfish Sailor. Some years ago, a Pacific steamer took fire. The burning vessel was headed for the shore, which was not very far off. The alarm and confusion among the passengers were terrible. Their only thought was how they could escape from suffering death, either by burning, or by drowning.

There was one man on board, who had been working for years in the mines of California. He had made a great deal of money, and was going back to his home, in New England, to enjoy it. He had already buckled his belt, containing a large amount of gold, around him. Then he fastened a life-preserver under his arms, and was getting ready to jump into the water, and try to swim ashore. Just then a little girl came up to him, and said:

"Sir, can you swim?"

"Yes, my child, I can," was his reply.

"Well, and won't you please, sir, save me?"

This request sent a thrill to the man's heart. He said to himself, "What shall I do? I cannot save this child and my gold too. One or both must be lost. Shall I give up the gold for which I have toiled so long, and on which I expected to live for the rest of my days? or, shall I give up the life of this dear child? She is worth more than gold to some one."

It was a hard struggle; but it had to be decided at once. There was no time to lose. But manhood, and unselfishness gained the victory. He said to himself: "I'll save the child's life!" Then he unbuckled his belt. He cast his gold away. It sank in the deep waters. And then, taking the little child in his arms, he jumped from the deck of the burning vessel into the ocean. The gold was lost; but the life of the child was saved. This was noble! That man was imitating the second point of Nehemiah's model. In the business of doing good he was unselfish.

I have one other story, under this point of our subject. It is a very sweet one. We may call it—

The Dying Girl's Penny. A little girl attended a missionary meeting, and sat upon her father's knee. While listening, with deep attention, to the missionary telling about the miseries, and cruelties, the poor heathen had to suffer, her father saw the tears trickling down her cheeks.

When they reached home she said: "Father, can't I do something to help to send the gospel to the heathen?"

"What can you do, my child?" said her father. "You are but a little girl, and you have no money to give."

"Mother gives me a penny a week," said the child; "couldn't I give that?"

"Yes, you can," said her father, "and I'll buy you a little box to put it in."

The next day her father bought her a little earthenware box, with a hole in the top of it, and every week the dear child dropped her penny into it.

Not many weeks after this, the little girl was taken ill, and died. Soon after her funeral, her father took the box to the minister. He placed it in his hands, and said: "This box belonged to my dear daughter, who was buried the other day. It contains what she was saving for the missionaries." Then he told him about the missionary meeting, and what she said on coming home from that meeting, and added:

"I hadn't the heart to break it myself; so I have brought it to you: if you will break it, you will find seventeen pennies in it."

The minister broke the box; but, on counting over the pennies, he found that there were *eighteen*, instead of seventeen. The father was surprised, and couldn't understand where the other penny came from. He asked the minister if it was not just seventeen weeks since that missionary meeting was held. The minister thought it over a little while, and then said: "Yes, it is just seventeen weeks." And there they had to leave it. But when the father reached home he told his wife about it, and asked her if she knew where the other penny came from?

"Oh, yes," she said, "I can tell you all about it. The day before our dear child died, a kind neighbor called in to see her. Observing how feverish, and parched her lips were, she said, on leaving—"Here, my child, is a penny to buy an orange, to moisten your lips with." When the neighbor was gone, our dear little one called me to her bedside, and said,— "Mother, 'tis true I am very thirsty, and the orange would be real nice; but I would rather you would fetch my missionary-box, that I may drop the penny in there." I carried her the box, and it was the last thing she did before she died. With a trembling hand, and a smile on her pale cheek, she dropped the money in, saying as she did so: "The heathen need the gospel more than I need an orange." And that penny made up the eighteen found in her box. How beautiful that was! That little girl was imitating this point of Nehemiah's model. In the important business of helping on the missionary work she was—unselfish.

In the third place, as a business man, Nehemiah was a model of—FAITHFULNESS.

The business he undertook to do at Jerusalem, was very trying and troublesome. But before starting in it, he made up his mind to be faithful, and go steadily on with it, whatever might happen. A long succession of difficulties met him, in attending to that business. His enemies began their efforts to hinder him, by making sport of what the Jews were doing. They said if even a fox should tread upon the wall, the Jews were building, it would tumble down. Yet Nehemiah did not care for their ridicule, but went steadily on with his work. Then his enemies tried to frighten him. They threatened to attack him and his friends, while they were working on the wall. But Nehemiah girded his sword by his side, and told his friends to do the same. They went to work in this way, and their enemies were afraid to attack them. Then the enemies of Nehemiah laid all sorts of snares and traps, to hinder him in his work; but he turned away from them, and went steadily on with what he was doing. Then they wrote to the king, his master, and charged Nehemiah with rebellion, against his authority. This made it necessary for him to go all the way back to Shushan, in order to explain matters to the king, and to prove to him that there was no truth in what his enemies had written about him. But even this did not discourage him. He made it all right with the king; and then returned to Jerusalem, and went bravely on with his work there. As a man of business, he was a grand model of faithfulness. And we must learn to be faithful too, in all we undertake, if we hope to be useful and successful in our work.

And now, for our encouragement, let us look at some other examples of faithfulness. The first example may be called—

Faithful in Obeying Orders. The late Lord Derby, in England, was having one of his country-houses decorated. The men were busy painting the walls and the floor of the great central hall. A young man, tall and strong, was at work on one of the walls. The Earl ordered a number of slippers, to be placed by the door-mat. He told this young man, if any one came in, he must order him to put on a pair of slippers, before crossing the passage; then he added, "And if anybody is not willing to do this, you must just take him by the shoulder and turn him out."

"I'll do it, sir," said the young man.

Soon after, a hunting party came to the house. Among them was the great Duke of Wellington. The Duke's boots were covered all over with mud. He opened the door, and was about to walk across the hall, when the young man, immediately jumped off from the ladder, on which he was painting. He offered the Duke a pair of slippers, but he declined to put them on. Then the young man seized the Duke by the shoulder, and fairly pushed him out of the house.

The painter said afterwards that the eagle eye of the Duke went right through him, and as he was not acquainted with him, he could not help wondering who it was.

In the course of the day, Lord Derby, on hearing what had taken place, called his household, into the library, with the men who were working for him, and demanded, who had the rudeness to push the Duke of Wellington out of his house.

The painter came forward, trembling, and said,—
"It was I, my lord."

"And pray," said his lordship, "how came you to do it?"

"Because, my lord," said the painter, "you told me

to put any one out, who should attempt to walk across the hall without putting on slippers; and I was only obeying your orders."

Then the Duke, who was present, turned round to Lord Derby with a smile; and taking a gold sovereign from his purse, handed it to the astonished painter, saying as he did so: "You are right, young man, to obey orders. Always be faithful to your orders, if you want to succeed in your business."

Our next story may be called—

Faithful to the Church. This story is told about a good, faithful Christian woman. She was a member of the Presbyterian church in a town in Illinois. The church to which she belonged, had run down so low, that it was thought to be dead; and the Presbytery, at one of their meetings, sent a committee to disband it. The committee arrived at the town, in which this church was located. They inquired for the church, and were told there was none. Then they inquired for the elders,—there were none; for the deacons,—there were none; for the male members,—there were none; for the female members,—there was but one. This was the good woman, of whom we have spoken. They found her out, and told her they had been sent there, by the Presbytery, to disband the church, or break it up. This excited her very much. She said to the gentlemen of the committee: "I am the only member of the church left here. But, I am entirely unwilling to be disbanded, or broken up."

"This is a pretty piece of business for the Presbytery. I am ashamed of them. My name is Jones.

You can go back and tell the Presbytery that Mrs. Jones positively refuses to be disbanded. The proper thing for them to do, is to send a good man here, to preach the gospel, and try to build up the church."

They tried to reason with her, but in vain. She had but one answer to all their arguments, and that was: "I will not be disbanded." They returned to the Presbytery and reported what Mrs. Jones said. *They* had the wisdom to see that Mrs. Jones was right. They sent a good minister to preach the Gospel there. God blessed his labors; and the result was, that the church was revived, and built up; and now, it is a flourishing, self-supporting church. It has a settled pastor, with more than one hundred and thirty communicants. And all these blessed results followed from the faithfulness of that good woman.

Let us all try to imitate Nehemiah's example, when, as a business man, we see him to have been—*a model of faithfulness.*

In the fourth, and last place, when we look at Nehemiah as a business man, we find him a model of— PRAYER.

In the opening chapter of the book, which is called by his name, and which contains the history of his great work, we learn that when he heard of the sad state of things among his countrymen at Jerusalem, the very first thing he did was to engage in prayer to God. We can turn to the first chapter of Nehemiah, and read this prayer. There we see how he began by asking God to make the king willing to let him go to Jerusalem, and build up its walls. That prayer was answered, and the way was opened for him to go.

And then, as he met with one difficulty after another, in carrying on his work at Jerusalem, we find him continually praying to God to remember him, and to help him.

We have a beautiful prayer of Nehemiah's in the 9th chapter of his book. This occupies almost the entire chapter, which is quite a long one. In reading this prayer we can judge of the way in which he used to pray for himself, and for his friends, who were helping in his work.

In the last chapter of his book, we find four short prayers. This shows us how he was in the habit of connecting prayer to God with all the work in which he was engaged. The very last sentence in the book of Nehemiah, is the prayer "Remember me, O my God for good."

And there is no one point, in the model of the business man, which Nehemiah has left us that is more important than this. He was a model of prayer, in everything that he did. If we hope to be successful in any work that we undertake, nothing is more important than to mingle prayer with it, as Nehemiah did. Let us be sure to imitate this point of the model he has left us. No limits can be put to the help we may get in answer to prayer. It is true, as the hymn says, that

> "Prayer makes the darken'd cloud withdraw;
> Prayer climbs the ladder Jacob saw;
> Gives exercise to faith and love,
> Brings every blessing from above."

Now let us look at some other examples of the help, and strength, and blessing that follow from the proper use of prayer. Our first story may be called—

Paying Rent by Prayer. A poor widow found that her rent was due, and she was very much troubled, because she had no money to pay it with. She talked with her little son George about it. He was a good boy, and was trying to be a Christian. After hearing what his mother had to say on the subject, George went out of the room, and his poor mother sat there, thinking what she was to do. In a little while she heard the sound of sobs coming from the next room. She went to the door of the room, and listened. She heard little George crying, and sobbing, and saying to himself: "Poor mother! what will she do?" Then he said to himself: "I'll ask God to help her." Then he kneeled down and offered this short and simple prayer: "O Lord, please help my dear mother to pay her rent, for Jesus' sake, Amen." His mother said nothing, but went away. This took place at the close of the day.

Early the next morning a kind lady came, and gave George's mother money enough to pay her rent. She had heard of her troubles, and came to help her out of them. So George's prayer was answered. He trusted in Jesus, and felt sure that all would be right, and so it was.

The Power of Prayer. Some years ago, in a western cabin, far away from any other habitation, a Christian mother sat rocking her babe to sleep. Her husband had been called suddenly away on business, without being able to get any one to stay with her. As she sat with her baby in her arms, on glancing round the room, she saw the feet of a man sticking out from under the bed. She knew he must be a robber. But she did not scream, or make any noise. She kept on rocking her baby till it went to sleep; when she gently laid it in the cradle. Then she quietly knelt down, and offered the following earnest prayer:—

"O Thou ever present God, who never slumberest, or sleepest, watch over our cabin this night. Keep me and my darling babe from all danger. Let no harm come near us. If there be those about who wish us ill, bring them to a better state of mind and feeling. O, Lord, have mercy on all wanderers, and upon all who do deeds of violence and death. Show them the error of their way. Lead them to repentance. Pardon and save them, for Jesus' sake, Amen." God heard this prayer. He caused it to touch the heart of that robber. As the mother rose from her knees she saw the man coming out from under the bed. He said:

"My friend, don't be alarmed. There will be no harm to-night to you, or your cabin. I thank you for that prayer. I am one of the wanderers that you spoke of. I have lived a very wicked life. But now, I wish to do better. Won't you please pray for God to help me." They kneeled down together, and she offered an earnest prayer, that God would have mercy on him, and help him to lead a better life. Then he thanked her, and went away.

Years passed by, and that good Christian mother heard nothing of the robber. In the meantime she had left her cabin in the West, and was living in Cincinnati. One day, she was attending a large public meeting in the cause of temperance, and reform.

Judge of her surprise, when in the principal speaker of that evening she recognized her robber friend. As he was going on with his speech, his eye rested on this good woman, and he recognized her. Then the memory of that night in her cabin came back to him with great power. He paused for a moment. His face turned pale, and he felt as if he would faint. But he rallied, and went on with his speech. When the meeting was over, he came up and shook her warmly by the hand, and said: "Oh, my friend, how can I ever thank you, as I ought, for your prayer that night? You saved me from going to ruin. You led me to the Saviour. I am now a minister. God has blessed me in my work. But I owe it all to you." Here we see the power of prayer.

I have one other story, under this part of our subject. We may call it—

The Influence of a Mother's Prayers. More than thirty years ago, one lovely Sabbath morning, eight young men, students in a law school, were walking along the banks of a stream that flows into the Potomac river, not far from the city of Washington. They were going to a grove, in a retired place, to spend the hours of that holy day, in playing cards. Each of them had a flask of wine in his pocket. They were the sons of praying mothers. As they were walking along, amusing each other with idle jests, the bell of a church, in a little village about two miles off, began to ring. It sounded in the ears of those thoughtless young men as plainly, as though it were only on the other side of the little stream along which they were walking. Presently one of their number, whose name was George, stopped, and said to the friend nearest to him, that he would go no further, but would return to the village, and go to church. His friend called out to their companions, who were a little ahead of him: "Boys! boys! come back here. George is getting religious. We must help him. Come on, and let's baptize him by immersion in the water." In a moment they formed a circle round him. They told him that the only way in which he could save himself from having a cold bath, was by going with them.

In a calm, quiet, but earnest way he said:

"I know very well, that you have power enough to put me in the water, and hold me there till I am drowned; and if you choose you can do so; and I will make no resistance; but, listen to what I have to say, and then do as you think best.

"You all know that I am two hundred miles away from home; but you do not know, that my mother is a helpless, bed-ridden invalid. I never remember seeing her out of her bed. I am her youngest child. My father could not afford to pay for my schooling; but our teacher is a warm friend of my father, and offered to take me without any charge. He was very anxious for me to come; but mother would not consent. The struggle almost cost her what little life was left to her. At length, after many prayers on the subject, she yielded, and said I might go. The preparations for my leaving home were soon made. My mother never said a word to me on the subject, till the morning when I was to leave. After I had eaten my breakfast, she sent for me, and asked if everything was ready. I told her all was ready, and I was only waiting for the stage. At her request I kneeled beside her bed. With her loving hands upon my head, she prayed for her youngest child. Many and many a night since then, I have dreamed that whole scene over. It is the happiest recollection of my life. I believe, till the day of my death, I shall be able to repeat every word of that prayer. Then she spoke to me thus:

"'My precious boy, you do not know,—you never can know, the agony of a mother's heart, in parting, for the last time, from her youngest child. When you leave home, you will have looked, for the last time, this side the grave, on the face of her who loves you, as no other mortal does or can. Your father cannot afford the expense of your making us visits, during the two years that your studies will occupy. I cannot possibly live as long as that. The sands in the hour-glass of my life have nearly run out. In the far-off, strange place to which you are going, there will be no loving mother to give you counsel in time of trouble. Seek counsel and help from God. Every Sabbath morning, from ten to eleven o'clock, I will spend the hour in prayer for you. Wherever you may be, during this sacred hour, when you hear the church-bells ringing, let your thoughts come back to this chamber, where your dying mother will be agonizing in prayer for you. But I hear the stage coming. Kiss me; farewell!'

"Boys, I never expect to see my mother again on earth. But, by the help of God, I mean to meet her in heaven."

As George stopped speaking the tears were streaming down his cheeks. He looked at his companions. Their eyes were all filled with tears.

In a moment the ring was opened, which they had formed about him. He passed out, and went to church. He had stood up for the right, against great odds. They admired him for doing what they had not courage to do. They all followed him to church. On their way there, each of them quietly threw away his cards, and his wine-flask. Never again did any of those young men play cards on the Sabbath. From that day they all became changed men. Six of them died Christians, and are now in heaven. George is an able Christian lawyer in Iowa; and his friend, the eighth of the party who wrote this account, has been for many years an earnest active member of the church. Here were eight men converted by the prayers of that good Christian woman. And, if we only knew all the results of their examples, and their labors, we should have a grand illustration of the influence of a mother's prayers.

And so, when we consider Nehemiah as the model of a man of business, we find four good points in the model he has left us. He was a model of *earnestness;* a model of *unselfishness;* a model of *faithfulness;* and a model of *prayer.*

Let us ask God for grace to imitate the points of this model, and then we shall be successful in our wordly business, and also in the business of serving God.

DANIEL, THE MODEL OF DECISION.

"O, Daniel, a man greatly beloved."—DANIEL x : 11.

ABRIEL, the angel of God, spoke these words to the prophet Daniel. In using them he meant to let Daniel know not only that he was beloved on earth, but that he was beloved in heaven. He meant that he was beloved of God, and beloved of the angels. What an honor this was! Who would not rather have an angel say this of him, than be permitted to wear the crown,—and sway the sceptre, —of the mightiest monarch on earth?

Daniel was one of the best, and wisest men of whom we read in the Bible. Most of these men, though generally very good, yet sometimes said, or did what was not right. But it was not so with Daniel. All through his life—so far as we can learn from the Bible —he never spoke a word, or did an act, that was not right and good. He began to serve God when he was quite young; and this, no doubt, was one thing that helped to make him so good a man. He was a very decided man. He always did what he knew was right, no matter what the consequence might be.

And so, we may speak of Daniel as *the model of—* DECISION. And we can see *three* great benefits that followed from his decision.

In the first place, Daniel's decision—*kept him from doing wrong*.

And if we learn to follow the model he has set us, it will do the same for us. We have a good illustration of this point of our subject, in the first chapter of the book of Daniel. When about sixteen years old, he was carried captive to Babylon, with a number of his countrymen. Daniel belonged to a princely family. After arriving in Babylon, he was chosen, with a number of other young Jewish princes, to stand in the king's palace. Among these were the three famous men—Shadrach, Meshach, and Abednego, who were afterwards cast into the burning fiery furnace, and came out unhurt. It is said of them that they were young men "in whom was no blemish; they were well-favored"—or good-looking—"skillful in all wisdom, and cunning in knowledge, and understanding science." Daniel and his companions had to go through a course of instruction, that they might understand the language and the learning of the people, among whom they had come to live. And in going through this course of training, Daniel was expected to eat and drink things that were forbidden by the Jewish law. Now most young men, situated as he was, would have said: "Well, I can't help this. Here I am in Babylon. I must do as the Babylonians do."

But Daniel did not think so. He felt sure that

what would have been wrong for him to do at Jerusalem, was wrong for him in Babylon; and he decided not to do it. He made up his mind that he would do what was right, and leave the result with God. He did so, and it all turned out well. I have not time now to tell the whole story. But read the first chapter of Daniel, and you will find it all there. And you will see how Daniel's decision kept him from doing wrong.

And then we have another illustration of the same thing, further on in Daniel's history. In the meantime he has risen to be the greatest man in the kingdom of Babylon. A man in such a high position always has some people about him who envy him, and become his enemies, just because he is so much better off than they are. And Daniel had a number of enemies of this kind. They envied him, and hated him, for no other reason than just because he was so good, and so great. They tried to find some charge to bring against him. But, he was so honest,—so true,—and so faithful, in all his duties, that they could not possibly find anything against him.

Then they determined to get up a charge against him on account of his religion. They knew how regular he was in praying to God, and they thought that they could succeed against him here. So they got the king to pass a law that no man should pray to any god for thirty days; and that if any one did so he should be cast into the den of lions. The law was passed. Daniel knew it. But he decided not to mind it. To stop praying to God was a wrong thing, and he determined not to do it, even though

DANIEL.

Engraved by C. Heinrichs after the Painting by Bastien Revois.

DANIEL, THE MODEL OF DECISION. 341

the consequence must be that he would be cast into the den of lions. He had been in the habit of praying to God three times a day. He kept on doing this, just the same as before. His enemies rushed into his chamber, and found him on his knees. They accused him to the king of breaking the law. He could not deny it. The king was sorry, for he loved Daniel very much. He tried all he could to save him; but that was impossible. So Daniel was cast into the den of lions. But God sent His angel to shut the lion's mouths, and they did not hurt him. The next morning he came out of the den safe, and unharmed. And here we see how Daniel's decision kept him from doing wrong.

And how many instances we find in which those who follow Daniel's decision, are kept from doing wrong, just as he was!

Let us look at some of these. Our first story we may call—

Decision in Telling the Truth. We find this story in Persian history. A little boy named Abdool Kader, had a dream one night, which made him feel that he must devote himself to the service of God. The carrying out of this dream would make it necessary for him to visit the sacred city of Mecca. The next morning he went and told his mother about it.

"She wept," he says, "when I told her of my dream, and where I was going. Then taking out eighty dinars, she said: 'This is all the family inheritance that remains to be divided between you and your brother. I give you forty dinars, which is the portion belonging to you. And now, promise me faithfully that wherever you go, and whatever happens to you, you will never tell a lie.' I promised her faithfully. Then she bade me farewell, saying: 'Go, my son; may God bless you, and permit us to meet again.'

"Then I started on my journey. All went on well, till one day our caravan was attacked by a large company of horsemen. One after another they plundered all our companions. At last one of them came to me. 'Little fellow,' said he, 'what have you got?'

"'Forty dinars,' said I, 'sewed up in the border of my coat.'

"The man laughed, and went away, thinking no doubt, that I was joking with him.

"Then another man came up to me. He asked the same question. I gave him the same answer. and he too went away.

"Then I was taken into the presence of the chief of the band, who was sitting under a tree. 'What property have you got, my little fellow?' he asked.

"'I have told two of your men, already,' I replied, 'that I have forty dinars, sewed up in the border of my coat, but they did not seem to believe what I said; and now, sir, I tell you the same.'

"He ordered the border of my coat to be ripped open, and there he found the money. He was very much surprised, and turning to me, he said: 'And how came you, my young friend, to speak so plainly, about your money that had been so carefully hidden?'

"'Because,' I replied, 'before leaving home I promised my mother that I would never tell a lie; and now, whatever happens I cannot break that promise.'

"'Brave boy!' said the robber. 'Can it be that you

have such a sense of your duty to your mother, at your early age, and yet I, at my age, am unmindful of the duty I owe to my God? Give me your hand, that I may swear repentance upon it.'

"A number of the band, impressed by his words and example, did the same.

"'You have been our leader in doing wrong,' they said to their chief,—'now be our leader in trying to do right.'"

And so, the example of that brave boy, and his decision in telling the truth, was the means of turning those robbers from their wrong doings.

Our next illustration shows us the evil that was prevented by—

Decision in Keeping the Sabbath. Some years ago, in one of the towns of Eastern Massachusetts, there was a livery stable kept by a Mr. D. He was a member of the church, and had such a regard for the Sabbath, that he never would allow any of his horses or carriages to be hired out on that day. One Sunday morning, three gentlemen from Boston, who were staying with their wives at the village hotel, said to the keeper of it, that they would like him to send over to the livery stable, and ask Mr. D. to let them have three single-horse buggies, as they each wished to take his wife and go to the camp-meeting about six miles off. "I would do so with pleasure," said the hotel keeper, "but it will be of no use, as Mr. D. never hires his horses out on Sunday."

"Well, I'll go over and see him about it," said one of the gentlemen. "You see if I don't get the horses. I never saw the man yet that could not be bought with money." So he went and rang the bell at Mr. D's door. Mr. D. answered the call himself, and invited the gentleman in.

Then the gentleman told him what he and his two friends wanted.

"I should be very glad to accommodate you, sir, if I could," said Mr. D., "but it is against my principles to hire my horses on the Sabbath day, unless it be a case of necessity."

"How much do you usually have a day for your single horses?" asked the gentleman.

"Two dollars and a half a day, sir, is our usual price," said Mr. D.

"Well, then," replied the gentleman, "here are three five-dollar bills; please take them, and let your man harness the horses, and we will go away very quietly, and will return just after dark without notice."

"Sir," said Mr. D., "I can only repeat what I have already said, that it is against my principles to hire out my horses on God's day, and so I must persist in declining your very liberal offer."

Then the gentleman stepped closer up to Mr. D., and slipping something into his hand, said to him: "There, take that, and let your man quietly harness the horses for us."

Mr. D. looked down at what was thus thrust into his hand, and saw that it was a new one-hundred dollar note on a Boston bank. *This* was a glittering prize. But, without a moment's hesitation, and with a decision which would have done honor to Daniel himself, he said, calmly, and emphatically:

"Sir, my principles in this matter are fixed; and if

you should offer me all the money in the city of Boston, it would not alter them. If you wish to attend worship our church-bell is now ringing, and I shall be most happy to show you a seat, but I cannot let my horses go out on the Lord's day;" and then he handed back the hundred dollar note.

The gentleman took the money which had been returned to him; then he looked Mr. D. admiringly in the face, and, stretching out his hand to him, he said:

"I want to shake hands with you. I have sometimes heard of such men; but this is the first time I ever met with a man who cannot be bought to do what he believes is wrong. I thank you for the example you have set me, and for the wrong you have kept me from doing." This is a fine illustration of decision, and of the wrong-doing it prevented.

I have one other illustration of this point of our subject. It is a story in verse, about a boy who had a struggle with his conscience, when tempted to take what did not belong to him. We may call it—

DECISION ABOUT STEALING.

BOY.

"Over the fence is a garden fair—
How I would love to be master there!
All that I lack is a mere pretence;
I could leap over the low stone fence."

CONSCIENCE.

"This is the way that crimes commence;
Sin and sorrow are over the fence."

BOY.

"Over the fence I can toss my ball,
Then I can go for it—that is all;
Picking an apple up under a tree
Wouldn't really be a theft, you see."

CONSCIENCE.

"This is a falsehood—a weak pretence;
Sin and sorrow are over the fence."

BOY.

"Whose is the voice that speaks so plain?
Twice have I heard it, and not in vain,
I never will do as I planned to day,
But always walk in the right, true way.

CONSCIENCE.

"This is the way that all crimes commence,
Coveting that which is over the fence."

Daniel was a model of decision; and the first great benefit he found in his decision was—that it kept him from doing wrong.

The second great benefit, Daniel found in his decision was that—IT HELPED HIM TO DO GOOD.

When he was a young man in Babylon, Daniel had three warm friends with him. Their names were Shadrach, Mesech and Abednego. They saw the decided way in which he acted, when he refused to eat, or drink anything that was forbidden by the law of Moses. Those young men admired Daniel's conduct on that occasion. They resolved to follow his example. They learned the lesson of decision then, and they never forgot it. And nobly indeed they practiced that lesson in after years.

The time came when Nebuchadnezzar, the king of Babylon, set up a golden image. At the same time he passed a law, requiring that everybody should fall down and worship this image, when they heard the instruments of music play; and stating that if any persons refused to do this, they were to be cast into a fiery furnace, and be burned to death.

These friends of Daniel had never forgotten the lesson of decision which he taught them so long before. They made up their minds that, whatever the consequences might be, they would not bow down, and worship this image. The instruments of music sounded. All the rest of the people fell on their faces, and worshipped the golden image. But Shadrach, Mesech, and Abednego, stood upright in their places. They refused to keep this law of the king of Babylon, because there was a higher law of the King of heaven, which forbade them to do any such thing.

The case was reported to Nebuchadnezzar. They were brought before him. He asked them if they were ready, when the instruments of music should sound again, to fall down and worship his golden image? They said decidedly: "No; we cannot do it." Then he ordered his servants to make the furnace seven times hotter than usual, and to throw these men in. They did so. But God wrought a miracle for their preservation. He took away from the fire, its power to hurt them. It just burnt the cords by which their limbs were bound, and then they walked up and down, amidst the roaring flames of the furnace, with as much ease, and comfort, as if they had been walking in a garden of roses.

The king looked on, with unspeakable amazement. He called them out of the furnace. They came out. Not a hair of their heads was singed; and even the smell of fire had not passed upon them.

This event, so strange, so wonderful, converted the king from his idolatry; and led him to publish a law, through all his vast dominions, in favor of the one true God whom Shadrach, Mesech, and Abednego worshipped. And all the good done by these three men, to the king of Babylon, and the people of his dominions, followed from the example of decision which Daniel set when he was a young man.

And we find many examples of the good which follows, in different ways, from the exercise of decision.

Here is a story about the decision of a young lady in standing up for Jesus, and of the good that followed from it.

At a fashionable evening party, some time ago, a young physician was present. He spoke of one of his patients who was in a very dangerous state. "I am very much annoyed," he said, "by some Christian people, who are all the time talking and praying with him. I wish these people would let my patients alone, and mind their own business. What's the use of all this fuss? Death is only an eternal sleep. The religion of Christ is all a delusion; and Christian people are simply mistaken."

A young lady, one of the gayest of the party, was sitting near, and heard all he said.

She at once answered him, saying: "Pardon me, doctor, but I cannot hear you talk thus, and remain silent. I am not a professor of religion myself, and I never knew anything about it by experience. But my mother was a Christian. Times without number she has taken me to her room, and with her loving hand upon my head has prayed that God would give her grace to train me for heaven. Two years ago my precious mother died, and the religion which she loved in life sustained and comforted her in death. She called us to her bedside, and with her face all radiant with glory, she asked us to meet her in heaven. And now," said the young lady, her voice choking with deep feeling, "can I believe that this is all a delusion? Does my mother sleep an eternal sleep? Will she never wake again on the morning of the resurrection? Shall I see her no more? No; I cannot, I will not believe it." Here her brother tried to quiet her, for, by this time all the company had gathered round her, and were listening to her earnest words. "No," she said: "brother, let me alone. I must defend my mother's God, and my mother's religion."

The physician made no reply, but soon left the room. He was found shortly after, walking up and down an adjoining room, in great distress of mind. "What is the matter?" asked a friend. "Oh!" said he, "that young lady is right. Her words have pierced my soul like an arrow. I, too, must have the religion I have despised, or I am lost forever." And the result of that conversation was, that both the young lady, and the physician, became earnest Christians, and spent all their days in doing good to those about them.

And here we see how much good was done by the decision of that young lady, in so nobly standing up for Jesus, and the truth as it is in Him.

The next illustration, is one that came under my own notice. We may call it—True Honesty; or—

Decision for the Right. One summer, some years ago, I was down at Cape May. As I was walking on the piazza of the hotel, a gentleman came up to me, and asked, "Is not this Dr. Newton?"

I said—"It is." "Do you remember me, Dr. N.?" he asked. I looked at him carefully, and replied, "No, sir, I do not."

"Well, sir," said he, "I can easily recall myself to your recollection. Do you remember, some years ago, when you were at St. Paul's Church, losing one day, a bank check, for $625?"

"Oh, yes!" I replied. "I never shall forget the fright, which that occasioned me."

"Very good. And do you remember giving a ten dollar gold-piece, to the young man who brought back the lost check to you?" "No, sir. I have no recollection of that." "Well, sir, you did. I am the person to whom you gave it; and a blessed ten dollar gold-piece that was to me. I had just come to Philadelphia, to try and get employment. I was in feeble health, and had not a dollar in the world. The day before, the offer had been made to me of a newspaper route, which was said to be very profitable. But they asked ten dollars for it; and this was more than I could raise. Immediately on receiving your ten dollar gold piece, I went and bought that newspaper route. It did prove profitable. From that day I have gone on and prospered. Now, I am well off; I am a member of the church, and the superintendent of a Sabbath-school; and I owe it all to your ten dollars."

"No, my friend," I said, "you are mistaken there. It was not that ten dollar gold-piece which has brought all this good to you; but, it was God's blessing on your honesty in returning the lost check, and your decision to do what was right, that has led to all the good which has followed you. You might have forged my name, on the back of that check, and have tried to get the whole of those six hundred and twenty-five dollars. Then you would have been taken up, and put in the penitentiary. But instead of that, you decided to do the fair, honest thing. And God's blessing has followed you ever since. Here we see the good to which a right decision leads.

I have only one other illustration under this head. We may call it—

A Boy's Decision About Drink. Many years ago, Mr. Hall, an English gentleman, visited Ireland, for the purpose of taking sketches of its most beautiful scenery, to be used in an illustrated work on Ireland, which has since been published.

On one occasion, when about to spend a day in the neighborhood of Lake Killarney, he met a bright young Irish lad who offered his services as guide, through the district.

A bargain was made with him, and the party went off. The lad proved himself well acquainted, with all the places of interest in that neighborhood, and had plenty of stories to tell about them. He did his work well, and to the entire satisfaction of the visitors. On their return to the starting point, after a day of great enjoyment, Mr. Hall took a flask of whiskey from his pocket, and drank some. Then he handed it to the boy, and asked him to help himself. To his great surprise the offer was firmly, but politely declined.

Mr. Hall thought this was very strange. To find an Irish boy, who would not touch or taste whiskey, was stranger to him than anything he had seen that day. He could not understand it; and he resolved to try the strength of the boy's temperance principles. He offered first a shilling; then half a crown; and then five shillings if he would taste that whiskey. But the boy was firm. A real manly heart was beating under his ragged jacket. Mr. Hall determined to try him further, so he offered the boy a golden half sovereign, if he would take a drink of whiskey. That was a coin seldom seen by lads of this class, in those parts. Straightening himself up, with a look of indignation in his face, the boy pulled out a temperance medal, from the inner pocket of his jacket, and holding it bravely up, he said: "This was my father's medal. For years he was intemperate. All his wages were spent in drink. It almost broke my mother's heart. And what a hard time she had to keep the poor childer from starving! But at last, my father took a stand. He signed the pledge, and wore this medal as long as he lived. On his death-bed he gave it to me. I promised him that I never would drink intoxicating liquor. And now, sir, for all the money your honor may be worth, a hundred times over, I would not break that promise." That boy's decision about drink was noble. Yes, and it did good too. As Mr. Hall stood there astonished, he screwed the top on to his flask, and flung it out into the water of the lake, near which they stood.

DANIEL, THE MODEL OF DECISION.

Then he turned to the lad, and shook him warmly by the hand, saying, as he did so:

"My boy! that's the best temperance lecture I ever heard. I thank you for it. And now, by the help of God, I will never drink another drop of intoxicating liquor while I live."

Daniel was a model of decision, and the second great benefit he found in his decision was, that it helped him to do good.

The third great benefit which Daniel found from his decision was, that—IT MADE HIM SUCCESSFUL.

He went to Babylon a poor boy, about sixteen or seventeen years old. But God blessed him for the decided way in which he always did, what he believed to be right. And this blessing brought success to Daniel, as it will do to everybody on whom it rests. He rose to one higher place after another, till he got to be —next to the king—the chief man in the nation. In the sixth chapter of Daniel, we read: "It pleased Darius to set over the kingdom an hundred and twenty princes, which should be over the whole kingdom. And over these three presidents, of whom Daniel was the first. Thus Daniel was preferred above the presidents and princes, because an excellent spirit was in him; and the king sought to set him over the whole realm." And when we see Daniel rise to so high a position as this, we realize how very successful he was. And he cotinued to occupy this honorable position, under the reign of four successive kings of Babylon. That was very remarkable. This shows us how wonderful the success was which followed Daniel's decision.

And we find illustrations of the same kind continually. Let us look at some of these. We may begin with the story of a young man in Boston. He had never learned to be decided about doing what was right, and his failure to do this, brought ruin on himself, and disgrace upon his family. He belonged to one of the first families of Boston. But he had cheated, and raised large sums of money in unjust ways. When his friends found this out, they advised him to leave the country, to save himself from being put in prison. He took passage on board a vessel that was to sail to a foreign country. Before the vessel sailed his father went down to the wharf to say "good-bye" to him. As they were shaking hands the young man said: "Father, I owe all this trouble to you. One day, when I was a boy, you stood by looking on, as I was playing a game of marbles with another boy. You saw me cheat him, and win the game by doing so. Then you praised me for my success in winning the game. You never said a word to me about the wrong I had done in cheating my companion. *That* was the rock on which I have made shipwreck. From the way you acted then, I thought it was right to cheat, if I could gain success by it. *This*, was what led me to do all the wrong things that I have done. This is what has brought ruin on me, and disgrace on all the family. But the blame rests on you. *You did it all.*"

Now here we see the failure and ruin, which came on that young man, because he had never learned to be decided in not doing what was wrong. For all the money in Boston I would not have been in that father's place.

A Little Boy's Decision. One day, a small boy

entered a store. The merchant looked at him, and asked: "Well, my little man, what will you have to-day?"

"Oh, please, sir, mayn't I do some work for you to-day!"

"Do some work for me, eh? Well, what sort of work, can a little chap like you do? Why, you can't look over the counter."

"Oh, yes, I can, and I'm growing please, growing very fast—there, now, see if I can't look over the counter!" said the little fellow, raising himself up on his tiptoes.

The merchant smiled, and then came round to the other side of the counter.

"I thought I should have to get a magnifying-glass to see you; but, I reckon if I get close enough, I can find out what you look like."

"Oh, I'm older than I'm big, sir," said the boy. "Folks say I'm very small of my age. You see, sir, my mother hasn't anybody but me; and this morning I saw her crying because she couldn't find five cents in her pocket-book. She thinks the boy that took the ashes stole it—and—I—haven't—had—any breakfast, sir."

Then his voice choked, and his blue eyes were filled with tears.

"I reckon I can help you to some breakfast, my little fellow," said the merchant, feeling in his vest-pocket. "Here—will this quarter do!"

The boy shook his head, saying:

"Thank you, sir, but my mother wouldn't let me beg, or take money, unless I did something for it."

"Indeed!" said the gentleman. "And where's your father?"

"He went to sea in the steamer City of Boston. The vessel was lost, and we never heard of him after that."

"Ah! that was bad. But you are a plucky little fellow, and I like you. Let me see," and then, after thinking for a few moments, he called out to one of the clerks—"Saunders, is the cash-boy No. 4 still sick?"

"He died last night, sir," was the reply.

"Ah! I'm sorry to hear that. Well, here's a little fellow that can take his place. What wages did No. 4 get?"

"Three dollars a week, sir," replied the clerk.

"Well, put this boy down for four dollars a week." Then turning to the astonished boy, he said, "There, my little fellow, go up to the clerk yonder, and tell him your name, and where you live; and then run home and tell your mother, you've got a place at four dollars a week; come back on Monday morning, and I'll tell you what to do. Here's a dollar in advance; I'll take it out of your first week's wages. Now go."

Little Tommy darted out of that store like an arrow. How he flew along the street! How nimbly he mounted the creaking stairs that led to his mother's room! As soon as he entered it, he ran across the room, clapping his hands, and jumping up and down, and crying out: "Mother! mother! I'm took!—I'm took! I've got a place at four dollars a week. There's the first dollar to get something to eat with. And don't you ever cry again; for I'm the man of the house now!"

But Tommy's mother did cry then. And how could she help it? She took the little fellow in her arms, and pressed him to her bosom. She wept tears of joy over him; and then she kneeled down, and thanked God for giving her such a treasure of a boy. Now here we see how decided little Tommy was, in doing what is right; and what success followed his decision.

I have just one other story to tell. We may call it—
The Story of a Grasshopper. If you ever go to London, of course, among the places of interest there, you will visit the public building known as—"The Royal Exchange." There is a cupola at the top of that building. Rising from that cupola is an iron rod, with a huge grasshopper on it, for a weather-vane. And there is an interesting story connected with that grasshopper. It is this: One day, more than three hundred years ago, a mother in England had an infant, a few months old, which she wanted to get rid of. So she wrapped it up in a shawl, and laid it down under a bush in a field, and left it there to die, unless somebody should find it, and take care of it.

Shortly after, a little boy was coming home from school. As he passed by the place, he heard a grasshopper chirping in the field. He stopped a moment to listen to it. Then he climbed over the fence to get it. But just as he was about to catch it he caught sight of the baby, which was close by. He let the grasshopper go; and taking the baby in his arms, he carried it home to his mother. She took charge of the baby and brought him up. He turned out to be a good, pious boy. He was always decided in doing what he knew was right, and in not doing what was wrong.

When a young man he went to London, and entered into business there. He was successful in business, and became rich. He was not only rich, but great. He was knighted, and is well known in English history—as—Sir Thomas Gresham. The Royal Exchange was built in honor of him. And he had the grasshopper put as a weather-vane on the top of it, in memory of the wonderful way in which, when an infant, his life was saved by the good providence of God.

This story has been put into simple verse. I will repeat it in this form, that you may remember it the better. The lines are headed—

THE GRASSHOPPER ON THE ROYAL EXCHANGE.

"What are grasshoppers good for?
   Child, come listen to me,
And I'll tell you about a grasshopper
   That hops in history.

"You have read of mighty London—
   Its wonderful sights, and strange—
Its castle, Abbey, and grand St. Paul's,
   Its Tower, and Royal Exchange.

"Well, on the topmost pinnacle,
   Of the Exchange, appears
A monster grasshopper weather-vane,
   That has hopped three hundred years.

"A woman once left a baby,
   In a summer field to die,
With a merry grasshopper chirping near,
   Its noisy revelry.

"A merry-hearted schoolboy,
   Listened as he skipped by;
And, running to catch the grasshopper,
   He heard the baby cry.

> Oh, 'twas a royal moment
>   For the lonely little one there;
> The boy carried that little one home
>   To a mother's loving care.
>
> "The baby grew up to manhood,
>   Decided, and good, and great;
> He was a true and noble knight,
>   In the service of the state.
>
> "And when the royal building
>   Was founded in his name,
> He lifted the humble grasshopper,
>   To its pinnacle of fame.
>
> "There, through the long, long centuries,
>   By breeze or tempest shaken,
> It tells, 'God heard the voice of the lad
>   By human love forsaken.'"

It was the decision of Sir Thomas Gresham which made him so successful.

Now we have spoken of Daniel as a model of decision. And we have seen the three great benefits that followed from his decision. The first was that—it *kept him from doing wrong*. The second was that,—*it helped him to do good*. The third was that,—*it made him successful*. Let us ask the Lord for grace to follow the model of decision which Daniel has set us, and then we shall share the same great benefits.

GOD, THE MODEL GIVER.

"He giveth to all, life, and breath, and all things."—
Acts xvii : 25.

IN the earlier part of this course of sermons, I had thought of taking Jacob as the model of giving. He is the first example we have in the Bible, of regular, systematic giving. When God appeared to him at Bethel, as he was just beginning his long journey to the home of his uncle Laban, in the far-off country of Mesopotamia, Jacob was a poor man. He was then setting out in the world, as we say, "to seek his fortune." God promised to be with him, and bless him, and make him a rich man. This made Jacob feel very happy. He thanked God for his goodness, and said: "Of all that Thou givest me I will surely give *the tenth* unto thee." This is a good example for giving. It is a proper thing for us to follow this example. I know some good Christian people who are in the habit of doing this. They set aside a tenth part of all the money they receive, and use it for charitable and religious purposes. They keep an account in their bank-book, which they call—"The O. P. J. Account," or the Old Patriarch Jacob account. In this they enter the tenth part of all the money they receive, and keep it as a fund sacred to God, and His cause. Jacob is a good example of giving. But if we wish to have the best example here, we must let Jacob go, and look up to Jacob's God, and *our* God, as the best example that we can set before us, in the matter of giving. And this is just what the apostle is doing when he utters the words of our text. Here he tells us that God—"giveth to all, life, and breath, and all things."

Here we have the best example of giving that can be named. Our subject now will be—"*God—the Model Giver.*" And there are three points in this model, of which I wish to speak.

And the FIRST *thing to notice in God, when set before us, as our model in giving, is that He is—a* CHEERFUL *—giver*.

Jesus said to His disciples: "Freely ye have received—freely give." But when He said they "received freely," He meant to show the way in which God gives. All that we receive we receive from Him. "He giveth to all, life, and breath, and all things." And all that He gives, He gives freely. He gives us life. But when the baby first begins to live, what does it have to pay for its life? Nothing. He gives us breath; and as we open our mouths to draw it in—what do we have to pay for it? Nothing. He gives us sunshine. And what do we have to pay for it? Nothing. He gives us pure, sparkling water from hundreds of springs and fountains, bubbling from the earth; and what do we have to pay for them? Nothing. He sent His blessed Son to die for us, and to "open the kingdom of heaven to all believers;" and what do we have to pay for Christ's entrance into our world, to save it? Nothing at all. What God gives to us, He gives freely. And this is the reason why God expects us to give as St. Paul says: "Not grudgingly, or of necessity; for God loveth a cheerful giver." He loves to have us give cheerfully, because this is the way in which He gives to us. God gives freely, or cheerfully, because He loves to give. And this is the only reason you can name why God gives at all. He is not *obliged* to give. If He should stop giving, no one could help it; and no one would have right to complain. But He gives because He loves to give. And when we do anything from love, we always do it freely, or cheerfully. God is the model Giver, because He gives cheerfully. And we find beautiful examples, of those who are trying to imitate the model of giving, which He sets before us, by giving cheerfully. Here are some illustrations of what I mean.

The first illustration we may call—

"*The Dowry.*" A clergyman, in England, was sent for to visit a young girl who was very ill. She was the only child of a widowed mother. The illness proved fatal. But the dear child was a Christian, and died rejoicing in the thought that she was going to be with Jesus. Then she left her poor mother alone in the world. A few days after her daughter's death, the widow called at the minister's house, and asked to see him. After talking awhile about the death of her dear daughter, she put into his hands a small parcel containing some money, and asked him to please give it for helping to send the Gospel of Jesus to the heathen. He opened the parcel and found that it contained twenty pounds, or a hundred dollars in our money. The minister was surprised to find so large a sum. He knew that the poor widow had nothing but her needle to depend upon for her living. He tried to persuade her that this was too much for her to give, and that she ought to take it back, and use it for her own support. She declined to take it back, and said: "Please sir, let me explain to you how I came to have so much money. When my child was born, I said to myself, 'Perhaps she'll live to get married, some of these days. Then I should like to have something to give her, as a dowry, or marriage portion.' So I thought I would begin to put by, what I could spare, from time to time against that day. I began with sixpence. Now it amounts to twenty pounds. You know what has happened, sir, within the last week. Well, I thought to myself, the Lord Jesus has come, as the heavenly Bridegroom. He has taken my dear daughter, to the bright home above, to be His bride. And so I thought, that as He has taken the bride, it is only right that he should have the bride's portion." This brought tears to the minister's eyes. He made no more objection, but took the money, and used it as the widowed mother desired. That was cheerful giving.

The Baptized Pocket-Book. Some time ago a rich merchant, who was going to join a Baptist church, was about to be baptized, as they are accustomed to do it, by immersion, or plunging the whole body under water. One of his friends, who saw his pocket-book in his pocket, suggested that he had better take it out, before going down into the water. But he shook his head and said, "No: no: I want my pocket-book to be baptized too!"

He meant by this, to say, that he wished it to be understood, that all his money, and everything he had, belonged to God. There are too many people who get baptized themselves, but their pocket-books are *not* baptized. They do not feel as if all that they have belongs to God. When people do feel in this way, and really have their pocket-books baptized, they will be *cheerful* givers.

Give, and It Shall be Given. "Cheerful giving," writes an aged minister, "is what God loves, and what brings down His blessing on the giver." And then he gives this illustration of the truth of his statement:

"A poor clergyman attended the annual gathering of the church to which he belonged, in a city far off from his own home. The railway company had supplied him with a return ticket. But when he attended the last meeting that was held, which was a missionary meeting, he found that a twenty-five cent piece was all the money he had left; and he would need more than that, to get himself something to eat on the long journey home. But he was a *cheerful* giver. And when the collection was taken up, he opened his purse, and threw in his last twenty-five cent piece. He gave it—*cheerfully.*

After the meeting was over he was invited, with a

GOD, THE MODEL GIVER. 365

number of the other clergy, to go home and dine, with a rich merchant, who belonged to the church. While they were at dinner, the gentleman of the house was called out of the room for a little while. When the dinner was over he spoke to the minister, of whom I am now telling, and asked him to come with him into the next room. When they were alone he said to the poor minister: "I was called from the table at dinner-time, by a man who has long owed me a small debt. I never expected to get it, and looked upon it as lost money. I don't know why he should have called just now, to pay me that old debt; except it be that the Lord wants me to give it to you. And so I beg you will accept it." And he thrust the envelope containing the money into his hands. This was all done so kindly, that the minister could not refuse to take what was offered to him. He took it, and thanked the good gentleman for his kindness. And when he was alone, and had an opportunity of looking into the envelope, he found to his surprise that it contained—*twenty-five dollars*. Thus God rewarded him a hundredfold, for the cheerfulness with which he gave away his last twenty-five cents. This shows us how true it is—that "God loves a *cheerful* giver."

Given to the Poor, Lent to the Lord. A worthy minister in New England, was appealed to for help, one morning, by a poor man, whom he knew very well. He asked his wife to give the poor fellow a trifle. She went to their money-bag, and found that forty-eight cents, were all they had left in the world. She gave the bag to her husband, and he gave the pennies to the poor man.

"Well, my dear," said the wife, "we haven't a single cent left for ourselves."

"Have faith in God, dear wife," said the minister. "If he sees best, how easily He could give us forty-eight dollars in place of those forty-eight cents." This minister was a cheerful giver. He loved to give. Now let us see what came of it.

About an hour after this, a friend of the minister's, who was very well off, and who lived some miles away, called to see him, with his servant. They had come to town on business. He stopped at the minister's house to get something to eat. But he noticed, while he was taking his lunch, how sad, and downcast the good minister's wife seemed. He inquired the reason; but she avoided giving an answer, and soon left the room. Then the gentleman asked his friend, the minister if they were in want of money? He smiled, but said nothing.

As soon as the gentleman was alone with his servant, he asked him if he had any money with him, and how much? They both looked into their pocket-books, to see what they had with them. The gentleman found that he had just forty-five dollars in his purse, and his servant had *three*. He wished very much, that one, or the other of them had two dollars more, so that they could have made up the round sum of *fifty* dollars. But *this* was all they had with them. Then the gentleman took the forty-eight dollars, and gave them to his friend the minister, saying: "I feel sure, my friend, that you are short of money. I would like to have made it up to fifty dollars; but this is really all we have with us."

The minister was overcome with surprise and joy. He counted the money out on the table, and then, calling in his wife, said to her:

"Look here, my dear, and see how soon that which I spoke of, as a thing, which God *could* do for us, *has been* done. He did not wait even till the day was past, but through our kind friend here, has sent us forty-eight *dollars*, for the forty-eight *cents* we gave to that poor man this morning."

Then they told their friend all about it; and he was delighted to find that he had neither more nor less, than what was just sufficient to repay the good minister a hundredfold, for what he had so cheerfully given to the poor man that morning.

This is a good illustration of the truth of the lines, which some one has written about giving, and which read thus:

> "Is thy cruse of comfort wasting?
>   Rise, and share it with another;
> And through all the years of famine,
>   It shall serve thee and thy brother.
> God Himself will fill thy storehouse,
>   Or thy handful still renew;
> Scanty fare for *one*, will often
>   Make a royal feast for *two*."

God is a *cheerful* giver, and we should try to follow, in this respect, the model he sets before us.

But, in the second place, God is—a VALUABLE—*giver, as well as a cheerful giver.*

And on *this* account too, we may well speak of Him as the model giver.

How nicely the words of our text come in to illustrate this point! "He giveth to all, *life*, and *breath*, and *all* things." What a valuable gift, the gift of life is! This is so valuable, that no one, in all the universe, has the power to bestow it in any case, but God himself. Wherever life is found existing, from the mightiest archangel to the tiniest insect, it is there as the gift of God. All the wisest, and best, and greatest men that ever lived could not bestow the gift of life on any creature. All the angels of heaven could not give life to the smallest worm, or insect. The life of an angel—the life of a human being—or of any meaner creature—is what none but God can give. But "He giveth *to all—life*." And life is one of the most valuable gifts that God bestows. It is so valuable, that it is quite true, as we read in the book of Job—"all that a man hath will he give for his life."

And then God gives the breath, by which life is sustained. Yes, and He gives—"all things" that help to make life pleasant, and happy. There is one passage in which Jesus spoke more beautifully about the value of God's gifts, than in any other to be found in the Bible. I refer here to the words spoken by Jesus to Nicodemus, when He said: "*God so loved the world, that He gave his only begotten Son*, that whosoever believeth in Him, should not perish; but have everlasting life." John iii: 16. If all the Bibles in the world were going to be destroyed, and I was called upon to choose one verse from the Bible, as the only one which could be preserved, I think I would take *this*, in preference to any other. We have the glorious Gospel of Jesus in a nutshell here. This verse deserves to be written in letters of gold, and hung up in

GOD, THE MODEL GIVER. 369

public places, so that every one might see it, and read it. There is nothing in the Bible, which shows us what a valuable giver God is, so well as this verse does. He is indeed a model giver, because his gifts are so valuable. And we should try to follow His example in this respect. And when we give that which helps to make Jesus and his salvation known to poor lost men, then we are following the model of giving which God sets us—and are giving valuable gifts.

Let us look at some examples of this sort of giving. The first illustration I have under this head, is a very nice one. It may be called—

"*The Consecrated Diamonds.*" This story is told of the Princess Eugenia of Sweden. She is an earnest Christian lady, and has for years been trying to do good among her people. She spends her summers at a beautiful home on the Island of Gothland. When there, she is accustomed to spend a good deal of her time in visiting among the poor. While doing this, she became very much interested in behalf of a number of poor women, who were suffering from complaints which could not be cured. And she felt the more for these poor sisters in their sorrow, because she herself was suffering in the same way. After thinking over it a good while, the idea came into her mind, how nice it would be to have a hospital home, for those poor women. Yes, indeed! but where was the money to come from! She was a princess, it is true, but she was already engaged in so many works, that all the money she could spare from her income was spent, and it would take a good deal to build this hospital. Still she kept on thinking about it, and wishing that it could be done. And you know the old proverb says: "*Where there's a will, there's a way.*" And so it proved here.

One day, while thinking about it, the question came into her mind: "Why can't I sell my set of diamonds for this purpose?" She asked God to guide her. Then she consulted her brother—the King of Sweden—about it. He gave his consent.

The diamonds were sent to London, for the Swedish ambassador to sell them. They were sold for many thousands of dollars. The money was sent back to the princess. The hospital home was built, and filled with poor sick women.

Several years passed away. The summer was drawing to a close. The time had come for the princess to leave her summer retreat, for her winter home in the city. She was going through the hospital to say—"Good-by" to the patients. As she entered one of the rooms, the matron pointed to a particular bed, saying: "The old woman who occupies that bed, used to be the hardest of all our patients to manage. Please speak a few kind words to her. You will find her wonderfully changed now."

The princess went to this bed, and spoke to the sufferer, who was now very near her end. These were the poor woman's words to her: "I thank God that the blood of Jesus Christ, His Son, cleanseth from all sin—and that *He has cleansed mine*." As she said this the tears were running fast down her cheeks. They were the tears of gladness which told of the gratitude she felt to Jesus for His love. The light of heaven was glistening in them. In speaking of them afterwards the princess said: "In those tears I *saw my diamonds again.*" That is true. Yes! and when Jesus shall give her the crown of glory, which she will wear forever in heaven, she will see those diamonds, in that crown, sparkling more beautifully than any ever seen in an earthly crown. It was a valuable gift, which the Princess Eugenia gave, when she sold her diamonds in order to build that hospital.

"Yes," some of you may be ready to say, "it's all very well for princesses, and those who have jewels to sell, or plenty of money, to give valuable gifts. But if you have no money to give, and no jewels to sell; then what are you to do?" Now I have two short stories here, which answer this question, and show that it is possible to give valuable gifts, even when we have very little money, or no money at all.

One of these stories is about a boy; and the other is about a girl. The boy's story is called—

The Bag of Farthings. They were taking up their anniversary collection, one day, at a Sunday-school in England, when a little boy, about seven years old, put a bag on the plate, that felt quite heavy. The collector opened it, and found that it contained two hundred and eighty-five farthings! And where do you think the little fellow got all those farthings? He hadn't found them; he hadn't begged them. No; but he had *earned* them. And how! Why, his mother was a poor widow, and kept a little store. He used to run errands for his mother, and she let him keep all the farthings he received in change at the different stores, to which he went. Instead of spending these farthings in buying candy, or fruit, or playthings, he kept them till their anniversary day came, and then he put them in the collection, which they always had on those occasions, for the missionary cause. That bag of farthings made up about six shillings of English money. They would make about a dollar and a half in our money. It was a valuable gift which that little boy offered in his bag of farthings.

And now for the girl's story. We may call it—

What Mary Gave. She had no money to give, not even farthings. But notice now, what she *did* give, in one day. She gave an hour of patient care to her little baby sister, who was cutting her teeth. She gave a string, and a crooked pin, to her little three-year old brother, who wanted to play at fishing. She gave Ellen, the maid, an hour's time to go and visit her baby at home; for Ellen was a widow, and she left her child with its grandmother, while she worked to get bread for them both. She could not have seen them very often, if this kind-hearted Mary had not offered to mind the door, and look after the fire, while she was away.

But this was not all that Mary gave. She dressed herself neatly, and was so bright, and kind and obliging, that every time her mother looked at her pleasant young face, it made her heart glad. Then she wrote a letter to her father, who was absent from home, in which she gave him all the news about the family, in such a cheery, pleasant way, that the letter made him perfectly happy, and he thanked his dear daughter in his heart. And then she listened patiently to her poor old grandmother, while she told one of her long and tiresome stories. Mary had heard the story many times before; but she listened as attentively as if it was all new. She laughed at the proper places, and when the story was ended, she made the old lady quite happy with a good-night kiss.

Now here was a little girl, who had no diamonds to sell, and not a penny in the world to give, but yet who gave valuable presents to *six* people, in one day, that helped to make them all happy.

God, the model giver, may well be so called because He bestows valuable gifts on His creatures; and if we try to imitate this part of the model He sets before us, whether we have much money, or little, or none at all, we shall find out many ways, in which, like little Mary, we shall be able to give valuable gifts, that will make those around us happy.

And then, in the third place, we may speak of God, as the model giver—because He gives—SELF-DENYING—*gifts.*

God is so great, and so rich; He has such an abundance of everything, that we do not think of what He gives as involving any self-denial on His part. And it is true that when He gives life, and breath, and such like things, *they* do not cost Him self-denial. But, when He gives the blessings of His grace, and His salvation, *then*, He is giving us that which cost Him more than we can ever tell. Before the least of these blessings, could be bestowed on us, it was necessary for God to give up His only begotten Son to death; even the death of the cross. This is what the apostle Paul teaches us, when he says: "He that spared not His own Son, but delivered Him up for us all, how shall He not with him also, freely give us all things?"

When God gave His Son for our redemption, He gave Him to be out of heaven, and away from His own bosom, for more than thirty years. He gave him to pass through untold sufferings,—and to die a dreadful death, of shame and agony. And this was a gift that involved such self-denial as we can never know. And we may well speak of Him, as "the Model Giver," because when He bestows upon us the blessings of His grace, and Gospel, He is giving us that which cost Him wonderful self-denial.

And we should try to imitate "the Model Giver," in this respect, when we give.

We have a good example of this kind of giving, in King David. When the pestilence was prevailing among the people, and they were dying by thousands, he was directed to go to a certain place, and offer a sacrifice. When he arrived there, he found Auraunah, the owner of the ground, engaged in ploughing. As soon as he found out what the king had come there to do, he generously offered him the oxen that he was ploughing with, for a burnt sacrifice, and proposed to break up the yoke on the neck of the oxen, and the plough they were using, for fire-wood. And he offered to give these to the king, freely, without any charge. The king thanked him for his kind offer, but said he would accept his offer only on *one* condition; and that was, that he should be allowed to pay for his oxen, and the things to be used for fuel, because he said he was not willing—"*to make an offering to God of that which cost him nothing.*" David was imitating "the Model Giver," when he did this.

Jamie Weston's Half Dollar. Jamie Weston had

fifty cents in his pocket, of his own earnings. He never had so much money of his own before, and he felt very rich. He saw his Cousin Sue coming towards him, and said to himself—"I must tell Sue how rich I am." But Sue had something to tell him; and before he had a chance to speak—"Jamie," she said, "I'm making up a box of nice things, to send to the missionaries. Have you anything to put in?"

Jamie hesitated a moment, and then said:

"I've got fifty cents, that I earned myself; take them and put something into the box for me."

And then, thrusting his chubby hand into his now empty pocket, Jamie hastened home.

His mother was a poor widow woman, who had a very hard time to get food and clothing for her children.

When Jamie came into the little cottage, where his mother was busy sewing, he said: "Mamma, I've given my half dollar to Cousin Sue, to buy something for the box she is making up for the missionaries."

Mrs. Weston stopped sewing when she heard this. Jamie saw the tears come into her eyes, as she said: "Oh, Jamie, I'm sorry you have done this! I wanted that money to help buy you a new jacket. The one you are wearing is old and thin, and I'm afraid you will suffer from the cold this winter."

Jamie threw his arms round his mother's neck, and said: "Don't cry, mother; God has always taken care of us; and He will send me a jacket, I'm sure."

In the afternoon, when Susie's work on the box was done, she sat down to tell her mother all about it.

"And mother, only think, Jamie Weston gave me

fifty cents, that he had earned himself, and that he was saving towards buying himself a winter jacket. I wish you could have seen his black eyes sparkle, when I told him about the box. I didn't want to take his money, when I found what he had been saving it for. But he made me take it, for he said, 'The heathen need the Gospel more than I need a jacket; and I'm sure God won't let me freeze this winter.' And then I took it."

"Let him freeze!" said Susie's mother, who was very much interested in what Susie had said about Jamie. "Of course not. I'll see to that. I'll send him a jacket this very evening. Yes, and not a jacket only, but a full suit, made out of the very best cloth in town."

And so it happened, that just as Jamie was lighting the lamp in their little room, that night, and drawing up the chairs around the fireplace, there came a rap at the door. When Jamie opened the door, a parcel was handed him, on which was written in plain letters, "For Master James Weston."

"What *can* it be, mamma?" he asked, with great wonder, as he laid the bundle on the table. It was soon opened, and was found to contain material for a full suit of nice, warm winter clothes.

Jamie fairly danced for joy. Tears of gladness filled his mother's eyes. Jamie threw his arms lovingly round her neck, and said softly to her—"I asked God for a jacket, mamma, when I gave the fifty cents for the missionary box; and I felt sure that it would come some time; but I didn't expect it so soon."

Now Jamie Weston was imitating the example of

"the Model Giver." What he gave involved self-denial on his part.

The Gold Dollar. A Secretary of the American Board of Missions, was once visiting in a town in Maine. He had held a meeting in one of the churches in that town one evening, and had given a very interesting account of the missionary work in heathen lands.

The next day, a little boy in the family where he was staying, came up to him, and began to talk to him. As he did so, the gentleman noticed that his right hand was clasped closely, as though he was holding something in it, very carefully.

"I want very much," said the little fellow, "to have a sled. Johnny has one, and Charley has one; but I haven't any, and I want one very much."

"I know boys are very fond of sleds," said the gentleman. "Both my boys have one, and they think a great deal of them. I hope you'll soon be able to get one."

He thought this little fellow wanted to beg from him the money to buy a sled with. But that was not what he wanted. For presently he held out his hand, and unclasped it; and there, lying on the palm of it, was a bright, gold dollar.

"I have been saving this gold dollar to get a sled with," said he; "but after hearing what you said about the heathen last night, I feel sure that they need missionaries to tell them about Jesus, more than I need a sled. And so I have made up my mind to do without a sled, and give my gold dollar to the Missionary Society."

The Secretary was very much touched with the speech, and the offering of the dear boy. He thanked him for his gift, and said he hoped he might soon have a nice sled given to him. He used to tell this story at missionary meetings, and he would wind up with saying: "Ah! my friends, if all Christian people would only learn to *deny themselves*, as this dear boy did, that they might have something to give to the cause of Jesus, how soon all the money needed for missionary work would be furnished!"

God, the model Giver, denied Himself, by giving His Son to die for us; and we should strive to imitate the model He sets for us, by giving in the same way.

And now we have spoken of *three* points in the model of giving which God sets before us. He is—*a cheerful* Giver—a *valuable* Giver—and *a self-denying* Giver.

Let us take this model, and keep it before us, till we learn to give according to it. Then we shall be such givers as God desires us to be. Then God will accept our gifts. They will do good to others, and will come back in great blessings to ourselves.

JOHN THE BAPTIST PREACHES IN THE WILDERNESS.

JOHN THE BAPTIST, THE MODEL OF GREATNESS.

"He shall be great in the sight of the Lord."—
LUKE i: 15.

ABRIEL, the angel, was sent by God to speak the above words to Zacharias the priest, the father of John the Baptist. It was in the temple at Jerusalem, while he was offering incense before the altar, that the angel appeared to him. He told him that he was about to have a son, and that he must call his name—John. Then he told him what sort of work he was to do. He was to go before Christ—the Messiah, as the morning star goes before the sun, to prepare His way before Him. And then he told him what sort of a man he should be: *"He shall be great in the sight of the Lord."*

And when our Saviour was on earth, in speaking of John the Baptist, one day, He said: "Of them that are born of women, there hath not risen a greater than John the Baptist." The angel Gabriel, and Jesus, the lord of the angels, both spoke of John the Baptist in the highest terms. They show us that, up to the time in which he lived, he was really the greatest man the world had known. And in view of what is thus said about him, when we come to put John the Baptist among the "Bible Models," we may well speak of him as—

The Model of Greatness. And in studying this model, there are *two* points of view from which we may look at it. One of these is—the *negative* view of it, or in what John's greatness did *not* consist. The other is—the *positive* view of it, or in what John's greatness *did* consist.

And in looking at this model from the negative point of view, there are *three* things to speak of. The first is, that—

John's greatness did *not consist in long life.* He was born about six months before our Saviour. He lived a private life, till he was thirty years of age. This was the age at which the Jewish priests and prophets, generally began their work in public. And it was at this age that John began his work, as the forerunner of Christ. He came among his countrymen, crying aloud: "Repent ye, for the kingdom of heaven is at hand." He told them of the coming of the long-promised Messiah—the Saviour of the world; thus he prepared the way before him. He began to preach, about six months before Jesus entered on his ministry; and he went on telling the people about Him, and pointing them to Him, for about a year longer. Then he was beheaded by the wicked Herod; and *that* was the end of John's ministry. About eighteen months was all the time he had to work for Jesus. And yet the angel said he should be—"great in the sight of the Lord." And he *was* thus great. But then we see that it was—*not long life* which made John the Baptist great.

Two things that helped to make John great, were—doing what he knew was right, and bringing souls to Jesus. And these things will make any one great in God's sight. But it does not require long life to do these things.

Here are some incidents to show how they may be done by very young persons.

Our first story may be called—

The Brave Boy. A little bootblack was standing near the entrance of a city hotel, waiting patiently for a job. Presently two fashionably-dressed young men came out of the hotel, smoking their cigars, and stood near the boy.

"Here, Boots," said one of them, placing his foot on the boy's box, and saying as he did so: "let's see if you are master of your trade."

The bootblack plied his brush with diligence and skill, and the boot was beginning to brighten under his ready touch. In the meantime the young men were trying to frighten him to make more haste, by swearing at him. The little fellow stood it as long he could. But, when one boot was finished, he stopped, and put his brushes in the box where he carried them.

"What now?" asked the young man.

"I won't finish your boots," answered the boy.

"Not finish them!" said the young man, with a dreadful oath; "then you won't get any money."

"I don't want your money," said the boy, "and I won't stay here and listen to your swearing."

"Let the boy alone," said the other young man, "and let him finish his job."

"Well and good," said the first speaker, "but it's a rare joke to find a bootblack who is afraid of swearing."

"I can't afford to swear," said the bootblack, looking reverently up to heaven.

"Do you mean to say that it costs anything to swear?" asked the young man in astonishment.

"Yes, sir," replied the bootblack, in an earnest, solemn manner: *"it would cost me my soul."* Now it was noble in that little boy to stand up so bravely in behalf of what was right. That would make him, like John the Baptist—"great in the sight of the Lord." It does not require long life to secure this sort of greatness. Doing what is right will make us great in God's sight.

And then—*bringing souls to Jesus will make us great in God's sight.* This was what John was doing all the days of his public ministry. And it was this which made him "great in the sight of the Lord." But children may do this as well as older people.

Here is a story about—

A Drunken Father Brought to Jesus by his Daughter's Sunday-school Hymn. A few years ago, in a city of Scotland, there lived a man, the father of a family, who was considered the wickedest man in that neighborhood. He seldom opened his mouth without uttering a terrible oath, and using the vilest language. His companions were the worst men to be found in the city. He was constantly drunk. He frequently beat his poor wife and children, and was the terror of all the people who lived near him. Late one Saturday night, he returned to his miserable home, perfectly wild with drink, and after swearing, and storming, and creating a terrible disturbance, he sank down upon his wretched bed and fell asleep.

He woke about eleven o'clock on Sunday morning, and called for more drink, with furious oaths. His sorrowing wife, fearing his ill treatment, was afraid to speak to him; but his little daughter Jenny, who was only eight years old, went up to him timidly, and said: "We haven't any money, father, and there is nothing in the house for dinner." Her mind was full of a sweet hymn she had learned at Sunday-school, and she said: "May I sing to you, father?"

"Yes," he replied, "you may sing if you like, but I want more drink."

With a quivering voice, which grew stronger and sweeter, as she went on, she sang:

> "I am so glad that our Father in heaven
> Tells of His love in the Book He has given;
> Wonderful things in the Bible I see;
> This is the sweetest—that Jesus loves me.
>   I am so glad that Jesus loves,
>   Jesus loves me—*even me.*"

When she had finished the hymn—"That is very sweet," he said; "you may sing it again."

As she was singing it the second time, the scalding tears began to trickle down her father's cheeks; he covered his face with his hands, and as soon as she stopped, he cried out: "Oh, Jenny! do you think that

Jesus loves *me?* Can He love such a wretch as I am? Will He love—even *me?*" Presently he fell upon his knees, and, for the first time in his life, the cry went up from his lips—"God be merciful to me a sinner!"

His prayer was heard. That miserable, drunken, swearing man, became an humble, earnest, useful Christian. What a change came over that family! And how often, in after years, he thanked God that his little Jenny had been a Sunday-school scholar!

Our Saviour has told us that one soul is worth more than the whole world. To be the means of saving a soul, is one of the greatest works that can be done. And so, when little Jenny was the means of bringing her father to Jesus, she did a great work. And though only eight years old, she was—"great in the sight of the Lord," as John the Baptist was. This greatness does not require long life.

In the next place, this greatness does not require—*great riches*.

John the Baptist was a poor man. We see this in the clothes he wore, when he began his ministry, and in the food on which he lived. We are told by St. Matthew (iii. 41), that—"John had his raiment of camel's hair, and a leathern girdle about his loins; and his meat was locusts and wild honey." This was just the kind of food and clothing which the poorest people of that country had. John owned no land. He never had a house of his own to live in. He had no money, with which to buy anything that was costly or expensive. And yet, in spite of his poverty, John was—"great in the sight of the Lord." And this sort of greatness we may all have, if we serve God as John did. Some men are rich without being great; and some are great without being rich.

Let us take one example of a man who was rich but not great, in the true sense. I refer here to the late William M. Tweed, of the city of New York. He was one of the richest men in that great city. He used to be called Boss Tweed, because he had the control of almost everything that was done in the government of the city. But he was an utterly bad man. Yet he felt so secure in his position, that if any one spoke to him about his wicked ways, he would say: "Well, and what are you going to do about it?" He felt as if he was perfectly safe in his position, and that nobody could touch him. But finally, the law took hold of him, and he was put in prison. He lost all his money. He died in prison; but before his death he made this sad confession—"My life has been a failure in everything. There is nothing that I am proud of." That is a sad illustration of a man who was rich, but not great.

And now let us take one or two examples of persons who were great, without being rich. The first we may call—

A Servant Girl's Greatness. One of the best and greatest men in England to-day is the Earl of Shaftsbury. He is well known through all the country, as the helper of the poor and the oppressed. He takes an active part in every good work. He has been for years, and still is, a blessing to the whole country: and every one who knows him is always ready to speak his praises. He is not only very good, and great, but also very rich; and he uses his riches to help others in many ways. But the Earl of Shaftsbury owes all his goodness and his greatness, under God, to a poor servant girl. When he was an infant, his mother had a faithful servant girl in her family, whose name was Mary Millas. His mother appointed Mary to be the nurse of the young Earl, and gave her the entire charge of him. She knew what an important position he would have to occupy when he grew to be a man, and she made up her mind to be faithful to the great trust committed to her charge. She felt very much as the mother of Moses did, when God, through Pharaoh's daughter, said to her—" Take this child away, and nurse it for me, and I will give thee thy wages." She was an earnest Christian, and she determined to do all in her power, to make that child a follower of Jesus. She prayed for him continually, with all her heart. She set before him a good example. As soon as he was able to learn, she taught him in a simple and attractive way, the story about Jesus, and the truth wrapped up in that story. She kept on doing this very faithfully till the young Earl was seven years old, and then she died. But the seed she had sown so carefully in his heart, took root there, and sprang up, and brought forth abundant fruit. He never forgot the example she had set before him, and the lessons she had taught him, in those early years of his life. He became a Christian, when he was quite young. He grew up in the way in which he had been so early led. And now for years, he has been known, and honored, all through England. No one can tell how much good he has been the means of doing. But the faithful work which Mary Millas did for the young Earl, was the cause of it all. She was truly great, in what she did for him. And we may well speak of that poor servant girl, as an example of greatness without riches.

I have one other example of a man who was great without being rich. We may call it—

A Beautiful Father. Two little boys came as new scholars to a mission school, in one of our large cities. They behaved very nicely; and at the close of school the teacher said to them: "Well, when you get home you can tell your mother that you have been very good boys to-day."

"Please, ma'am," said one of the little fellows, whose name was Tommy, "we haven't any mother."

"Ah, indeed!" said the teacher; "then pray tell me who takes such good care of you? for your clothes look very nice."

"Father does," said Tommy. "We've got such a beautiful father! Oh, ma'am, you ought to see him!"

"But who takes care of you when he is at work?" asked the teacher.

"Why, father takes all the care of us before he goes off in the morning, and after he comes back at night. He's a house-painter, but there isn't any work this winter, so he's doing laboring-work till spring comes. He says he won't let us eat charity food, and wear other people's old clothes, while he is well and strong. He leaves us a warm breakfast when he goes off; then we have bread and milk for dinner, and a good warm supper when he comes home at night. Then he tells us stories, and plays on the fife, and whittles out pretty things for us with his jack-knife. Oh, you ought to see our home, and our father—they are both so beautiful!"

The teacher said she would come and see them in their home, as soon as she could. Before long she found time to do so. She called one day to see that home and that father.

The room was a poor garret room. But it was perfectly neat and clean. It was ornamented with cheap pictures, and autumn leaves, and other nice little things that cost nothing.

When the teacher called at the children's home, it was at the close of the day. The father was busy at the time preparing the evening meal for his motherless little ones. As the lady first looked at him, there seemed to be nothing pleasing about him. He was a rough-looking man. His clothes were old, and coarse, and stained with paint. But, before she had been very long there, that garret room seemed to be turned into a palace; and the teacher thought that rough-looking working-man, appeared to her almost like an angel. His children did not know that they were poor. And indeed they were not, with such a brave and loving father to take care of them, and to fight the battles of life for them. There were no rich man's children in that city, who were really happier, than were the children of that rough, hard-working laboring-man.

If he could not get work at his trade, he was ready to saw wood, or sweep the streets, or do anything to provide for his children, rather than let them live on charity. And his cheerful spirit spread sunshine round his home, which would otherwise have been dark and gloomy. He was training his boys to be honest, industrious, and useful, as they grew up; and was teaching them how, as the catechism says, they were to—" do their duty in that state of life, in which it might please God to call them." And any man who acts, as this humble house-painter did, though he may have no riches, will yet, like John the Baptist—"be great in the sight of the Lord."

But again, *the greatness of John the Baptist did not consist of "the honor that cometh from man."* Men often call persons great, when they are really not so at all.

There was a famous person, of whom we read in history. He lived in the time of Henry VIII., King of England, and was known as Cardinal Woolsey. He was a poor boy, the son of a butcher. But he got into college. He entered the ministry. He was rector of several churches. He became a favorite with King Henry VIII., who made him his Prime Minister. Then he was made Bishop; then Archbishop of York; then he was made Lord Chancellor; and finally the pope of Rome appointed him Cardinal—which was the highest office he had in his power to give to any one. Thus Cardinal Woolsey had all the honor that cometh from man. But what good did it do him? In a single day he lost it all, and all his riches too, and died—a poor, miserable, heart-broken creature. And just before he died, he is said to have spoken these words to a friend who was near him:

> "O Cromwell! Cromwell! had I but served my God
> With half the zeal with which I've served my king,
> He would not now have forsaken me."

The greatness of John the Baptist was very different from that of Cardinal Woolsey. Men had nothing to do with it. He was great in the sight of the Lord. And this is the only greatness that is worth having.

And this greatness we can all have, if we seek it in the right way. Let us look at one or two illustrations of this kind of greatness. The first story may be called—

The Name of the Good Samaritan. Many years ago a good and faithful minister, whose name was Oberlin, was laboring among the high Alps. On one occasion he was traveling on foot in the winter time. The snow was deep, and the weather very cold. Weary with his journey, faint, and hungry, and overcome by the cold, the poor minister felt that he could not struggle any longer. He dropped on the snow and fell asleep. If he had been left there a little while, he never would have wakened again in this world. But he had not slept long, before he was roused by some one shaking him, and calling to him.

It was a Swiss peasant who had seen him, as he was driving by in his sleigh, and had stopped to help him. He gave him some wine to drink, and some food to eat, and then lifted him into his sleigh, and drove him to the next village.

Mr. Oberlin felt that he owed his life to the great kindness of this stranger; and he was at a loss how properly to thank him for what he had done. He offered him money, but he refused to take it.

"It is our duty to help one another," said the peasant, "and it is almost an insult to offer to pay a man for any such service."

"Well," replied Oberlin, "at least tell me your name, that I may tell it to the Lord in my prayers."

"I see you are a minister of the Gospel," said the peasant. "Will you please tell me the name of the good Samaritan?"

"I can't do that," said the minister, "for his name was never told."

"Then let my name go with his," was the peasant's reply: "we'll leave them both together with the Lord."

That good Swiss peasant, and the good Samaritan, had neither of them any of "the honor that cometh from man," but, like John the Baptist, they had the honor which cometh from God. They were "great in the sight of the Lord," and that is the best sort of greatness.

Thus we have taken the *negative* view of John's greatness, and have tried to show *in what it did* NOT *consist.*

It did not consist—*in long life—in great riches*—or *in the honor that cometh from man.*

And now, let us take the *positive* view of John's greatness, or in what it *did* consist. And there are three things to speak of under this head.

One thing that helped to make John great, in the sight of the Lord, was—*his humility*. John was very humble. We see this in several things. We see it in what he said of himself, when the Jews sent messengers from Jerusalem, after he had been preaching some time, to ask him who he was. His answer was: "I am the voice of one crying in the wilderness." He did not say—I am a prophet, or—I am the forerunner of Christ. He simply said: "I am a *voice*"—a little breath put in motion—that's all. How humble John was!

And we see his humility again in what he said about Christ. "After me," said he, "cometh one mightier than I: one who was preferred before me; whose shoes-latchet I am not worthy to unloose." How humble John was!

And then, we see his humility again, in what took place before the baptism of our Saviour. When he first applied to John to baptize him, he declined and said: "I have need to be baptized of thee, and comest thou to me?" But when Jesus said: "Suffer it to be so now;" then John baptized him. All these things show us the humility of John; and this was one of the things that helped to make him great.

Solomon says: "Before honor is humility." And Jesus says: "He that humbleth himself shall be exalted." Here is a story called—

Nature's Lesson on Humility. A farmer took his little son into the wheat-field during harvest.

"See, father," said the boy, "how straight those stems hold up their heads! They must be the best ones. Those that hang down their heads I don't think are good for much."

The farmer plucked a stalk of each kind, and said: "Look here, my child. This stalk, that stood so straight, is light-headed, and good for nothing; but this, which hung down its head, so modestly, is full of precious grain."

And so we cannot always tell what people are by the way they hold up their heads. Empty heads are often the straightest—because they haven't sense enough to weigh them down.

Here are some sweet lines called—

JOHN THE BAPTIST, THE MODEL OF GREATNESS.

THE REWARD OF HUMILITY.

"The bird that soars on highest wing,
   Builds on the ground her lowly nest;
And she that doth most sweetly sing,
   Sings in the shade when all things rest;
In lark and nightingale we see
What honor hath humility.

"The saint that wears heaven's brightest crown,
   In deepest adoration bends;
The weight of glory bows him down
   The most, when most his soul ascends;
Nearest the throne itself must be
The footstool of humility."

Here is a good missionary story, which shows how humility leads to honor and greatness.

One time, when Dr. Morrison, the celebrated missionary to China, found the work there too much for him, he wrote home to his friends in Scotland, and asked them to send him out an assistant. The managers of the missionary society inquired for a suitable person to send out to China. Their attention was directed to a young man of Aberdeen, who was said to be a person of great piety, and industry.

He was called before the committee who had charge of this business. They had a long talk with him. Then he withdrew from the committee, and left them to talk it over among themselves.

After he was gone, one of the gentlemen of the committee said: "I don't think that young man will answer our purpose at all. He's too plain and rough."

Finally, one of them suggested, that even if they did not send the young man out as a missionary, it might do very well to send him out as a servant, to help Dr. Morrison in his work. The committee all agreed about this. Then the gentleman who had made the suggestion, was requested to see the young man and talk with him about it. He did so. He told him that the committee were not willing to send him out as a missionary; but they would be very glad to have him go out as a servant to Dr. Morrison, if he was willing to go.

Now many a young man, would have been offended at this, and would have risen up in pride and anger, and said: "No, I can't consent to that. If I can't go out as a missionary, I won't go at all." But it was different with this young man. When asked if he was willing to go as a servant—without a moment's hesitation, and with a bright smile, he replied: "Yes, sir, certainly. I am willing to do anything, so that I am only at work for Jesus. To be 'a hewer of wood, or drawer of water' is too great an honor for me when the Lord's house is building." That young man went out to China as a servant. But he was well known afterwards as—the Rev. Dr. Milne—one of the best and most successful missionaries that ever was. And it was his humility which made him great.

But the last and best illustration of this subject to be found anywhere, we have in our blessed Saviour. There never was such humility as we find in Him. He humbled Himself to come down from the throne of heaven, and take our nature upon Him. He humbled Himself to live a life of poverty and shame. He humbled Himself to suffering and death—"even the death of the cross." "Therefore," as St. Paul says, "God hath highly exalted Him, and given Him a name which is above every name; that at the name of Jesus every knee should bow, of things in heaven, and things on earth, and things under the earth; and that every tongue should confess that Jesus Christ is Lord, to the glory of God the Father."

There never was such humiliation as that to which Jesus stooped. And there never will be any greatness like that to which He has already risen; and to larger measures of which He will rise hereafter.

One thing that had to do with the greatness of John the Baptist, was his humility.

Another thing that had to do with John's greatness in the sight of the Lord—was *his unselfishness*.

One day, some of John's disciples came to him and said: "He that was with thee beyond Jordan, and to whom thou didst bear witness, behold the same baptizeth, and all men come to him." They were feeling jealous for their master, and they wanted him to do something to show his importance. But John had no idea of setting himself up in opposition to Jesus. Just listen to what John said to his disciples:

"A man can receive nothing, except it be given him from heaven. Ye yourselves bear me witness, that I said, I am not the Christ, but I am sent before him. He that cometh from above, is above all. He must increase, but I must decrease." How beautifully John's unselfishness shows itself here! He was willing to be lost sight of, and to be counted as nothing, so that Jesus might be exalted. His unselfishness, was one of the things that helped to make him great. And we must learn this lesson too, if we wish to be—"great in the sight of the Lord."

Let us look at some other examples of persons who were made great by their unselfishness. Our first story is about—

An Unselfish Boy. Harry had seen some boys flying their kites from the top of a house, and he thought it would be nice fun if he could do so too. So he came to his aunt and said: "Aunt Mary, can't I go up to the top of the house, and fly my kite?"

No, Harry, my boy; I think it would be a very dangerous sort of sport. I'd rather you wouldn't do it."

"All right," said Harry; "then I'll go out, and play on the bridge."

His aunt smiled, and said she hoped he would always be as obedient, and as unselfish, as he was then.

"Harry, what are you doing?" said his mother to him one day.

"Spinning my new top, mother."

"Oh, well, can't you take the baby out to ride? Get the carriage, and I'll bring him down."

"All right," shouted Harry, as he put the top away in his pocket, and hastened to obey his mother.

"Uncle Willie," said Harry, one morning, "may I go over to your shop, after breakfast? I want very much to see those baskets again, that I was looking at yesterday."

"Oh, yes, Harry," said his uncle, "I shall be very glad to have you do so."

"But I can't spare you, Harry," said his mother.

"I want you to go with me to-day. You can go and see the baskets some other day."

"All right," said Harry, and went on cheerfully with his breakfast.

No matter what Harry was asked to do, or what refusal he met with, in asking for anything, his constant reply was: "All right." He never stopped to worry, or to tease. He had learned not only to obey, but to obey in a pleasant, cheerful way. He was a good example of an unselfish boy. And we may be sure that his unselfishness would help to make him—"great in the sight of the Lord."

Our next story is about—

An Unselfish Engineer. One day, not long ago, a long train of cars left Jersey City on the Pennsylvania Railroad. There were six hundred and twenty passengers in that train. It went on increasing its speed, till it was flying along at the rate of forty miles an hour. Presently the engine and the tender connected with it, were found to be on fire. The speed, with which the train was flying along, drove the smoke and flames into the other cars. The engineer and the fireman were driven from their posts. The passengers were dreadfully frightened. And well they might be. The train was rushing on like the wind, and no one had any control of it. What was to become of them? The only prospect before them was that of being dashed to pieces.

The name of the engineer on that train, was Gustavus Seig. He was an unselfish, noble-hearted man. He saw that unless something was done, the train would be wrecked, and many lives would be lost. At the risk of his own life, he resolved to try and save the train. He rushed through the flames, to get at the air-brake, and stop the train. His clothes caught fire; but still he went on. He reached the brake. He put it in operation. He stopped the train. By this time his clothes were all in flames. Then he plunged into the water-tank to stop the burning of his clothes. He did stop it, but not till it was too late. He died from the effect of his burns. But, by losing his own life, he saved the lives of more than six hundred passengers on that train. This was one of the noblest actions ever performed.

The unselfishness of that engineer made him great, not only in the sight of the Lord, but in the sight of men.

And then there was one other thing that helped to make John great, and that was his—*courage*.

John was a very brave man. At the time when he was preaching, Herod was the king of Judea. He was fond of John, and became his friend. We are told that he took great pleasure in hearing John preach, and did many things that he told the people to do. But Herod was a very bad man. He had taken the wife of his brother Philip to be his wife. This was very wrong. It was breaking God's law. John made up his mind to speak to Herod about it.

Many a man would have been afraid to do this. He would have said to himself: "I had better let this matter alone; for I shall surely lose the friendship of the king, if I say anything to him about it." But John was not afraid. His rule was always to do what was right, no matter what the consequences might be.

So he told the king one day, that it was not lawful for him to have his brother's wife. This made Herod very angry. He had John cast into prison; and not long after, at the request of his wife, he ordered him to be put to death. But John's work was done. And when he died, he went into the presence of that Lord, in whose sight he was great. And one thing that helped to make him so, was his courage.

And we must learn to follow his example in this respect, if we hope to be great in the sight of the Lord, as he was.

Let us look at some other examples of courage, and see how it makes those great who have it. The first story is about—

A Brave Chinaman. Two young Chinese lads attended the services of a mission chapel, in the city of Canton. One of them was named Wah Lee, and the other Ah Wing. They were very much interested in what the missionary had told them about Jesus, and his love for poor sinners. But they could not feel quite easy about giving up the idols, they had been taught to worship. They had many long talks together on the subject. If they could only feel satisfied that their idols were not real gods, they would be willing at once to give them up, and become Christians. But they could not quite make up their minds about it. Wah Lee was a youth with a great deal of courage, and always ready to do whatever he believed was right. But Ah Wing was very timid, and afraid of taking any decided step. But, one day, they concluded to go to the Joss House, which is the name given to the place where their idols are worshipped, and see if they could not make up their minds, whether those idols were real gods, or not.

When they reached the Joss House, Ah Wing was afraid to go any further than just inside the door. But Wah Lee walked up to the altar, and standing boldly before the idol he said: "You no god. You only block of wood." Ah Wing trembled when he heard this. But Wah Lee grew bolder, and turning to his companion, he said: "Me ask Jesus help me; then me pull the idol's beard." Poor Ah Wing was dreadfully frightened when he heard this. But Wah Lee was not afraid. He went up close to the idol. It was made of wood, about two feet high, in a sitting position, on an altar. As usual, it had on its chin a long beard, made of horse-hair. As Wah Lee stepped up to the idol, Ah Wing held his breath. It was a bold thing his friend was going to do. If that idol was a real god, he expected that Wah Lee would be struck dead on the spot. But the brave young man was not afraid. He stood boldly up before the idol. He took firm hold of its beard, and gave it a good pull. The idol toppled over, and fell to the ground, resting on its head. For a moment the young men were both speechless. They waited to see if anything would happen. But there was nothing.

Then Wah Lee cried out: "Now me sure he no god. He only block of wood. Now me give up idols, and take Jesus for me God." And Ah Wing did the same. The courage of Wah Lee made him great. It proved a great blessing both to himself, and to his friend, Ah Wing. Let us try to have courage like this, and it will be a blessing to us.

I have one other story to illustrate this part of our subject. We may call it—

The Brave Soldier. It is a story connected with the late war. General Kershaw, of South Carolina, tells the story, and the brave Sergeant Kirkland, to whom it refers, was a soldier in his brigade. It was the day after the battle of Fredericksburgh, that this incident took place. That was not a decided battle. Neither side had gained the victory. The two armies lay within sight of each other, and the broad plain between them was covered with dead and wounded soldiers, who had fallen in the battle of the previous day.

Soon after breakfast that morning, Sergeant Kirkland came up to General Kershaw, very much excited, and said: "General I can't stand this any longer."

"Can't stand what?"

"Why, the cry of those poor wounded fellows. 'Water! water! water! for God's sake give me water!' I've been hearing all night, and all morning. I can't stand it any longer; and I've come to ask, sir, if you will allow me to go and take them some water?"

The General looked at him with wondering admiration. Then he said: "Kirkland, don't you know, that the moment you step over the lines, you will be in danger of having a bullet put through your head?"

"Yes, sir, I know it," said the brave fellow, "but, if you'll allow me, I am willing to try it."

"Kirkland," said the General, "I ought not to allow you to run such a risk; but the motive which influences you is so noble, that I cannot refuse your request. I pray God to take care of you. You may go."

"Thank you, sir," said the Sergeant, as he made his bow with a pleasant smile. Then he hastened away. With a bucket of water, and a tin-cup in his hand, he started. How anxiously he was watched, as he stepped over the lines, on his errand of mercy. Unharmed he reached the nearest sufferer. Kneeling beside him, he tenderly raised his drooping head, rested it gently on his own noble breast, and poured the cool, refreshing, life-giving water down his fever-parched throat. Then he laid him tenderly down,—placed his knapsack under his head, straightened out his broken limb, spread his overcoat over him, filled his empty canteen with water, and left him as comfortable as he could be, while he turned to another poor sufferer.

By this time, his object in going out among the wounded, was understood by both armies, and he was safe. As he went on with his work, fresh cries were heard from all parts of the field—"Water! water! for God's sake, water!" For an hour and a half that noble-hearted soldier kept on with his blessed mission. Like an angel of mercy, nay, like the Lord of the angels, he was "going about doing good." And he never stopped in his work, till all the wounded in that part of the field, were relieved. How well we may say that the courage of that brave soldier made him great, not only in the sight of the Lord, but in the sight of men too!

Now, where is our text to-day? St. Luke, first chapter and 15th verse. What are the words of the text? "He shall be great in the sight of the Lord." What is the sermon about? *John the Baptist, the Model of*

Greatness. From how many points of view did we look at John's greatness? Two. What was the first? The *negative* view; or in what it did *not* consist. It was not—*in long life—not in great riches—and not in the honor that cometh from man.*

And what was the second view from which we looked at John's greatness? The *positive* view; or in what it *did* consist. It was *his humility—his unselfishness—and his courage*—which made John great.

Let us pray for grace to follow his example in these respects, and then, we may hope to be great in the sight of the Lord, as John was.

THE APOSTLE PAUL, THE MODEL OF EARNESTNESS.

"I press toward the mark."—PHILIPPIANS iii : 14.

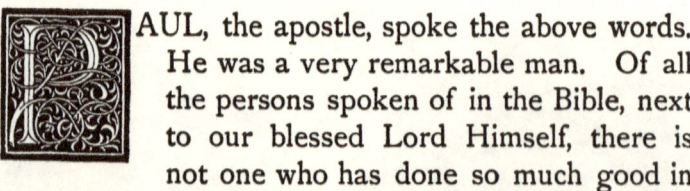AUL, the apostle, spoke the above words. He was a very remarkable man. Of all the persons spoken of in the Bible, next to our blessed Lord Himself, there is not one who has done so much good in the world as St. Paul. And I suppose that the chief thing that helped to make him so useful was the—*earnestness*—which marked his character. And, in putting him among our *Bible Models*, we cannot do better than to consider him as—*the model of earnestness*.

This feature of character belonged to him by nature. Before he became a Christian, he was earnest in getting an education. He left his home at Tarsus; in Asia Minor, for this purpose, and was brought up at the feet of Gamaliel, the greatest teacher of that age. None but an earnest young man would have done this.

And then we see how earnest he was in persecuting

PAUL STRUCK BLIND BY A LIGHT FROM HEAVEN.

the followers of Jesus, when he thought *that* was the right thing for him to do. He got letters from the chief priests, and then travelled all the way from Jerusalem to Damascus—a very long journey in those days—that he might make prisoners of the Christians there, and bring them bound to Jerusalem. But it is chiefly in St. Paul's character, after he became a Christian, that we find his earnestness exhibited. And there are three things about the Christian life of St. Paul, in which his earnestness appears. These are—the *beginning;* the *continuance;* and the *results* of that life.

St. Paul showed his earnestness in the way in which he BEGAN his Christian life. We see what that beginning was in the prayer which he offered, when Jesus appeared to him on his way to Damascus. He found that he was utterly wrong in the course of life he was pursuing. He saw that it would be necessary for him to make an entire change. He knew not what to do. So he offered the prayer: "*Lord, what wilt* THOU *have me to do?*" This showed that he was ready to begin his Christian life by doing whatever God wanted him to do.

In answer to this prayer, God told him through Ananias, who baptized him, that—"he was a chosen vessel unto Him, to bear His name before the Gentiles, and kings, and the children of Israel. And that He would show him what great things he must suffer for His name's sake." This would have been enough to discourage, and alarm many persons. But Paul was neither alarmed, or discouraged. It was an answer to his prayer. He saw now what the will of God concerning him was, and he began his Christian life by resolving at once to do that will. And we read that: "Straightway he preached Christ in the synagogues, that He was the Son of God. And all that heard him were astonished, and said: 'Is not this he that destroyed those that called on this name in Jerusalem, and came hither for that intent, that he might bring them bound to the chief priests?' But Paul increased the more in strength, and confounded the Jews that were at Damascus, proving that this is the very Christ."

Here we see what a model of earnestness, Paul was in the way in which he *began* his Christian life. And all who desire to follow this model must begin their Christian life as he did, by resolving to do just what God wants them to do.

Here is an example of earnestness in a little girl, who was trying to be a Christian.

Her name was Lutie Goldsborough. It was the custom in their family, when they had prayers in the morning, for each of the children to repeat a text of Scripture. Lutie was the youngest of the children, a bright little blue-eyed child, about seven years old. One morning her verse was: "Inasmuch as ye have done it unto one of the least of these, my brethren, ye have done it unto me."

After prayers were over she came up to her father, saying: "Papa, I don't understand the verse I repeated this morning; what does it mean?"

"Well, it means this," said her father: "if you were going along the road, and saw a poor ragged beggar sitting under the hedge, and you should stop and give him a cup of cold water, or a piece of bread, it would be the same as if you had given it to the blessed Saviour Himself. Don't you understand now, my dear?"

"Yes, papa, I do. Thank you.

A few days after this, there was a church fair being held in the village; and one afternoon, Mrs. Goldsborough said to her little daughter: "Lutie, my dear, you have been such a good, obedient girl lately, that mamma wants to reward you. Here's a purse with some money in it; you may take it, and go over to the fair, and buy anything you like for yourself and little May."

"Anything I like!" said the little girl, as she danced up and down, feeling perfectly delighted. "Oh, let me start this very minute!"

"You may start as soon as you please," said her mother. So Lutie put on her bonnet, and set off, with her precious purse in her pocket, thinking of the lovely things she would buy.

As she neared the village, she saw an old woman sitting under a tree, with a basket in front of her, filled with boxes of matches, shoe-strings, tapes, papers of pins, and such like things.

"Buy some matches, little lady, please," said the poor woman, as Lutie stopped a moment to look at her. "I haven't sold enough all day to buy a loaf of bread; and I'm awful hungry."

"Oh, I can't buy anything," said Lutie; "I'm going to spend my money at the fair;" and then she ran away, as fast as her little feet would carry her, until she reached the bridge, near the village. There she stopped and looked back.

"If I should buy some of that poor woman's matches, and help her to get a loaf of bread," she said to herself, "'twould be the same as if I'd done it to the blessed Saviour."

She hesitated a little while, jingling the money in her purse, and looking wistfully towards the building in which the fair was being held. Then she turned and went slowly back.

"Buy some matches, my pretty dear," said the old woman, as the child drew near to her.

Lutie went up to her, and putting the purse into her hand, said: "Take this, poor woman, and buy yourself some supper." And then, before the woman could give her anything from her basket, she ran away.

"Mamma," said Lutie that night, when her mother came to kiss her before she went to sleep, "I don't mind about the fair one bit. To lie here and think that I've done a kind thing for the Lord Jesus to-day, makes me happier than if May and I had all the pretty things in the world."

How sweet this was! That little girl was imitating Paul's model, by showing *earnestness* in *beginning* her Christian life.

I will close this part of our sermon, with some sweet lines which embrace all that I have been trying to say on this subject. They are headed—

TEACH ME TO LIVE.

"Teach me that hardest lesson—*how to live*,
 To serve Thee in the darkest paths of life;
 Arm me for conflict now; fresh vigor give,
 And make me more than conqueror in the strife,

> "Teach me to live for self and sin no more;
>   But use the time remaining to me yet,
> Not mine own pleasure seeking as before,
>   Wasting no precious hours in vain regret.
>
> "Teach me to live! No idler let me be,
>   But in thy service hand and heart employ;
> Prepared to do thy bidding cheerfully;
>   Be this my highest and my holiest joy.
>
> "Teach me to live! and find my life in Thee,
>   Looking from earth and earthly things away;
> Let me not falter, but untiringly
>   Press on, and gain new strength and power each day.
>
> "Teach me to live! with kindly words for all;
>   Wearing no cold, repulsive brow of gloom;
> Waiting with cheerful patience till Thy call
>   Summons my spirit to its heavenly home."

These lines well express the earnestness with which St. Paul *began* his Christian life.

But *secondly, we see what a model of earnestness St. Paul was—in the way in which he*—CONTINUED—*his Christian life, after it was begun.*

We see this illustrated in the words of our text, in which he says: "*I press towards the mark.*" In the use of this language, St. Paul has reference to the public games, which were practiced in his days.

One of these was the game of racing. A long race-course was prepared, in one of the public squares of the great cities. At the end of this race-course, the laurel crown, to be given to the victor, was hung on the top of a high pole, so that all the racers could keep it in sight. The men who were going to join in the race, would put off their unnecessary clothing, and with their loins girded, would stand all ready to start, as soon as the signal was given. The moment they heard the signal—they would be off. Each one would keep that crown in view, while, forgetting everything else, he would strain every nerve, as he "pressed toward the mark," in the earnest endeavor to win the prize.

And when St. Paul said: "I press toward the mark," he meant to say that he compared his Christian life to a race. The mark, or prize, at the end of this race, which he kept in view, and towards which he was pressing all the time, was the crown of life and glory which Jesus has promised to give to all His faithful followers. This was what he meant when he said—"I press toward the mark." And in doing this, he showed the earnestness with which he was *continuing* the Christian life which he had begun.

We see the earnestness of St. Paul in *the way in which he preached;* and in *the way in which he worked.*

This great apostle showed his earnestness in *the way in which he preached.*

In writing to the Corinthians, about his preaching, he said: "*I determined not to know anything among you save Jesus Christ, aud Him crucified.*" He felt that he was sent to preach the gospel, or to tell men that the only way of salvation was through Jesus Christ. And *this*—was all he had to say to them.

Wherever he went, he had nothing else to tell but what was a *new* story then, though we call it now,—"the old, old story, of Jesus and His love." He never got tired of telling this story, all his days.

Some ministers give up preaching about "Jesus

and Him crucified;" and preach about history, and philosophy, and science and learning. But St. Paul never did this. And if he had lived right straight on through all the past eighteen hundred years, to the present time, he never would have changed the subject of his preaching. And he showed his earnestness in the way in which he preached.

But then, he showed it, too, by *the way in which he worked*. He spent his life in taking one missionary journey after another, till he had gone all round the world, as it was then known. And in pursuing these journeys, no one ever worked harder, or suffered more than he did. *This* is his own account of what he passed through in carrying out his Christian life, after it was begun. In his Epistle to the Corinthians, he says that he had been—"in labors more abundant, in stripes above measure, in prisons more frequent, in deaths oft. Of the Jews five times received I forty stripes save one. Thrice I was beaten with rods, once I was stoned, thrice I suffered shipwreck, a night and a day have I been in the deep; In journeyings often, in perils of waters, in perils of robbers, in perils by mine own countrymen, in perils by the heathen, in perils in the city, in perils in the wilderness, in perils in the sea, in perils among false brethren; In weariness and painfulness, in watchings often, in hunger and thirst, in fastings often, in cold and nakedness. Beside those things that are without, that which cometh upon me daily, the care of all the churches."

How great his earnestness must have been, to make him willing to go on all his days, suffering and laboring in such a way as this! In all the history of the church, from the days of St. Paul to the present time, I suppose there never has been another servant of Christ, who has passed through such an experience as he had. And as we think of the way in which he worked, we see how well he may be spoken of as the model of earnestness!

We may finish this part of our sermon with an illustration of earnestness, which may be called—

The Earnest Boy. In a little town in Germany, lived a poor widow. Her husband had died, leaving her nothing but the care of her three young sons. She found it very hard to support herself and them; yet she managed to do so, sparingly, but honestly. The two elder sons at last were old enough to leave home, and do something for their support: but the youngest remained with his mother still, and went daily to school.

Then the war broke out, and there was a time of great trouble and distress. Collections were made, all over the country, for thousands of the poor wounded soldiers, and the cry for help reached even to the little town where this poor widow lived. The list of contributors to this work of mercy was carried from house to house. One day, the collectors called at this poor widow's house. She had given her little mite to them, and they were going away, when her little boy took up a pen, and quietly wrote down his name on the list for three dollars; and then counted out the money into the hand of the astonished collector. This was more than many of the people in the town, who were quite well off, had contributed. And where did this money come from? For several years this little fellow had been longing to own a watch; and every time that his mother, or one of his elder brothers, would give him a small piece of money, he would put it carefully away. When he got enough pennies, he would change them into a silver piece, and great was his joy when his money had increased so much that he had his first whole dollar. But now, at last, it had increased to three dollars; and very soon he was expecting to have the great pleasure, to which he had been looking forward so long,—the pleasure of feeling that he had *his own watch in his pocket.* But he gave up this long-expected pleasure, and readily parted with all his money, in the earnestness of his desire to help the poor wounded soldiers.

This was real noble in that boy. It showed that he had just the same spirit which St. Paul had, when he was such an example of earnestness in his Christian life. It was this earnestness of spirit, which led the great apostle of the Gentiles to continue his Christian life, in the same way in which he had begun it.

But, in the third place, we see what a model of earnestness St. Paul was, when we look at the RESULTS WHICH— FOLLOWED—*from his Christian life.*

We see one of the results of St. Paul's earnest life, in his *labors* for the cause of Christ. His missionary journeys took him to the utmost ends of the world, as it was then known—east, and west, and north, and south. Probably no man ever preached the Gospel to such multitudes of people as St. Paul did. If we only knew how many thousands, and hundreds of thousands of persons there were, who had heard the Gospel from him, how surprising it would be!

And if we could have an account of the multitudes of people who were converted by his preaching; and then of the multitudes who were converted *by them*, and so on, all the way down, from that day to this, we should no doubt find numbers of Christians laboring in the church to-day, as the direct result of his labors, before he went to heaven eighteen hundred years ago. While he was still alive St. Paul said that the Gospel "had been preached to *every creature under heaven*," and this was mainly the result of his labors. And when we think of all this, we may well say, that he was indeed a model of earnestness, in view of the results which followed from his labors.

But we see the result of St. Paul's earnestness in his *writings*, as well as in his labors.

There are twenty-one Epistles in the New Testament. Of these St. Paul wrote *fourteen*, or two-thirds of the whole. These Epistles are filled with the precious truths of the Gospel. Ever since St. Paul wrote them, ministers of the Gospel have been taking texts from these Epistles, and preaching sermons from them. And through these sermons multitudes of souls have been converted; those in ignorance have been instructed; those in trouble have been comforted; those who were doubting have been encouraged, and an amount of good has been done, which will never be known, till that great day of judgment shall come, when all that is now secret shall be made known.

And so, when we think of the results of St. Paul's Christian life, both in his *labors* and in his *writings*, we may well speak of him as a model of earnestness.

Now let us look at some illustrations of earnestness in the Christian life, and the good that has resulted from it. We may begin with the story of—

An Earnest Child, and the Good she did. A young man who had graduated at college, was on his way home, riding in a stage-coach. Among the passengers in that stage, was a Christian mother with her little girl, who was beginning very young to be a Christian. The young man took the little girl upon his knee, and tried to get into conversation with her. He was pleased with her bright, innocent face, and was very much struck with her intelligence. All at once the little one turned the full gaze of her sparkling eyes, directly towards her new-found acquaintance, and asked the simple, touching question: *"Does you love God?"* That young man was living a giddy, careless life. The little one's question touched him very much. He tried to turn the conversation to some other subject. But the child seemed to take no interest in what he was saying; and every little while she would repeat her question: "Does you love God?" He could not answer the question, for he seldom went to church, and thought little about God.

Before long, the stage reached the home of the little girl and her mother, and they got out, while the young man continued his journey.

He had not answered the little girl's earnest question; but he could not get rid of it. Wherever he went, it followed him. The last thing at night, as he laid his head on his pillow; and the first thing in the morning, as he opened his eyes on the light of another day, it would come up to him afresh. It made him think of his sinfulness in not loving God. It led him to repentance, and he never rested till he became a Christian, and made up his mind to study for the ministry.

Several years after this, that young man was passing through the same part of the country. He stopped at the home of the little one, whom God had made the means of his conversion. He met at the door, a lady looking very sad, and recognized her as the mother of the little girl, with whom he had travelled in the coach. He asked to see her child. With the tears streaming down her cheeks, she said:

"My precious one has been taken from me. She has gone to dwell in heaven with Jesus, whom she loved; and has left nothing behind her, but these little toys, which I keep as sacred to her memory."

"Pardon me, my friend," said the young man, whose eyes were also filled with tears; "but you are mistaken there. These toys are not *all* that your darling little one has left behind. Do you remember the earnest question she put to me, as we were riding in the stage together: 'Does you love God?' That question led to my conversion. I am about to enter the ministry; and whatever good may follow from my future life in this blessed work, will be due to your darling child. It will be the result of the earnestness with which she pressed on me that question."

Our next story may be called—

A Missionary's Earnestness, and What it Led to. One hot day in July, 1839, Dr. Hamlin, of the American Mission at Constantinople, and so long at the head of Robert's College in that city, while passing by the Custom House, saw a crowd of people gathered there. Forcing his way through it, he found a poor sailor, lying by the side of the wall, apparently dying of cholera.

"Do you speak English?" asked Dr. Hamlin.

"Yes," said the man, following the word with an oath.

"Are you an Englishman, or an American?"

"American," he replied with another oath.

Still more terrible curses showed that profanity had become his mother-tongue.

Dr. Hamlin secured assistance, and had him removed to the home of one of the missionaries.

For several weeks he was kindly nursed, and taken care of by the missionaries. Then he recovered. One morning he called on Dr. Hamlin to say good-by, as he was about to sail for Boston. Lingering for a moment at the door, he said, with great feeling:

"I never shall forget your kindness to me, Dr. Hamlin. I have been a very wicked man, and have done all the evil in the world I could. But now, by the help of God, I am going to turn round, and try to do all the good I can. God bless you! Good-by."

Three years afterwards Dr. Hamlin received a letter from him, which read thus:

"DEAR DR. HAMLIN:—Thank God I still live. I am here workin', and blowin' the Gospel-trumpet on the Eri Kanal."

When the Rev. Dr. Goodell, the missionary, saw this letter, he asked that he might begin the answer to it, and taking a sheet of paper, he wrote as follows:—

"DEAR MR. BROWN:—Blow away, brother! blow! Yours in blowing the same Gospel-trumpet,
"WILLIAM GOODELL."

Twenty-five years after this, Dr. Hamlin was dining one day, at a hotel in the city of Paris, when an American gentleman came up to him, and said: "Sir, I am just from Honolulu, in the Sandwich Islands. I knew a man there by the name of Brown, who is acting as missionary, or Bible reader, and who has done a wonderful amount of good among the sailors. He can go anywhere, and everywhere, among them. He told me that he was once a wretched blaspheming sinner, dying in the streets of Constantinople, when you kindly took him to your home, and was the means of saving both his body and his soul. This seemed to me too strange to be true. Was it so?" asked the gentleman, "or is it only a sailor's yarn?"

"It *is* a sailor's yarn, indeed," said Dr. Hamlin, "but it is a good yarn, and every word of it is true. And I am glad to know that in showing kindness to that poor blaspheming sinner, I was enlisting a trumpeter who not only sounded the Gospel-trumpet on what he called the 'Eri Kanal,' but is now doing the same from the Atlantic coast to the Golden Gate of California, and among the islands of the Pacific."

This faithful missionary was imitating Paul's model of earnestness; and we see what great good resulted from his labors.

I have just one other illustration of the good results that follow from earnestness in the missionary work. This was given by a Chinese convert, whose name was Paul Ah Fat. He lived at New Bendigo in Australia. This story may be called—

Before and Now. This Chinaman was asked, one day, what good had been done by missionary work, in seven years among his countrymen, at New Bendigo. He gave his answer in this way—

"*Before* missionary come, no one understood God's word. Good many work Sunday all same as week-day. *Now*, no work done on Sunday, by my countrymen at New Bendigo. No matter how poor, every one no work on Sunday.

"*Before* missionary come, all worship idols. Idols in every house. *Now*, only ten houses and stores at New Bendigo with idols in them.

"*Before* missionary come, nearly all Chinese steal fowls, steal everything. *Now*, no more steal; every one work; go get job.

"*Before* missionary come, Chinaman learn to fight every night. *Now*, none learn to fight. All learn God's word.

"*Before* missionary come, no Chinaman read God's word; he not know, not care. *Now*, good many people like read God's word.

"*Before* missionary come, all have too much time; nothing to do. *Now*, no more waste time. When no work, love to read the Bible.

"*Before* missionary come, good many make fun of God's word, and laugh. Papers put up outside of stores, make laugh at Christian. When men baptized, papers put up on door of house to make laugh. *Now*, heathen men no more make fun. Feel Christian right. Like to be one. All quiet now."

Here we see the blessed results that follow from earnestness in Christian work.

And when we think of the way in which St. Paul *began* his Christian life; of the way in which he *continued* it; and of the *results* which followed from it, we may well speak of him as a model of earnestness.

Let us pray God for grace to follow the example of St. Paul's earnestness in our Christian life and labors. Then we shall be useful and happy while we are here, and at last, "we shall come to those unspeakable joys which God has prepared for such as unfeignedly love Him, through Jesus Christ our Lord, Amen."

JESUS, THE MODEL OF PERFECTION.

"*Made perfect.*"—HEBREWS v : 9.

T. PAUL, the writer of this Epistle, is speaking here of Jesus, our blessed Saviour. He tells us what He is to be to His people, and what He is to do for them. Jesus will make all His people perfect in heaven, though He does not make any of them perfect here, in this world. Jesus Himself, is the only perfect Being who ever lived on our earth. And in finishing this course of sermons, on "Bible Models," I know not how to conclude it better than by considering Jesus as—

The Model of Perfection. His doings are perfect. His thoughts and plans are perfect. Everything connected with Him, is perfect. He is like a jewel with many surfaces. Each is different from the rest, but all are perfect in their kind. He is a perfect Friend; a perfect Guide; a perfect Protector; and as embracing everything else in one, He is a *perfect Saviour*.

And *this* is the point of view, from which we desire to look at the character of Jesus. He is the model of perfection as a Saviour. And when we come to examine this model, there are three things in it, which show the perfection of Jesus as our Saviour. We see it *first—in the perfect example He sets us. Secondly, in the perfect help He affords us. And thirdly, in the perfect home He is preparing for us.*

In the *first place, we see the perfection of Jesus as our Saviour—in the*—PERFECT EXAMPLE—He sets us.

We have a great many examples in the Bible that are very good. Noah was a good example of obedience; for when he was building the ark, we are told that—"all that the Lord commanded him so did he." Job was a good example of patience; Abraham of faith; Moses of meekness; David of piety; and Peter of courage. But none of these were perfect examples. They all failed, at one time or other, in their lives. Yes, and they each failed in the *very thing*, for which he was spoken of as an example. But it is different with Jesus. He is an example not of *one* point of character only, but of *every* point. And He is perfect in them all. He never failed in any of them. He said, when He was on earth—"I came down from heaven, not to do mine own will, but the will of Him that sent me." God, His Father in heaven, is perfect in all things. Jesus came down from heaven to tell us about His Father, and to show us what a perfect Saviour should be. He has left us an example of perfect submission to His Father's will,—of perfect obedience to His Father's commandments, —an example of perfect humility,—of perfect gentleness,—of perfect patience,—of perfect courage,— and a perfect example of everything that we are expected to do, and to be. And, we are required to follow His example; and to endeavor,—"daily to tread in the blessed steps of His most holy life." This was what St. Paul was doing when he said: "For me to live is Christ." He meant by this to say, that he was trying to follow the perfect example which Jesus had set. His aim was to—"have the same mind which was in Christ;" to think, and feel, and speak, and act like Him in all things. And if we wish to be true Christians, *this* is what we must try to do. We cannot do this of ourselves, but we can all do it, by the help of God's grace. And the sooner we begin to do this, the easier, and the better it will be for us. Let us all begin at once, and try to follow the perfect example which Jesus has set for us.

Here are some incidents that illustrate this part of our subject. The first we may call—

Copying a Blot. "Mother," asked a little boy, who was looking round for a good example, "which, of all the big boys I know, would you like for me to pattern after?"

"Which should you think?" asked his mother. "You know the boys better than I do."

The little fellow thought awhile. Then he said: "Well, there's Dan Park; he's a good fellow, but he smokes; there's Bill Jones, he swears; Sam Jay, he drinks; Bill Parker, he has an ugly temper; Jim Wood, he's lazy, and hates study; Charley Doe, he goes a-fishing on Sunday; and Tom Smith, he tells lies. Mother, there isn't one of them, that if I copy, I shouldn't have to copy a blot from."

"Then my dear," said his mother, "suppose you

let them all go, and take the blessed Saviour, for your pattern. He came on purpose, as the apostle says, to—'leave us an example that we should follow his steps.' And we can do this with entire safety. In Him you will find a perfect example. And there are no blots to copy here."

Our next story may be called—

A Christian in Little Things. A boy, named Willie, was about twelve years old. One winter there was a good deal of religious interest, in the church which he attended. Willie had been trying to be a Christian, for some time. The season for Confirmation in that church was approaching, and he expressed an earnest desire to be confirmed, and join the church. He was rather young to take such an important step. His parents were earnest Christians. They felt sure that Willie understood this matter, and that he was trying, with all his heart, to be a Christian, and they consented to his being confirmed.

This solemn step was taken, and the next Sunday he went forward to the holy Communion, for the first time. That was the happiest day Willie had ever spent. And yet, in the midst of his happiness, he felt that he had taken solemn vows upon himself, and that he would need the help of God, to enable him to keep those vows. In the prayer, which he offered, before going to bed that night, Willie showed how earnest his desire was, to be a *true* Christian. He did not know that his mother was near him then; but she was, and she heard him offer this prayer: "O God, make me a Christian in *little* things." He meant by this, that he wanted God to help him to be

JESUS, THE MODEL OF PERFECTION. 425

a Christian, not only on Sunday, and at church, but on week-days too; at home, at school, and at play. Wherever he was, and whatever he was doing, he wished to keep the example of Jesus before him, and to be asking himself the question—How would Jesus have me feel? and what would Jesus have me say, and do? And, like this dear boy, we must try to be Christians in *little* things, if we hope to be true Christians.

A young man had a situation as clerk, in a mercantile house, in one of our large cities. In writing home to his mother one day, he said: "I have been connected in business, at different times, with a number of merchants, all of them members of Christian churches; but, I must say, that Mr. Johnson, with whom I am now employed, is the best of them all, in the way in which he governs himself by his religion, in all his business affairs. I take great pleasure in watching how faithfully he does this. I must say of him, that he is *a Christian—all over.*" It was a great honor to this good merchant, that one of his clerks, should feel obliged to speak thus of him. Now let us remember these last two illustrations; and let us all try to follow the example, which Jesus sets us, in such a way, that we may be *Christians in little things*—and *Christians all over.*

Jesus is a *perfect Saviour*, in the first place, *because He sets us a perfect example.*

He is so, *in the second place, because He gives us—* PERFECT HELP.

There are three things about Jesus, which make Him a perfect Helper. One of these is—that He is

—a NEAR *helper*. Many persons, when they are in need of help, can think of their friends at home, who would be glad to help them. But they are far away, and it is impossible for them to do anything in the way of helping. There was the Prodigal Son. He went off into a far country, and spent all his money, "in riotous living." Then he hired himself out to a man, who sent him into the fields to feed swine. He was so hungry, that he was ready to eat the husks on which the swine were feeding. But no one gave him anything to eat, and he was in danger of starving. Then he thought of his home, and said to himself: "How many hired servants of my father's, have bread enough and to spare, while I perish with hunger." He needed help. His father could have given him just the help he needed, if he had only been near him; but he was far away, and help from him was impossible.

And it often happens so now. We are in need of help. We have kind, loving friends. They would be glad to help us, if they were only near. But they are far away, and it is impossible for them to do anything for our relief. But how different it is with Jesus! He is in every place. He is *always near*. "He is a God"—a Helper—"at hand, and not afar off." And this is one thing that makes Him a perfect Helper—*He is* NEAR *to help*.

Another thing that does this—is *that He is*—ABLE TO HELP. It sometimes happens that though our friends are near us, in our troubles, yet they are not able to help us. Take an illustration. There is a very rich family. They have a daughter—their only

JESUS, THE MODEL OF PERFECTION.

child. She is taken sick with scarlet fever. The doctor is sent for. He does all that is in his power to do; but he finds that he cannot save the child's life. Other physicians are called in. They are told to spare no expense. Thousands of dollars would be freely spent, if only by any means, that dreadful disease could be checked. But the doctors say that to do this is impossible. They have no ability to render the help that is needed. In spite of all that they can do—the child must die.

But it is not so with Jesus. Nothing is impossible with Him. His ability to help is perfect. St. Paul tells us that—"He is able to save," and to help—"*unto the uttermost.*" "He is able to do exceeding abundantly above all that we can ask, or think." "Nothing is too hard for the Lord." Nothing is impossible with Him. He is a perfect Helper, because He is able to help in every time of need.

And then, there is one other thing which shows what a perfect Helper Jesus is, and that is—that He is *willing to help*. As one of our beautiful Collects says: "He is more ready to hear than we to pray, and is wont to give more than either we desire or deserve." We read in the Bible that God—"is ready to pardon;"—"ready to forgive;"—"ready to save;" that—"He waiteth to be gracious." He says of His people,—"Before they call, I will answer; and while they are yet speaking, I will hear." And then He says to each of His people—"I *will* help thee." These passages show us, how willing He is to help us when we are in trouble. And when we put these things together, and think how *near* He is to help;

how *able* He is to help; and how *willing* He is to help, we may well say that He is indeed—a *perfect Helper*.

I have one illustration to give, of each of the three points just spoken of. The first story shows Jesus to us as—

A Near Helper. The incident related in this story, took place many years ago, in the military academy at West Point. The Rev. Charles P. McIlvaine, afterwards Bishop of Ohio, was then the chaplain of the academy. While he was chaplain there, a revival of religion took place among the students. Many of them were converted, and became Christians. Among these was a young man, whose name was Leonidas Polk. He afterwards became the Bishop of one of our Southern States, and was eminently useful there. Before his conversion, he was a very careless young man, and had neglected his studies. But as soon as he became a Christian, he gave up those careless habits, and was known as one of the most diligent, and industrious students in the academy. But he could not, all at once, make up for the studies he had neglected. Not long after this, the final examination in the studies of that year, came on. He was very anxious about this examination. The fear that he might fail, and so lose his place in the class, and bring disgrace on the cause of Christ, with which he was now connected, made him feel very uncomfortable. The branch of study that he had particularly neglected, was that of mathematics. The examination began. He was called to the blackboard, and a problem was given him to solve. It was one he had never studied. He knew nothing about it. He stood there utterly at a loss to know what to do. The thought of the disgrace which failure would bring upon himself, and the reproach to the cause of Christ, distressed him greatly. He lifted up his heart in earnest, silent prayer, to his new-found Friend in heaven, for help. Then he picked up the chalk, and began to work upon the problem, but he was all in the dark about it. Presently he saw his way clear to make a beginning, and went slowly on, till he got through. But he was afraid it might not be right, and felt anxious to know what the professor would say about it. Presently, his turn came to be examined. He went on, and explained what he had done. While doing this, he saw the professors whispering to each other, and he feared they had found something wrong about it. But he got through with his work, and then waited, in fear, to hear what would be said about it.

"Mr. Polk," said the professor in charge, "where did you get that solution?"

"Is it not right, sir?"

"Right!" he replied. "It is not only right, but it is the most beautiful demonstration of that problem ever given. It is new, sir. *It does not appear in any of the books.*"

This was wonderful. That young man needed help, in the examination-room. He prayed to Jesus for it, and found Him *near to help*, even there. Truly He *is* a perfect Helper.

Our next story shows that He is—

An ABLE *Helper*. A little ragged boy, named Jim, belonging to a mission school, received one day, a card on which were printed the words—"*Mighty to*

Save." He put it in the pocket of his ragged jacket, carried it home, and at night, before going to sleep, he tried to spell it out, but he could not understand it. He resolved to ask his teacher about it next Sunday, and he did so. Jim was a weak-minded little fellow. The rude boys in the court called him—"Soft-headed Jim." Yet he was trying to be a Christian, and was a very good-natured boy.

His teacher tried to show him that—"Mighty to Save" referred to Jesus, and that the meaning of those words was, that He would put His arms round us, and would always help us when we were trying to do right. Jim made up his mind to try and do some good at home, and hoped that the one—"Mighty to Save" would help him. So when he woke the next morning, he was thinking how he should begin. His father and mother were both drunkards. They lay there sleeping heavily. His little brother Tom, whose legs had been broken by his father, in one of his drunken sprees, and who after weeks of suffering, was just able to sit up, was leaning on his elbows, longing for something to eat.

"Jim," said little Tom, "I'm awful hungry. Couldn't yer get me something to eat?"

"I wish I knowed where to get it, Tom," said Jim. Just then a thought came into his mind. "Wait a bit, Tom. I shouldn't wonder if I could do it," said Jim. "I've just got 'quainted with one that can help."

Then he went over, to the other corner of the room, and kneeling down, he offered this simple prayer: "Oh, dear Jesus, mighty to save, will yer show a poor feller how to get a few crusts of bread, or somethin' for his little brother, who is sick and starvin'? Do, dear Jesus, and do it quick. Amen." Then he ran out of doors, and got into the street. The pavements were covered with snow. A lady opened the front door of one of the houses, and said to her little girl, "Who can we get to clear the snow off the pavement?"

"Oh, ma'am, can I clear off the snow?" said little Jim.

"You! why you are such a little fellow?"

"Yes'um, I'm little, but I'm strong. And Him that's mighty to save, is going to help me."

The lady did not know what he meant.

"Come into the hall, my boy," she said. "It's too cold to stand talking here." While Jim was warming himself by the stove, she asked him what he meant by what he had just said. In a simple, earnest way, Jim tried to explain his meaning. While he was speaking the lady's heart was touched, and her eyes were filled with tears. Then she went into the kitchen, and returned with a lunch. "Eat this, little Jim," she said, "and then you can clean the pavement."

"I will clean the pavement first, ef you please, ma'am. I'm in a hurry to get back to poor Tom."

The pavement was soon cleaned, and Jim returned to the door. There he received a package, which the lady said was to pay for his service.

Jim ran home, as fast as he could go. Tom saw him enter the room, carrying a bundle. "Oh, Jim, hev yer got something for me?" he asked.

Jim opened the box, and as he saw the nice things in it, he had to shout for joy. As for Tom, tears and smiles were chasing each other, over his pale, eager face; he clasped his hands for joy, and asked: "Oh, Jim, where did yer get all these good things?" and then his voice grew sad, as he added: "Jim, yer a good brother, an awful good brother, and I love yer; but yer didn't steal them, did you? Remember the commandment yer learned at school, and taught me."

"No, little Tom, I'd starve 'fore I'd steal; an' Tom, much as I love yer, I'd rather y'ud starve too, cause then we'd go up there, you know," said he, pointing upwards. "Eat away, Tom; Him that's mighty to save, helped me to get these."

"Where does he live? Is he an angel?" asked Tom, while eagerly devouring one of the nice sandwiches which Jim had brought.

"He's better and stronger than all the angels. He's the King of heaven," said Jim, reverently.

"Why, Jim, where could you a seen him?" asked Tom, in a great wonder.

In answer to this Jim explained about the One mighty to save; how he had gone to Him, and prayed for help, to find bread for his starving brother. "An' Tom," said he, "I'll never be afraid of nothin' while I live—no nothin'."

"Not of pa knockin' yer over the head, and throwin' sticks, and the poker, and the ugly iron chair at yer? Oh, Jim, ye'll be afraid of that, won't yer?"

"No, never! Why, Tommy, didn't I tell yer that the arm of Him that is mighty to save is aroun' me? Ef father sh'ud kill me," and his voice sank lower—"it wouldn't be me layin' here with the blood spurtin' on the white face and the rags. I'd—I'd be—oh, Tommy, I'd be up in the arms of Jesus. Just think of that! ain't it comfortin', awful comfortin', to think of Him that's mighty to save?"

The boys thought their parents were fast asleep, but they had been awake for some time with their eyes shut, listening to all the little ones were saying.

Tom lay back on his bed, feeling very comfortable after eating three nice sandwiches.

Jim said: "Let's save these big slices, with the nice meat 'tween 'em, for father and mother."

"I'm willin'," said Tom, "but they'd rather have somethin' to drink."

"Poor father! poor mother!" said Jim.

"Does yer pity 'em, Jim?" asked Tom.

"Pity 'em, and love 'em too," said Jim.

"How *can* yer, when they're so cruel to us,—beatin', and jawin', and poundin' everythin' aroun'?"

"I do, 'cause I ought," said Jim; "an' Tom, mebbe Him that's mighty to save, will do somethin' for them. I'm prayin' for them."

"He wouldn't for them, Jim; they're too bad."

"Teacher said He'd save to the *uttermost*. I can't remember all she said; but I think *they's the uttermost*, an' ef Him that's mighty to save 'ud put His arms about 'em, He'd lift 'em up. But, Tom, I'm goin' out now, to get somethin' for father, and mother, with the money that kind lady gave me."

Before going out, he noticed that his father and mother had turned their faces to the wall, but he didn't know that they were weeping bitterly. While the boy was out buying some coal, and coffee, and milk, and sugar, they lay there thinking of their wicked lives, and of those wonderful words—"*Mighty to save.*"

Jim came back. The hot coffee was soon ready. He and Tom had drank a cup of it, and were waiting for their father and mother to wake up.

"I wish they'd wake up, Tom."

"Mebbe they'll pound you when they do."

"I ain't 'fraid, yer know, with the Mighty One to help me."

"Jim! little Jim!" his father called. He hastened to him, thinking something strange had happened, for his father had never spoken to him so gently. "Jim, God bless you! Jim, Him that's mighty to save is near me, boy. I'm going to follow Him too." And so he did. And the mother did the same.

This led to a blessed change in that family. It became a very happy family, and it was all brought about by the help which Jesus gave to that dear little boy, Jim.

I have one other story, much shorter than the last. This shows us that Jesus is—

A Willing Helper. A soldier, who had lived a long life in sin, lay on a hospital cot, sick, and full of trouble. A kind nurse stood near. She saw that the patient was restless, and asked what she could do to make him feel better.

"I don't know: I want something," answered the sick man. "I feel dreadfully."

The nurse brought a cup of water, saying, "Wouldn't you like a drink?"

The soldier took the cup in his trembling hand, but said: "No, this isn't what I want."

"It is almost time for the surgeon to come," said the nurse kindly. "Perhaps he may be able to do something for you."

JESUS, THE MODEL OF PERFECTION. 435

"Well, he can't do much for me," sighed the poor man. "It ain't such help that I need. Oh, I'm a dreadful wicked man; and the way before me is dark—all dark."

The nurse was a Christian; and by this time she understood what was the matter with the patient; so she sat down beside his bed, and asked him if he wouldn't like to hear what the Bible has to say to sinful men, who want something which the surgeon, or the nurse, cannot give.

"Oh, yes!" moaned the sick man, "that's it; but there's no use in it. It's a long time since I've had anything to do with the Bible, and I'm the greatest sinner in the world; and it's all dark ahead—*very dark!*"

"But Jesus is always able and willing to help poor sinners. Now listen to what He says," and opening the Bible, at the third chapter of St. John, she began to read. The man listened attentively, until she had finished the sixteenth verse: "God so loved the world, that He gave His only begotten Son, that whosoever believeth in Him should not perish, but have everlasting life."

"Stop!" said he. "Read that again."

She read it again.

"But what does that—'*whosoever*'—mean?" the sick man eagerly inquired.

"It means," said the nurse, "anybody or everybody."

"No, not everybody. Not such a sinner as I am," said he.

"Yes, just so," was her answer.

"One so vile and hardened?"

"It is just such that Jesus came to save. There are none so wicked, or so low, and so miserable but that they can have Jesus if they want Him. 'Whosoever' is willing, may be saved."

"Read that verse once more?" and the sick man looked into the nurse's face with the most intense earnestness. When she stopped, his face lighted up with hope and joy as he exclaimed: "'*Whosoever* believeth'—then it *does* mean me! Oh! the *wonderful willingness* of Jesus to save, and to help!"

But, *in the third place*, *He is a perfect Saviour*, because *He prepares for His people*—a PERFECT HOME—*in heaven*.

He will make their bodies perfect, after the pattern of His own glorious body, as it appeared on the Mount of Transfiguration. He will make their souls perfect. They will be entirely free from sin forever. He will put them in a perfect home. Before He left this world, Jesus said to His disciples,—"I go to prepare a place for you." If we wish to know what sort of a place this will be, we must read the last two chapters of the book of Revelation. There we have a full description of it. It is called—"the heavenly city—the New Jerusalem." It will be a city such as no one ever saw before. Its gates will be made of pearl. Its walls and its foundations, will be made of jewels, or precious stones. Its streets will all be of gold, as clear as crystal. The throne of God will be in it. The angels will be our companions there. No pain; no sickness; no crying; and no sin will be there. And in that blessed place we shall have our home forever.

We shall be better off then, than the angels will be. For Jesus will wear our nature, amidst the glory of that heavenly state, but He will not wear the nature of angels, and this must bring us nearer to Him than they can ever be.

And then, we shall be able to sing the song of praise—"to Him who hath loved us, and *washed us from our sins in His own blood*." But the angels can never sing that song; because they have not been washed in that blood. They have heard about—"the riches of redeeming love;" but they can never experience the joy which that love imparts. And so we need not be surprised, when we hear some good people say, that they would not be willing to change places with the angels. The happiness which Jesus—the perfect Saviour—is preparing for His people in heaven, is greater than that which the angels will have there. Here are some sweet lines on this subject. They may be called—

THE HIGHEST PLACE IN HEAVEN.

"It may be wrong—but yet I would not be
An angel, formed in spotless purity;
It may be strange, yet with my sins and cares,
I would not change this lot of mine for theirs.
They, in the light of God have ever shone,
Yet joys are *mine*, which they have never known.
They, since He made them first, have ever been
Viewing His love, no earthly veil between;
In that, from age to age, they still abide,
Drink of its fulness, and are satisfied;
Yet even *they*, bend down new depths to see,
New depths of love, the love that rescued me.
Sweet are their songs, yet not to them is given
To sing the song of the redeemed in heaven.

Bright are their crowns, their harps are shining gold,
Yet in their hands no victor's palm they hold,
No wreath they wear, such as shall clasp the brow
Of those who pass through tribulation now.
Their robes are white, yet they shall fade, beside
The robes that Jesus' blood hath purified.
They near Him stand, but for His Bride alone,
Remains the place the nearest to His throne;
To her alone, it shall be given to rest
Upon His arm, and lean upon His breast.
Blest thought! Each conflict here, each bitter strife,
Shall then add sweetness to the cup of life.
Each heavy stroke, shall but his child prepare,
To be a pillar in His temple there;
There, where the things which darkly now I see,
Shall be in perfect light revealed to me.
Then be it so; a sinner though I am,
Yet will I boast and glory in the Lamb."

And when we think, of the three things, of which we have spoken, *the perfect example*, He sets before His people; *the perfect help, He affords them* in following that example; and *the perfect home*, He is preparing for them—we see how truly He may be spoken of as a perfect Saviour—or as—*the Model of Perfection.*

INDEX.

Abel, the Model Speaker, 7
Abel, a Model in the Matter of his Speaking, 8
Abel's Sacrifice spoke about Christ's Death, 9
Abel, a Model Speaker in the Manner of his Speaking, 13
Abel, by his Actions—a Loud Speaker, 16
A Good Deed Rewarded, 18
A Duke Taught by the Act of a Boy, 19
A Sailor's Act, and how Loudly it Spoke, 21
Abel by his Actions an *Effectual* Speaker, 21
A Safe Walk, 30
A Little Act Useful, 33
A Little Talk with Jesus, 40
A Noble Boy, 60
A Real Hero, 60
A Cure for Anger, 73
A Beautiful Example, or Lady Stanley, 76
Abraham a Model of Obedient Faith, 93

A Child's Faith in her Father, 96
Abraham's a Model of Conquering Faith, 98
A Sailor's Conquering Faith, 100
A Child's Faith, 101
Abraham's Faith a Comforting Faith, 105
A Wife's Comforting Faith, 107
A Hair-dresser's Faithfulness to God, 113
A Faithful Aunt, 120
A Faithful Mother, 120
A Brave Sailor-boy, 143
A Little Girl's Usefulness, 157
Abraham the Model of Faith, 88
Abraham the Model of Simple Faith, 89
A Christian Mother's Faith in God, 90
An Example of Thanksgiving, 184
A Little Girl's Lesson of Praise, 186
An Anchor to the Soul, 222
A Lesson from a Cow, 224
A Loving Friend, 235
A Little Hero, 236

INDEX.

A Patient Sufferer, 260
A Child's Life Saved by Trust, 264
A Poor Colored Woman's Confidence, 265
A Ray in the Dark, 274
A Scene in a Railway Station, 282
A Woman's Love, 299
A Young Lady's Decision, and the Good it did, 348
A Boy's Decision about Drink, 351
A Little Boy's Decision, 354
A Beautiful Father, 387
An Unselfish Boy, 396
An Unselfish Engineer, 397
A Brave Chinaman, 399
A Little Girl's Earnestness, 406
A Drunken Father brought to Jesus, 382
A Servant Girl's Greatness, 385
An Earnest Child, and the Good she did, 415
A Missionary's Earnestness, and its Result, 416
A Christian in Little Things, 424
A Christian All Over, 425
A Near Helper, 428
An Able Helper, 429
A Willing Helper, 434

Blood The, on the Door-posts, 11
Bless, and Curse Not, 33
Bessie and her Mission, 75
Brave Ben's Faithfulness to Himself, 116
Bishop Doane's Perseverance, 169
Bishop Randall's Perseverance, 170
Betsey Brown, or the Power of Kindness, 303

Christ's Sacrifice—Important to Talk about, 9
Christ's Sacrifice—Important because we cannot be Good without it, 9
Christ's Sacrifice—Important because we cannot be Happy without it, 10
Christ's Sacrifice—Making an Indian Happy, 10
Christ's Sacrifice—We cannot be Safe till we Know about it, 11
Conduct—The Effect of a Boy's, 23
Certainly I will be with thee, 205
Courage in telling the Truth, 268
Cardinal Woolsey's Honor from Man, 389
Copying a Blot, 423

Don't Worry, 137
David the Model of Praise, 176
David a Model of Praise for Temporal Blessings, 177
David a Model of Praise for Spiritual Blessings, 183
David a Model of Growing Praise, 189
David a Model of Universal Praise, 194
David the Model User of God's Word, 200

David Used God's Word for Meditation, 203
David Used God's Word for Light, 205
David Used God's Word for Cleansing, 210
David Used God's Word for Strength, 214
David Used God's Word for Joy, 218
David Used God's Word for Trust, 221
David Used God's Word for Peace, 224
David's Great Sin and its Results, 228
Damon and Pythias, 236
Do It, 276
Daniel the Model o. Decision, 338
Daniel's Decision kept him from Doing Wrong, 339
Decision in Telling the Truth, 341
Decision in Keeping the Sabbath, 343
Decision about Stealing, 345
Daniel's Decision Helping him to do Good, 346
Daniel's Decision Made him Successful, 353
Dr. Milne's Humility, 393

Example, The Influence of, 17
Enoch the Model Walker, 27
Example, The Power of, 44
Examples of the Use of God's Word, 203

Every-day Blessings, 179
Elijah the Model Reformer, 252
Elijah a Model of Promptness, 253
Elijah a Model of Patience, 258
Elijah a Model of Confidence, 262
Elijah a Model of Courage, 266
Elisha the Model Helper, 272
Elisha a Ready Helper, 273
Elisha a Kind Helper, 277
Elisha a Useful Helper, 281
Elisha a Powerful Helper, 285
Ebed-Melech the Model of Kindness, 296
Earnestness in Conquering a Bad Habit, 320

Faithfulness to God, A Worthy Example, 112
For Mamma, 162
Feasting on the Word, 204
Faith in Mother, 91
Faith The, of a Fireman's Daughter, 97
Faithfulness and its Reward, 125
Faithful in Obeying Orders, 327
Faithful to the Church, 329

Giving, The Profit of, 44
God the Model Giver, 360
God a Cheerful Giver, 361
God a Valuable Giver, 367
God a Self-denying Giver, 373
Give, and it shall be Given, 364
Given to the Poor, Lent to the Lord, 365

INDEX.

Helping a Fellow Up, 275
How Actions Speak, 21
How Example Speaks, 22
Hidden and Safe, 31
Home Piety, The Influence of, 69
How Children can show Piety at Home, 70
How she Knew, 92
Hold of Papa's Hand, 106
How a Student Resisted Temptation, 217
Helping and Thanking, 298
How God Works, 312
How Charley Built the Church, 318
How Kate was Taught to be Thankful, 181
How Many Mercies in a Year, 192
How the Bible kept Billy Jones from Stealing, 216
Him that is Mighty to Save, 429
Henry Martyn's Company in God's Presence, 133

I Can't Afford It, 118
It Says so in the Book, 72
I Like to Help People, 278
Influence The, of a Mother's Prayer, 334

Job the Model of Piety, 67
Job the Model of Home Piety, 68
Job the Model of Practical Piety, 74
Job the Model of Patient Piety, 77
Job the Model of Rewarded Piety, 81
Jamie the Gentleman, 174
Joseph the Model Realizer of God's Presence, 132
Joseph found Company in his Loneliness—from God's Presence, 132
Joseph found Comfort from God's Presence, 134
Joseph found Strength in God's Presence, 142
Joseph found Victory over Temptation in the Thought of God's Presence, 146
Jesus an Example of Patient Piety, 80
Jonathan the Model Friend, 232
Jonathan a Loving Friend, 233
Jonathan a Generous Friend, 240
Jonathan a Faithful Friend, 245
Jacob's Example in Giving, 360
Jamie Weston's Half Dollar, 374
John's Greatness—not in Long Life, 380
John's Greatness—not in Great Riches, 384
John's Greatness—not in the Honor that cometh from Man, 389
John's Greatness—in his Humility, 391
John's Greatness—in his Unselfishness, 395
John's Greatness—in his Courage, 398
Jesus the Model of Perfection, 421

INDEX. 443

Jesus gives Perfect Help, 425
Jesus a Near Helper, 426
Jesus an Able Helper, 426
Jesus Prepares a Perfect Home, 436

Kindness is Profitable, 308
Kindness Rewarded, 310
Kind Words, 279

Living Alone, 37
Little Scotch Granite, 127
Learning the Lesson of Praise, 190
Light Out of Darkness, 196
Light on the Traveller's Path, 206
Luther's Confidence, 264

Moses the Model of Faithfulness, 110
Moses Faithful to God, 110
Moses Faithful to Himself, 115
Moses Faithful to his Family, 119
Moses Faithful in All Things, 124
Minding Orders, 121

Never Out of Sight, 152
Nehemiah the Model Man of Business, 316
Nehemiah the Model of Earnestness, 317
Nehemiah the Model of Unselfishness, 326
Nehemiah the Model of Faithfulness, 326
Nehemiah a Model of Prayer, 330
Nearness The, of God, 137

Nature's Lesson of Humility, 392
Noah the Model Worker, 47
Noah a Ready Worker, 48
Noah a Persevering Worker, 51
Noah a Thorough Worker, 55
Noah a Courageous Worker, 59
Noah a Successful Worker, 63
Noble Engineer The, 244
Negro Servant, The Faithful, 251

Obedient Faith, 95
Obeying Orders, 58
One Day at a Time, 260

Pedler, A Little, 14
Please Help me, 43
Perseverance in Prayer, 53
Prayer Over Lessons, 63
Profitable Giving, 82
Piety Rewarded, or Telling the Truth, 84
Preaching a Sermon with a Shovel, 158
Poor Mary, 185
Prayer turned to Praise, 193
Promptness leading to Success, 254
Paying Rent by Prayer, 331

Recommendations, The Best, 13
Reward The, of Humility, 393

Shaking a Finger, The Good done by, 34
Sunshine the Best, 38
Strong Faith, or Light in Darkness, 38
Strings, Two, 42

INDEX.

Stroke on Stroke, 54
Susie's Faith, or the Tolling Bell, 103
Spoiling his Trade, 147
Samuel's Call, 154
Samuel a Model of Usefulness, 155
Shovel The, and the Snow-drift, 53
Secret The, 138
Soldier, The Dying, 226
Substitute, The Little, 238
Soldier, The Confederate, 243
Samuel a Model of Happiness, 159
Samuel a Model of Perseverance, 165
Samuel a Model of Honor, 172
Soldier, The Brave, 401
St. Paul the Model of Earnestness, 402
St. Paul Earnest in Beginning his Christian Life, 405
St. Paul Earnest in Continuing his Christian Life, 409
St. Paul Earnest in Preaching, 410
St. Paul Earnest in his Work, 411
St. Paul Earnest in the Results of his Life, 413
St. Paul Earnest in his Writings, 411
Singing-school, The Deacon's, 306

The Price Paid, 83
The Thought of God's Presence, 145

The Thought of God's Eye, 147
Those Four Words, 148
The Faithful Fisherman, 57
The Left-hand Letter, 64
The Power of Example, 69
True Comfort, 74
The Two Sailors, 162
The Christian's Triumph, 163
The Persevering Boy, 167
The Story of a Bootblack, 168
The True Gentleman, 173
The Contented Shepherd-boy, 178
The Little Scotch Boy, 179
The Causes for Thankfulness, 182
The Love of Jesus, 187
The Man with One Leg, 196
The Blessing of Affliction, 198
The Great Problem, 207
The Wonderful Lamp, 208
The Power of God's Word, 211
The Hidden Treasure, 218
The Secret of Happiness, 219
The Faithful Servant, 122
Thank God for the Bible, 220
The Watchword, 225
The Dying Soldier, 226
The Arab and his Horse, 246
The Faithful Comrade, 248
The Faithful Dog, 247
The Minute-boy, 255
Ten Minutes' Delay, 256
The Pansy, 261
The Brave Boy, 269
The Boy with his Toad, 280
The Good One Man can do, 284
The Cabin-boy Hero, 290
To Show Kindness is Easy, 297

INDEX.

The Baby's Sermon, 301
To Show Kindness is Useful, 303
The Beggar-boy and the Flower, 309
The Unselfish Brother, 322
The Unselfish Sailor, 323
The Dying Girl's Penny, 324
True Honesty, 350
The Story of a Grasshopper, 357
The "O. P. J. Account," or Jacob's Rule of Giving, 361
The Dowry, 362
The Baptized Pocketbook, 363
The Consecrated Diamonds, 369
The Bag of Farthings, 371
The Brave Boy, 381
The Name of the Good Samaritan, 390
The Humility of Jesus, 394
The Earnest Boy, 411
The Good Results of Missionary Work, 418
The Perfect Example of Jesus, 422
Teach me to Live, 408
The Mind Stayed on God, 139
The Companionship of Jesus, 134
The Presence of Jesus, 135

The Visits of Jesus, 136
True Comfort, 74
The Power of Prayer, 332
The Little Girl and her Bible, 288
The Evil of Indecision, or You Did it All, 354

Walking with God a Useful Walk, 31
Walking with God a Pleasant Walk, 36
Walking with God a Profitable Walk, 41
Walking with God a Safe Walk, 28
We have God too, 45
Whole-hearted Christians, 56
What a Child did, 156
What we should Praise God for, 198
What did the Angels Blot it out with? 212
Willie Winkie's Sacrifice, 241
What Mary gave, 372
With all your Might, 257
What are you Doing? 282
Willie's Prayer, 288

OTHER SOLID GROUND TITLES

In addition to *BIBLE MODELS*, Solid Ground Christian Books is honored offer many other uncovered treasure, many for the first time in more than century, and several from Richard Newton:

THE MOTHER AT HOME by John S.C. Abbott
THE CHILD AT HOME by John S.C. Abbott
THE FAMILY AT HOME by Gorham Abbott
THE PUBLICATIONS OF THE AMERICAN TRACT SOCIETY
BIBLE PROMISES: *Sermons for Children* by Richard Newton
BIBLE WARNINGS: *Sermons for Children* by Richard Newton
BIBLE ANIMALS: *Lessons for the Children* by Richard Newton
BIBLE JEWELS: *Lessons for the Children* by Richard Newton
THE KING'S HIGHWAY: *10 Commandments for the Young* by Richard Newton
HEROES OF THE REFORMATION by Richard Newton
HEROES OF THE EARLY CHURCH by Richard Newton
SAFE COMPASS AND HOW IT POINTS by Richard Newton
RAYS FROM THE SON OF RIGHTEOUSNESS by Richard Newton
THE LIFE OF JESUS CHRIST FOR THE YOUNG by Richard Newton
FEED MY LAMBS: *Lectures to Children on Vital Subjects* by John Todd
TRUTH MADE SIMPLE: *Attributes of God to Children* by John Todd
THE STILL HOUR: *Communion with God in Prayer* by Austin Phelps
THE SECRET OF COMMUNION WITH GOD by Matthew Henry
CALVINISM IN HISTORY *by Nathaniel S. McFetridge*
OPENING SCRIPTURE: *Hermeneutical Manual by Patrick Fairbairn*
THE ASSURANCE OF FAITH *by Louis Berkhof*
THE PASTOR IN THE SICK ROOM *by John D. Wells*
THE POWER OF GOD UNTO SALVATION *by B.B. Warfield*
THE LORD OF GLORY *by B.B. Warfield*
SERMONS TO THE NATURAL MAN *by W.G.T. Shedd*
SERMONS TO THE SPIRITUAL MAN *by W.G.T. Shedd*
A PASTOR'S SKETCHES 1 & 2 *by Ichabod S. Spencer*
IMAGO CHRISTI: *The Example of Jesus Christ by James Stalker*
THE SHORTER CATECHISM ILLUSTRATED *by John Whitecross*
THE CHURCH MEMBER'S GUIDE *by John Angell James*
THE SUNDAY SCHOOL TEACHER'S GUIDE *by John A. James*
CHRIST IN SONG: *Hymns of Immanuel from All Ages by Philip Schaff*
COME YE APART: *Daily Words from the Four Gospels by J.R. Miller*
DEVOTIONAL LIFE OF THE S.S. TEACHER *by J.R. Miller*

Call us Toll Free at 1-866-789-7423
Send us an e-mail at sgcb@charter.net
Visit us on line at www.solid-ground-books.com
Uncovering Buried Treasure to the Glory of God

www.ingramcontent.com/pod-product-compliance
Lightning Source LLC
Chambersburg PA
CBHW030330240426
43661CB00052B/1583